## Plausible Crime Stories

*Plausible Crime Stories* is not only the first in-depth study of the history of sex offences in Mandate Palestine but it also pioneers an approach to the historical study of criminal law and proof that focuses on plausibility. Doctrinal rules of evidence only partially explain which crime stories make sense while others fail to convince. Since plausibility is predicated on commonly held systems of belief, it not only provides a key to the meanings individual social players ascribe to the law but also yields insight into communal perceptions of the legal system, self-identity, the essence of normality and deviance and notions of gender, morality, nationality, ethnicity, age, religion and other cultural institutions. Using archival materials, including documents relating to 147 criminal court cases, this socio-legal study of plausibility opens a window onto a broad societal view of past beliefs, dispositions, mentalities, tensions, emotions, boundaries and hierarchies.

**Orna Alyagon Darr** is a senior lecturer at the law schools of Sapir Academic College and Ono Academic College. She is the author of *Marks of an Absolute Witch: Evidentiary Dilemmas in Early Modern England* (2011). Her work explores evidence law, criminal law and criminal procedure in their cultural, social and historical context, and her articles have been published in leading academic journals such as *Law and History Review, Law and Social Inquiry, Continuity and Change* and *Yale Journal of Law and the Humanities.*

## The Law in Context Series

*Editors* William Twining (University College London), Maksymilian Del Mar (Queen Mary, University of London) and Bronwen Morgan (University of New South Wales).

Since 1970 the Law in Context series has been at the forefront of the movement to broaden the study of law. It has been a vehicle for the publication of innovative scholarly books that treat law and legal phenomena critically in their social, political and economic contexts from a variety of perspectives. The series particularly aims to publish scholarly legal writing that brings fresh perspectives to bear on new and existing areas of law taught in universities. A contextual approach involves treating legal subjects broadly, using materials from other social sciences, and from any other discipline that helps to explain the operation in practice of the subject under discussion. It is hoped that this orientation is at once more stimulating and more realistic than the bare exposition of legal rules. The series includes original books that have a different emphasis from traditional legal textbooks, while maintaining the same high standards of scholarship. They are written primarily for undergraduate and graduate students of law and of other disciplines, but will also appeal to a wider readership. In the past, most books in the series have focused on English law, but recent publications include books on European law, globalisation, transnational legal processes, and comparative law.

### Books in the Series

Acosta: *The National versus the Foreigner in South America*
Ali: *Modern Challenges to Islamic Law*
Anderson, Schum & Twining: *Analysis of Evidence*
Ashworth: *Sentencing and Criminal Justice*
Barton & Douglas: *Law and Parenthood*
Beecher-Monas: *Evaluating Scientific Evidence: An Interdisciplinary Framework for Intellectual Due Process*
Bell: *French Legal Cultures*
Bercusson: *European Labour Law*
Birkinshaw: *European Public Law*
Birkinshaw: *Freedom of Information: The Law, the Practice and the Ideal*
Brownsword & Goodwin: *Law and the Technologies of the Twenty-First Century: Text and Materials*
Cane & Goudkamp: *Atiyah's Accidents, Compensation and the Law*
Clarke & Kohler: *Property Law: Commentary and Materials*
Collins: *The Law of Contract*
Collins, Ewing & McColgan: *Labour Law*
Cowan: *Housing Law and Policy*
Cranston: *Legal Foundations of the Welfare State*
Darian-Smith: *Laws and Societies in Global Contexts: Contemporary Approaches*
Dauvergne: *Making People Illegal: What Globalisation Means for Immigration and Law*
Davies: *Perspectives on Labour Law*

Dembour: *Who Believes in Human Rights?: Reflections on the European Convention*
de Sousa Santos: *Toward a New Legal Common Sense*
Diduck: *Law's Families*
Estella: *Legal Foundations of EU Economic Governance*
Fortin: *Children's Rights and the Developing Law*
Ghai & Woodman: *Practising Self-Government: A Comparative Study of Autonomous Regions*
Glover-Thomas: *Reconstructing Mental Health Law and Policy*
Gobert & Punch: *Rethinking Corporate Crime*
Goldman: *Globalisation and the Western Legal Tradition: Recurring Patterns of Law and Authority*
Haack: *Evidence Matters: Science, Proof, and Truth in the Law*
Harlow & Rawlings: *Law and Administration*
Harris: *An Introduction to Law*
Harris, Campbell & Halson: *Remedies in Contract and Tort*
Harvey: *Seeking Asylum in the UK: Problems and Prospects*
Hervey & McHale: *European Union Health Law: Themes and Implications*
Hervey & McHale: *Health Law and the European Union*
Holder & Lee: *Environmental Protection, Law and Policy: Text and Materials*
Jackson & Summers: *The Internationalisation of Criminal Evidence: Beyond the Common Law and Civil Law Traditions*
Kostakopoulou: *The Future Governance of Citizenship*
Lewis: *Choice and the Legal Order: Rising above Politics*
Likosky: *Transnational Legal Processes: Globalisation and Power Disparities*
Likosky: *Law, Infrastructure and Human Rights*
Lunney: *A History of Australian Tort Law 1901–1945: England's Obedient Servant?*
Maughan & Webb: *Lawyering Skills and the Legal Process*
McGlynn: *Families and the European Union: Law, Politics and Pluralism*
Moffat: *Trusts Law: Text and Materials*
Monti: *EC Competition Law*
Morgan: *Contract Law Minimalism: A Formalist Restatement of Commercial Contract Law*
Morgan & Yeung: *An Introduction to Law and Regulation: Text and Materials*
Nicola & Davies: *EU Law Stories: Contextual and Critical Histories of European Jurisprudence*
Norrie: *Crime, Reason and History: A Critical Introduction to Criminal Law*
O'Dair: *Legal Ethics: Text and Materials*
Oliver: *Common Values and the Public–Private Divide*
Oliver & Drewry: *The Law and Parliament*
Picciotto: *International Business Taxation*
Probert: *The Changing Legal Regulation of Cohabitation, 1600–2010*
Reed: *Internet Law: Text and Materials*
Richardson: *Law, Process and Custody*
Roberts & Palmer: *Dispute Processes: ADR and the Primary Forms of Decision-Making*
Rowbottom: *Democracy Distorted: Wealth, Influence and Democratic Politics*
Sauter: *Public Services in EU Law*

Scott & Black: *Cranston's Consumers and the Law*
Seneviratne: Ombudsmen: *Public Services and Administrative Justice*
Seppänen: *Ideological Conflict and the Rule of Law in Contemporary China*
Siems: *Comparative Law, 2nd Edition*
Stapleton: *Product Liability*
Stewart: *Gender, Law and Justice in a Global Market*
Tamanaha: *Law as a Means to an End: Threat to the Rule of Law*
Turpin & Tomkins: *British Government and the Constitution: Text and Materials*
Twining: *Globalisation and Legal Theory*
Twining: *Rethinking Evidence: Exploratory Essays*
Twining: *General Jurisprudence: Understanding Law from a Global Perspective*
Twining: *Human Rights, Southern Voices: Francis Deng, Abdullahi An-Na'im, Yash Ghai and Upendra Baxi*
Twining & Miers: *How to Do Things with Rules*
Ward: *A Critical Introduction to European Law*
Ward: *Law, Text, Terror*
Ward: *Shakespeare and Legal Imagination*
Wells & Quick: *Lacey, Wells and Quick: Reconstructing Criminal Law*
Zander: *Cases and Materials on the English Legal System*
Zander: *The Law-Making Process*

**International Journal of Law in Context: A Global Forum for Interdisciplinary Legal Studies**

The *International Journal of Law in Context* is the companion journal to the Law in Context book series and provides a forum for interdisciplinary legal studies and offers intellectual space for ground-breaking critical research. It publishes contextual work about law and its relationship with other disciplines including but not limited to science, literature, humanities, philosophy, sociology, psychology, ethics, history and geography. More information about the journal and how to submit an article can be found at http://journals.cambridge.org/ijc

# Plausible Crime Stories

## The Legal History of Sexual Offences in Mandate Palestine

ORNA ALYAGON DARR
Sapir Academic College and Ono Academic College

CAMBRIDGE
UNIVERSITY PRESS

**CAMBRIDGE**
**UNIVERSITY PRESS**

University Printing House, Cambridge CB2 8BS, United Kingdom

One Liberty Plaza, 20th Floor, New York, NY 10006, USA

477 Williamstown Road, Port Melbourne, VIC 3207, Australia

314–321, 3rd Floor, Plot 3, Splendor Forum, Jasola District Centre, New Delhi – 110025, India

79 Anson Road, #06–04/06, Singapore 079906

Cambridge University Press is part of the University of Cambridge.

It furthers the University's mission by disseminating knowledge in the pursuit of education, learning, and research at the highest international levels of excellence.

www.cambridge.org
Information on this title: www.cambridge.org/9781108497237
DOI: 10.1017/9781108667128



First published 2019

Printed and bound in Great Britain by Clays Ltd, Elcograf S.p.A.

*A catalogue record for this publication is available from the British Library.*

*Library of Congress Cataloging-in-Publication Data*
Names: Orna, Alyagon Darr, author.
Title: Plausible crime stories : the legal history of sexual offences in mandate Palestine / Orna Alyagon Darr, Sapir Academic College and Ono Academic College.
Description: Cambrdige, United Kingdom ; New York, NY, USA : Cambridge University Press, 2018. | Series: Law in context
Identifiers: LCCN 2018037324 | ISBN 9781108497237 (hardback)
Subjects: LCSH: Sex crimes – Law and legislation – Palestine – History – 20th century. | Trials (Sex crimes) – Palestine – History – 20th century. | Palestine – History – 1917–1948. | BISAC: LAW / Criminal Law / General.
Classification: LCC KMQ1420 .D37 2018 | DDC 345.5694/0253–dc23
LC record available at https://lccn.loc.gov/2018037324

ISBN 978-1-108-49723-7 Hardback

In memory of Miriam, Yosef, Aliza & Emmanuel

# Contents

# Acknowledgements

This book has benefited from the help and generosity of many people. Assaf Likhovski read parts of it and offered criticism and support at critical stages of the writing process. My thanks also go to Nehama Darr, Thomas Duve, Lena Foljanty, Gershon Gontovnik, Adam Hofri-Winogradow, Ofri Ilany, Ruth Kannai, Amalia Kessler, Nomi Levenkron, Michael Lobban, Tammy Razi, Anat Rosenberg, Daphne Rozenblatt, Christopher Tomlins, Steven Wilf and Yuval Yonay for comments and suggestions on drafts of various sections.

I am grateful to Orit Rozin, who encouraged me to explore the realm of law and emotions. William Twining, who views evidence law as part of a broader social context, was a source of inspiration, and I feel especially privileged to have had his support and encouragement as a series editor. My thanks also go to Amos Megged, a mentor and a friend.

I am grateful to Linda Forman, who edited the text and rooted out the many linguistic peculiarities of a non-native English speaker. I am fortunate to have worked with her. I thank Rouda Morcos, a linguist as well as a lawyer, who helped me translate Arabic transcripts and expressions.

Huge thanks are due to the editorial staff of Cambridge University Press, especially Tom Randall, and Penelope Harper, the book's copy-editor. I would also like to thank the anonymous reviewers of the manuscript for their most helpful comments.

I frequented the Israel National Archives over a period of several years. I would like to express deep appreciation to archive staff members, who were always accommodating. I am especially indebted to Helena Vilensky, whose help was invaluable, and to Galia Weisman. I am also grateful to staff at the Hagannah Archives, the Israel Supreme Court Archive, the Haifa District Court Archive and the Queensland Parliamentary Service for their assistance. I thank the City Museum, Haifa, for the archival assistance and permission to use the cover illustration. In researching the history of the cover photo I benefited from the kind and generous help of Nathan Brun, Nurit Lifshitz, Alber Nahas and Debbie Usher from Middle East Centre Archive, St Antony's College, Oxford.

An earlier version of Chapter 2 appeared in *Law and History Review*, and an earlier version of Chapter 6 appeared in the *Yale Journal of Law and the Humanities*; I use material from those chapters by permission. During the years I conducted the research on which this book is based, I benefited from the feedback of many colleagues in various fora where I presented aspects of my work. My appreciation goes to the participants in the 2012 Conference of the Association for Israel Studies (Haifa); 2012 Conference on the Legal Histories of the British Empire (Singapore); 2013 Conference of the Association for the Study of Law, Culture and the Humanities (London); 2013 David Berg Summer Institute for Law and History (Shfayim, Israel); 2013 Max Planck Summer Academy for Legal History (Frankfurt am Main); Tenth Annual Conference of the Israeli Association of Legal History (Jerusalem, 2014); Fourth European Congress on World and Global History (Paris, 2014); Eighth Global Conference on Sex and the State/Persons and Sexualities (Oxford, 2015); 2015 Conference of the Israeli Law and Society Association (Haifa); 2016 Resistance and Empire conference organized by the ICS-ULisboa Research Group 'Empires, Colonialism, and Post-colonial Societies' (Lisbon); 2017 Shaming Conference IDC (Herzlia, Israel); 2017 Evidence of Feelings Workshop, Center for the History of Emotions, Max Planck Institute for Human Development (Berlin); 2018 Queer History Conference (Haifa); 2018 Legal Histories and Empire conference (Barbados); the Hebrew University Faculty of Law colloquium; Shaarei Mishpat Law School colloquium; Carmel Academic Center colloquium; IDC Herzlia Law School colloquium; and Sapir Academic College colloquium.

Finally, I am deeply grateful to my family. My husband Asaf was the first to hear, and often to challenge, nascent ideas during my research and writing. He was a partner in endless stimulating discussions, a sharp commentator on my drafts and someone who made me laugh even at difficult times. He remains the best life companion I could wish for. To my children Rimon and Adam, thank you for many joyous moments and for constantly reminding me, simply by being there, what is really important.

# Introduction

In 1944 the Haifa District Court in Mandate Palestine acquitted twenty-five-year-old Nimr Razek of attempting to commit an indecent act upon nineteen-year-old Nafiseh, a married woman from his village of Kafr Kare.[1] Nafiseh testified that on the night of 16 June 1944, while her husband was away, she had been sleeping with her baby daughter on the roof of her house. She had been awakened by a man who grabbed her and tried to take off her 'drawers', and she had recognized his voice as that of her neighbour, Nimr Razek. Nafiseh began to shout profusely and managed to tear Nimr's shirt as he escaped. In addition to her testimony, the evidence introduced at trial included a torn shirt, the testimony of her father, to whom Nafiseh immediately reported the attack, and the testimony of Khalil, Nafiseh's husband's brother. Khalil testified that he had been sleeping in the family compound and had been awakened by Nafiseh's loud screams. He saw a man running from Nafiseh's roof to Nimr's house. He then heard Nimr's mother ask 'Who is that?' followed by Nimr urging her to be quiet. The court did not believe Nafiseh's story. In a revealing paragraph, the British President of the Haifa District Court, Judge Curry, reasoned as follows:

> The story of the complainant I find strange in one or two particulars. It seems to me unusual for a married woman to be sleeping alone although I appreciate it is not impossible, but I feel it is strange for a man in the middle of the night, to come to commit an indecent act upon a woman unless there has been some friendship or some encouragement to hope that he would not be badly received. Naturally if they were together with her consent and something happened to alarm her, she would give the alarm, to save her own honour.[2]

Clearly, Judge Curry's considerations were not strictly legalistic. But what made him find Nafiseh's story unconvincing? Why did the story of a courtship that crossed the line and ended with a fabricated accusation make more sense to him? Was the 'plot' of Nafiseh's testimony deficient in some way? Was her story contradicted by other evidence? Judge Curry was a high-ranking figure in the British colonial administration, and Nafiseh was

[1] ISA/RG 30/Law 2036 (original docket # Cr.C 208/44).

[2] See the judgment given 16 December 1944.

a young Muslim villager and a colonial subject. Did their respective political positions and ethnic identities influence the judge's assessment of the young woman's testimony and, if so, how? To what extent was the scrutiny of Nafiseh's story conditioned by gendered patterns? Was Judge Curry's incredulity anchored in the particularities of her story, in his presumptions regarding the sexual mores of Arab villagers in Palestine or in his more general beliefs about the way the world operates?

In this book I attempt to determine what makes one story convincing and another doubtful, inside and outside the criminal courtroom. In doing so, I employ 'plausibility' as an analytical framework that provides valuable insight into the practice of factual determination. In theory, the establishment of true facts inside the courtroom is based on information and materials that are admitted through proper application of the rules of evidence. The doctrinal rules, however, only partially explain what stories make sense in practice. Nafiseh's story, although supported by other pieces of evidence, was found implausible. Why? Because, I contend, its plausibility depended to a large degree on the social context in which it was told. I argue that persuasion relies on socially constructed knowledge, reasoning and sentiments that are shared by the members of a given society in a given time and place. Therefore, rather than seek to define plausibility in universally applicable human psychological or philosophical terms, my research takes a 'law in action' approach that deciphers persuasion in a particular historical and socio-cultural setting.

Evidence and procedure are typically perceived as quite technical in nature, while substantive norms are widely recognized as expressing broad social interests and values. The socio-legal history of plausibility can shed light on actual practice as an integral mechanism in the process of proof, and it highlights the socially constructed nature of the supposedly neutral and technical mode of factual determination. Despite extensive awareness of the distinction between 'law on the books' and actual practice, evidence scholars usually shun 'in action' analysis of legal proof and evidence law and of their role in legitimizing social institutions and in disguising the interests behind legal regimes.[3]

[3] While no mainstream evidence scholars have engaged in full-blown 'in action' analysis, a few leading scholars have questioned the basic axiom of the truth-finding rationale and have offered a contextual rather than a strictly doctrinal perspective. Alex Stein, for example, points to risk sharing by and cost reduction for contending parties as major considerations in the constitution of evidence law. However, Stein perceives society as a homogenous entity, whose members share similar ideas about the constitution of well-being as well as similar concepts of 'utility', 'fairness' and 'morality'. Another exceptional voice is that of Ian Dennis, who regards legitimization, and not truth-finding, as the ultimate basis of evidence law. By pointing to legitimization, Dennis implies that power relations constitute evidence law, but he does not pursue the significance of his conclusion, as he does not explain who seeks legitimization, by what means and for what purpose. Most contextual is the work of William Twining, who calls for a multi-disciplinary study of evidence from a broad theoretical and historical perspective. See I. H. Dennis, *The Law of Evidence*, 4th ed. (Sweet & Maxwell: London, 2010); Alex Stein, *The Foundations of Evidence Law* (Oxford: Oxford University Press, 2005); William Twining, *Rethinking Evidence: Exploratory Essays* (Cambridge: Cambridge University Press, 2006).

Although a broad treatment of proof 'in action' is still wanting in the field of evidence law, several legal historians point to the gap between doctrine and practice and the social and cultural foundation and uses of legal proof.[4] Legal historians who study sex offences have been particularly sensitive to proof as a locus that reveals the gap between 'law on the books' and 'law in action' and have underlined proof's embodiment of cultural norms and social interests. In her study of illicit sex crimes in Ottoman Aleppo, Semerdjian demonstrates that a flexible use of evidence (sometimes to the extent of bending Sharia rules by allowing hearsay and circumstantial evidence) was a significant channel through which the court accommodated the local community.[5] Kolsky's examination of evidentiary standards in rape cases in colonial India demonstrates how the requirement of 'corroboration' through application of medico-legal standards was based upon ethnical and gendered prejudices against native female complainants, which made it difficult for victims to successfully prove their complaints. The proof of rape allegations, Kolsky shows, was not merely a technical legal issue but part of colonial and gendered politics.[6] Backhouse's work on the history of sexual assault law in Canada and Australia analyses corroboration as a doctrine that lends credence to guilty men at the expense of female and child victims.[7]

Awareness of the social role of evidence in the area of sex offences was first raised by feminist theoreticians who explored rape as a means of subjugating women and who scrutinized cultural myths scaffolding the patriarchal treatment of sexual assault. Consequently, feminist critique of evidentiary

[4] Several scholars have placed the historical study of evidence law at the heart of their research. Mnookin examines criteria of admissibility of scientific evidence such as DNA and fingerprints in relation to cultural beliefs about the reliability and legitimacy of various ways of knowing. She also analyses the relation between the structure of the adversarial system and the nature of scientific evidence (and, more specifically, the problems of partisanship and epistemic competence of expert witnesses). See Jennifer L. Mnookin, 'Fingerprint Evidence in an Age of DNA Profiling', *Brooklyn Law Review* 67, no. 1 (2001); 'Expert Evidence, Partisanship, and Epistemic Competence', *Brooklyn Law Review* 73, no. 3 (2008). Sengoopta explores the cultural context in which fingerprinting was developed in India under the Raj and was then exported to Victorian England. See Chandak Sengoopta, *Imprint of the Raj: How Fingerprinting Was Born in Colonial India* (London: Macmillan, 2003). Blum concludes that procedural and evidence rules in Mandate Palestine reflect colonial authorities' changing ideas about and stereotypes of the natives as well as their own evolving political interests. See Binyamin Blum, 'Evidence Rules of Colonial Difference: Identity, Legitimacy and Power in the Law of Mandate Palestine, 1917–1939' (JSD dissertation, Stanford University, 2011). My own work has investigated the affiliation between socio-cultural context and the development of evidentiary techniques in early modern English witch trials. See Orna Alyagon Darr, *Marks of an Absolute Witch: Evidentiary Dilemmas in Early Modern England* (Farnham, UK: Ashgate, 2011).

[5] Elyse Semerdjian, *'Off the Straight Path': Illicit Sex, Law, and Community in Ottoman Aleppo* (New York: Syracuse University Press, 2008), xxiv, 87, 97–98, 138, 147, 150.

[6] Elizabeth Kolsky, '"The Body Evidencing the Crime": Rape on Trial in Colonial India, 1860–1947', *Gender & History* 22, no. 1 (2010); 'The Rule of Colonial Indifference: Rape on Trial in Early Colonial India, 1805–57', *The Journal of Asian Studies* 69, no. 4 (2010).

[7] Constance Backhouse, 'The Doctrine of Corroboration in Sexual Assault Trials in Early Twentieth-Century Canada and Australia', *Queen's Law Journal* 26 (2001); *Carnal Crimes: Sexual Assault Law in Canada, 1900–1975* (Toronto: Osgoode Society 2008),173–83,190–92.

mechanisms based on 'rape myths' highlighted the social embeddedness of the process of proof of sex crimes. Feminist writing pointed to the proof of consent, corroboration, the recent complaint requirement and other evidentiary doctrines and methods as gendered and as part of the social power grid.[8] Some works pointed to the intersection of gender, race and colonial difference in the manner of proof.[9]

In this book, I explore persuasion in the context of sex offences in Mandate Palestine. The site and the topic offer several methodological advantages. Both legal history and feminist scholarship demonstrate that sexual crimes are fertile ground for the study of social embeddedness of legal proof. The criminal prohibitions regulating sexuality are soaked in moral and cultural perceptions and therefore provide a convenient platform for conducting socio-legal research. In the arena of sexuality, social, cultural and religious norms and practices are no less binding than the criminal law is, and perhaps are even more so. They are pertinent to a variety of issues: Who is a legitimate partner for sex? Under what conditions? What sexual practices are permissible? What practices are considered illegitimate? What establishes consent to a sexual act? The answers may depend on social attributes of the participants in an act, such as their age, gender, religion, nationality, race, ethnic origin, marital status and social status. The answers given by law and culture can overlap, conflict or diverge. Socially constructed perceptions of sexuality and sexual offences can shape both the finding of facts and the application of legal rules, as demonstrated in Judge Curry's opinion above.

Mandate Palestine (1918–1948) offers a socially and culturally heterogeneous site for research into plausibility. The territory's residents included British citizens, Jews and Arabs; Muslims and Christians; people of religious conviction and atheists; urban dwellers and peasants; colonial rulers and their subjects. In this land of social, ethnic and political cleavages, one can expect to find a range of attitudes towards, beliefs about and perceptions of sexuality and its regulation. In this complex environment, with a plurality of narrators and audiences, the question of what establishes a convincing as opposed to an unconvincing story becomes acute. Moreover, the region's different ethnic and national communities, to a large extent, were socially and culturally distinct

8 For a collection which contains articles on the practice of evidence from a feminist perspective, see Mary Childs and Louise Ellison, eds., *Feminist Perspectives on Evidence* (London: Cavendish, 2000). A prolific writer on the gendered regime of evidence is Aviva Orenstein, whose work includes: Aviva Orenstein, '"My God!": A Feminist Critique of the Excited Utterance Exception to the Hearsay Rule', *California Law Review* 85, no. 1 (1997); 'Special Issues Raised by Rape Trial', *Fordham Law Review* 76, no. 3 (2007); 'The Seductive Power of Patriarchal Stories', *Howard Law Journal* 58, no. 2 (2015); Aviva A. Orenstein, 'No Bad Men!: A Feminist Analysis of Character Evidence in Rape Trials', *Hastings Law Journal* 49 (1998). See also Kathy Mack, 'Continuing Barriers to Women's Credibility: A Feminist Perspective on the Proof Process', *Criminal Law Forum* 4, no. 2 (1993).

9 Kathy Mack, 'An Australian Perspective on Feminism, Race and Evidence', *Southwestern University Law Review* 28 (1999); Christine Stewart, 'Men Behaving Badly: Sodomy Cases in the Colonial Courts of Papua New Guinea', *Journal of Pacific History* 43, no. 1 (2008).

and often even hostile to each other. The colonial framework and national tensions sharpened and accentuated the differences. With its heterogeneous population, Mandate Palestine makes a perfect setting for the study of plausibility in a multi-cultural environment.

Furthermore, in a colonial context, one might expect the colonizers' hegemonic view of native subjects and their sexuality to be more transparent and explicit than in the home country. Given the differences between their beliefs and perceptions and those of their subjects, and their sense of superiority over the natives, colonizers are likely to explicate their worldview to an extent that would not be deemed necessary at home, where judges and other participants in legal proceedings, diverse as they might be, share many cultural and ideological attributes. Such transparency, which was evident in British colonial courts, assists in the exploration of stories that did and did not make sense in the period under study and renders some the mechanisms of plausibility more visible. Methodologically, the degree of separation between communities in Mandate Palestine facilitates the tracing of distinctive ethnic voices and interpretations in court records. Nevertheless, while Mandate Palestine makes an excellent site for the study of plausibility, one must keep in mind that socially constructed phenomena may take different forms across time, cultures and places. While the general mechanisms of plausibility may be similar from society to society, their particular manifestations may vary across cultural and national boundaries. The primary materials on which this book leans offer another methodological advantage. The Mandate court records contain information about the ethnic and national groups to which the participants in legal proceedings belonged. With only a few exceptions, the ethnic origin of the participants practically leaps off the pages of the court files: it can be easily deduced from names (most are identifiably Arab, Jewish or British), and often the religion of a witness or a party is plainly noted in trial transcripts, investigative reports or indictments. Thus, the attempt to affiliate ethnicity or nationality with notions of plausibility is much facilitated.

Law and society are not distinct or separate spheres but are interconnected and mutually influence each other.[10] While this study assumes that the process of proof is socially and culturally embedded, I make no presuppositions regarding the particular manner in which the culture and norms of any one social group or segment are manifested in the process of proof. When I inquire what makes a particular story plausible, I do not make assumptions based on what is already known about the social players under study in terms of their

[10] For discussion of their interconnectivity, see Assaf Likhovski, 'Chasing Ghosts: On Writing Cultural Histories of Tax Law', *UC Irvine Law Review* 1, no. 3 (2011); Robert W. Gordon, 'Critical Legal Histories', *Stanford Law Review* 36, no. 1/2 (1984); Christopher Tomlins, 'How Autonomous Is Law?', *Annual Review of Law & Social Science* 3, no. 1 (2007); Austin Sarat and Thomas R. Kearns, 'The Cultural Lives of Law', in *Law in the Domains of Culture*, ed. Austin Sarat and Thomas R. Kearns (Ann Arbor: University of Michigan Press, 2001); Naomi Mezey, 'Law as Culture', *Yale Journal of Law & the Humanities* 13, no. 1 (2001)

social and cultural identity. Rather, my aim is to detect indications of socially embedded elements of plausibility within the primary documentary sources. I use secondary literature on the norms or cultures of various groups merely to evaluate and further probe my findings, which are always grounded in the primary sources. Research into plausibility focuses on the meeting point of culture and law within the process of proof.

At the centre of this investigation of how stories make sense in the law lies the term 'plausibility', through which I study the traits that make one story appealing and another unconvincing. In so doing, I also probe the meaning of the term 'plausibility' itself, to which the legal literature often relates in an indiscriminate and incoherent manner. The scholarly uses of the terms 'plausibility' and 'implausibility' vary and are often theoretically indistinct. These terms may play into the chances of the prosecution to convict,[11] theories of a crime[12] or the proportionality of a prison sentence.[13] In this book I call for more precise use of 'plausibility' to denote a rhetorical quality that pertains to whether a story makes sense, whether it is persuasive.

Indeed, the plausibility of a story describing an alleged crime can vary when that story is considered by different actors in different sites and from various angles. Substantive law sets forth the elements of the offence, and no finding of guilt can be made unless each element is substantiated by evidence. The fact finders determine which witnesses should be believed and which evidence is unreliable. Police investigators' intuition as to the likelihood of an occurrence may influence the direction of an investigation or the sifting of cases before they reach court.[14] Media coverage embraces and propagates some storylines while rejecting others. Which stories of alleged crimes make sense? Can the same story strike one audience as implausible and make sense to others? Which stories are explicitly told and which are implicitly transmitted? The answers to these questions, as we shall see, draw on criminal law, procedure and evidence as well as on social and cultural narratives and norms.

This book explores various planes of plausibility, a domain that involves complex relations between law and society. The term 'plausibility' should be distinguished from the juridical terms 'credibility' and 'probability', which also set standards for the evaluation of statements and facts. In the next two sections, I clarify the differences between these related concepts, which are widely used in the legal arena.

[11] Willem Albert Wagenaar, P. J. van Koppen and Henricus Florentine Maria Crombag, *Anchored Narratives: The Psychology of Criminal Evidence* (Hemel Hempstead, UK: Harvester Wheatsheaf, 1993), 62.

[12] Travis Hirschi and Michael Gottfredson, 'Age and the Explanation of Crime', *American Journal of Sociology* 89, no. 3 (1983): 567.

[13] Andrew Ashworth, *Sentencing and Criminal Justice*, 6th ed. (Cambridge: Cambridge University Press, 2015), 290.

[14] Racial profiling is an extreme case in point.

## The Difference between 'Probability' and 'Plausibility'

Despite its statistical ring, in its common legal usage the term 'probability' is not a quantitative measure of likelihood, and the mathematical formula is a metaphor for desired certainty rather than a computational tool.[15] The logician Jonathan Cohen even claims that the mathematicist analysis of probability is not applicable to judicial proof in Anglo-American courts acting in accordance with existing legal standards and procedures.[16] Cohen believes that ordinary jurors and judges are competent to assess judicial proof on the basis of inductivist analysis and practical commonsense reasoning.[17]

The term 'probability' conveys two opposed notions regarding the possibility of knowing facts with certainty. On the one hand, it implies the impossibility of absolute certainty. Knowledge of a 'probable' fact is necessarily an inference. On the other hand, probability implies the possibility of reaching a high level of assurance about facts not directly observed. Shapiro describes how these notions, which the ancient Greeks and Romans perceived as dichotomous, became less distinct in early modern England.[18] 'Science' in that setting was no longer strictly syllogistic or mathematical, and knowledge had become more empirical and more concerned with matters of fact. English thinkers in different fields no longer believed that absolute certitude was humanly possible. By the end of the seventeenth century, satisfying knowledge of the 'truth' could be highly probabilistic, relying on observation of facts and experience.[19] Early modern English legal thought shared this epistemological turn, reflected in growing emphasis on assessments of probability, degrees of certainty and the formation of standards such as 'reasonable doubt'.[20]

The rise of empiricist thought coincided with a significant procedural change transferring adjudication from the hands of God to those of lay jurors. Resolving questions of proof and evidence involved acknowledging human fallibility and the impossibility of possessing certain knowledge. In the early days of jury trials, self-informed jurors could reach a decision based on their knowledge of most of the facts, common sense and common knowledge.[21] However, growing reliance on witnesses made necessary the assessment of

[15] For references to evidence scholars lamenting the innumeracy of lawyers and judges, see William Twining, 'Narrative and Generalizations in Argumentation About Questions of Fact', *South Texas Law Review* 40 (1999): 353 fn. 7.

[16] L. Jonathan Cohen, *The Probable and the Provable* (Oxford: Clarendon Press, 1977),117–18, §§ 14–39.

[17] Ibid., 274–275. Cohen distinguishes between Pascalian and Baconian probability. Pascalian probability estimates chances on the basis of the frequency of examined occurrences in a given set of cases or on the basis of the personal experience of the fact finder. Baconian inductive probability expresses a degree of belief and evaluates the extent to which the available evidence in a particular case corresponds to the issues under review. See also Stein, 41–44.

[18] Barbara J. Shapiro, *Probability and Certainty in Seventeenth-Century England: A Study of the Relationships between Natural Science, Religion, History, Law, and Literature* (Princeton, NJ: Princeton University Press, 1983), 1.

[19] Ibid., 2–3, 9–10. [20] Ibid., 11. [21] Ibid., 177.

evidence. The fact finder could not be certain of some fact merely because a witness had attested to it. In the words of Stein, '[a]djudicative fact-finding is about probabilities, not about certainties'.[22]

Although English jurors were permitted to base their verdicts on circumstantial evidence, in their attempt to grade the value of evidence, they borrowed from their Continental counterparts the concept of the classification of proof. Roman-canon doctrine, dating at least as far back as the 1150s, ranked presumptions with respect to three evidentiary levels, customarily named 'violent', 'probable' and 'light'.[23] Ironically, Continental juridical terminology of degrees of certitude was employed to facilitate convictions in hard-to-prove cases such as witchcraft.[24] Short of direct evidence, conviction on the basis of aggregated fragments of proof was made possible. The notion of degrees of certainty legitimized the use of circumstantial evidence and enabled its classification according to varying degrees of probative strength. In fact, James Whitman argues that the nascent standard requiring assurance 'beyond a reasonable doubt', despite its certitude-conveying rhetoric, actually enabled fact finders to soothe their consciences when convicting despite lingering uncertainty. Through the application of this standard jurors could convict without risking the salvation of their souls.[25]

By the beginning of the eighteenth century the basic rules of evidence had formed.[26] Thereafter, the Anglo-American legal system gradually developed an intricate matrix of evidentiary rules, with exclusionary mechanisms, many exceptions and exceptions to the exceptions. To enter the record, evidence must be admissible. In addition, its credibility and weight must also be considered. Prevailing legal theory regards the rules of evidence as a rational and objective means of getting closer to truth.[27] The view of probability as a means of evaluating an empirical truth is rooted in basic concepts and standards such as 'reasonable doubt', 'balance of probabilities' and 'probable cause'.

Assessments of probability are made by fact finders whose minds are 'stocked with a vast number of commonplace generalizations about human acts, attitudes, intentions, etc., about the more familiar features of the human environment, and about the interactions between these two kinds of factor,

[22] Stein, 35. [23] Alyagon Darr, 80. [24] Ibid., 81–85.

[25] James O. Whitman, *The Origins of Reasonable Doubt: Theological Roots of the Criminal Trial* (New Haven, CT: Yale University Press, 2008).

[26] John H. Langbein, *The Origins of Adversary Criminal Trial*, Oxford Studies in Modern Legal History (Oxford: Oxford University Press, 2003).

[27] As expressed in the classic treatise by John Henry Wigmore, *Evidence in Trials at Common Law*, 4th ed., 10 vols., Vol. 1, *Wigmore on Evidence* (Boston: Little, Brown and Company, 1983), xx, 8, see also 9, fn. 5. While the discovery of truth is the paramount objective, other values entrenched in the rules are 'economizing of resources, inspiring confidence, supporting independent social policies, permitting ease in prediction and application, adding to the efficiency of the entire legal system, and tranquilizing disputants' (Judge Weinstein as quoted by Stein, 36).

together with an awareness of many of the kinds of circumstances that are favourable or unfavourable to the application of each such generalization'.[28] These generalizations are the product of culture and socialization.[29]

Like plausibility, probability is predicated on communality, and both concepts hinge on shared societal knowledge. However, while probability pertains to 'truth', the correspondence of the evidence with empirical reality, plausibility addresses the rhetorical level and the ability to persuade. Determination of probability rests on factual finding that is inferred from the evidence. The analysis of plausibility examines this process of inference and probes the communality on which inferences rely. Inferences, which may be accurate or mistaken, are based on socially valid knowledge that establishes plausibility. This book thus maps out the various elements that establish plausibility; the question it addresses is not what makes a story real or true but what makes a story acceptable or convincing.

## The Difference between 'Credibility' and 'Plausibility'

Another concept that is closely related to but that should be distinguished from 'plausibility' is 'credibility', or 'reliability'. The credibility of a witness guarantees the accuracy and truthfulness of his or her testimony. It speaks to the witness's perception, intelligence, communication skills and honesty. The assessment of credibility is intended to ensure that fact finding and judicial decisions rest upon truthful witnesses.

To achieve the goal of keeping liars out of the courtroom, the old common law relied mainly on competence.[30] 'Infamous witnesses' who belonged to a list of dubious categories were not qualified to testify under oath.[31] As it was given without oath, their testimony had little value. The English judicial notion of truthfulness was transformed during the early modern era in response to growing doubts about the value of oath-taking and a rising empiricist worldview that emphasized observers' ability to perceive facts and convey their observations accurately. As early as the seventeenth century, Matthew Hale, while still referring to categories of incompetence,[32] made a distinction between the competency and the credit of testimony.[33] The emergent concept

[28] Cohen, 274. [29] Ibid., 275.

[30] Colin Tapper, *Cross & Tapper on Evidence*, 12th ed. (Oxford: Oxford University Press, 2010), 223.

[31] Among these categories were infidels, convicted felons, those convicted of perjury or conspiracy, the insane, those 'not of discretion', interested parties, and champions in a writ of right who became recreant or coward. William Nelson, *The Law of Evidence*, 1st ed. (London: B. Gosling, 1717), 20.

[32] Sir Matthew Hale, *Pleas of the Crown* (London: William Shrewsbury and John Leigh, 1678), 263.

[33] Sir Matthew Hale, *Historia Placitorum Coronae. The History of the Pleas of the Crown, by Sir Matthew Hale . . . Now First Published from His Lordship's Original Manuscript, and the Several References to the Records Examined by the Originals, with Large Notes. By Sollom Emlyn . . .*

of credibility emphasized the individual qualities of the witness rather than stereotypes attached to social categories. Most of these categories were formally abolished by the Evidence Act 1843 (6 & 7 Vict c. 85). Matters of fact had to be based on credible witnesses, and mere oath was no longer sufficient to establish reliability. Nevertheless, a true story from the mouth of a credible witness was not necessarily a plausible one.

Despite the plummeting significance of the competency rules, credibility of witnesses is still partly socially constructed. It is still predicated not only on individual qualities such as intelligence and perceptiveness but also on the plausibility of the narrative the witness unfolds and of his or her role in it. For example, in a judgment rendered while sitting on the Palestine Supreme Court, Judge Curry doubted the testimony of a female rape victim who did not become hysterical and was not reduced to tears after the alleged rape.[34] In this example, plausibility depended on the social identity of the witness (a female complainant in a rape case) and the cultural expectation about how she should fulfil her social role. Credibility, one may say, is predicated on both individual qualities (such as the ability to perceive) and roles and expectations that are attributed to the social category to which the witness belongs. The latter of these two factors belongs to the realm of the 'plausible'. In other words, 'plausibility' is that part of the credible that is socially constructed.

While both probability and credibility relate to 'true' stories, plausibility pertains to stories that make sense. Twining points to several attributes of 'good' stories: internal structure and coherence, fitness for purpose, and effect on an audience. A story may also be appealing if it fits into a familiar pattern. A story may not strike hearers as good if it ends in an anti-climax, ceases to have a point or is not memorable, truthful as it may be.[35] The narrative conventions apply to storylines and stock characters.[36] In a criminal trial, when fact finders need to choose between alternative narratives, they may prefer the one that appears to better solve the crime.[37] The same logic applies to journalistic crime stories – interesting and persuasive ones may be preferred over factually accurate and boring ones.[38]

*To Which Is Added a Table of the Principal Matters. In Two Volumes. . . .* (London: F. Gyles, T. Woodward, and C. Davis, 1736), I 635.

34 'I am extremely surprised that a girl of 19½ was not in a much more distressed state after having been raped by three ruffians than this girl apparently was. One would have expected the reaction to have made her hysterical and to have reduced her to tears . . . '. See the minority opinion of Acting Justice Curry from the Palestine Supreme Court in Cr.A 31/47.

35 Twining, 'Narrative and Generalizations in Argumentation About Questions of Fact', 360, fn. 38.

36 Joseph E. Davis, *Accounts of Innocence: Sexual Abuse, Trauma, and the Self* (Chicago: University of Chicago Press, 2005), 15.

37 Wagenaar, Koppen and Crombag, 59.

38 Twining, 'Narrative and Generalizations in Argumentation About Questions of Fact', 360, fn. 38.

Wagenaar et al. argue that to be plausible and convincing evidence must be 'anchored' in safe commonsense rules.[39] They provide many illuminating examples to demonstrate that the acceptance of some facts and the rejection of others depends on the 'goodness' of stories. They study this phenomenon as a psychological process. Yet 'common' sense is a social and cultural creation, and fact finders' reasoning in legal proceedings is inextricably entrenched in social and cultural perceptions of the world. Ayelet Ben-Yishai stresses that facts, as much as norms, acquire their meaning and persuasiveness through communal approval and that the empirical concept of the fact is challenged and undermined by a communal one.[40] What may seem at first glance to be two separate worlds, one of pre-existing facts that are revealed through empirical means in the legal process and one of constantly generated social facts, are inseparably intertwined. An example of such entanglement is found in an empirical study of what prosecutors in England and Wales look for when conducting pre-trial interviews with witnesses to determine if a realistic prospect of conviction exists. The six considerations that the researchers identify blend empirical reality and social facts: (1) the nature of the offence (a mixture of empirical reality and a reified concept of the 'offence'); (2) circumstances surrounding the complaint (empirical facts that are selected and viewed through a socially constructed prism of 'relevancy'); (3) 'missing information' – gaps in a witness's story; (4) the 'inherent implausibility' of stories that do not 'ring true' or 'add up'; (5) conflicting or otherwise problematic evidence; and (6) complex evidence, in which case the prosecutor endeavours to clarify the events by fitting them into a clear and logical narrative.[41] These categories are based on the experience and worldview of the prosecutors, who measure witnesses' stories against stereotypical patterns of behaviour. Statements that look good 'on paper' may turn out to be unconvincing.[42] Interestingly, examples from rape cases figure prominently in all six categories, which may imply that narratives of rape are especially susceptible to social and cultural considerations of plausibility.

Plausibility leans on socially constructed knowledge and may sometimes be coupled with empirical or legal truth. Furthermore, the establishment of true facts inevitably rests on an epistemological foundation, which changes across place and through time. Moreover, even within a given culture and time, different social actors may not share the same impressions of the plausibility of the same stories. Socio-legal inquiry concerning plausibility, which probes what is considered to be socially valid knowledge, therefore should take place

[39] Wagenaar, Koppen and Crombag, 35–41.
[40] Ayelet Ben-Yishai, *Common Precedents: The Presentness of the Past in Victorian Law and Fiction* (Oxford: Oxford University Press, 2013), 117, 32.
[41] Paul Roberts and Candida Saunders, 'Piloting PTWI – a Socio-Legal Window on Prosecutors' Assessments of Evidence and Witness Credibility', *Oxford Journal of Legal Studies* 30, no. 1 (2010).
[42] Ibid., 123.

within a specific social and historical context, not just within the walls of the courtroom.

Participants in legal proceedings make arguments and tell stories imprinted by both legal and socio-cultural influences. The identification of the socio-cultural elements that affect the constitution of plausibility can provide insight into varied perceptions, dispositions and beliefs and allows the observer to track how participants in the proceedings mobilize these elements in the courtroom. To avoid circular explanation, one should not make assumptions in advance about the nature of the social factors affecting the construction of plausibility but rather scrutinize the primary sources for cues, indications and markers of such social embeddedness. Such investigation takes place in the rhetorical dimension. It targets the interweaving of law and culture and need not address the causal relationship between these spheres.

An additional methodological advantage of searching for the socio-cultural elements of plausibility within primary sources is that, beyond providing a glimpse into the way certain social players perceive the world, it also occasionally reveals how they believe others perceive them. For example, Chapter 4 demonstrates how Arab lawyers tailored arguments for mitigating circumstances on the basis of what they deemed to be judicial British prejudice against their local Arab clients.

The existence of widely accepted cultural narratives does not preclude individual narration, and individual stories vary in the degree to which they correspond to collective stories. Yet individual experience is mediated, configured and interpreted through culturally pervasive narratives. Some narratives stand in oppositional relation to others, as in the case of 'counter-narratives' or 'subversive stories' produced by marginal social players, such as victims.[43]

## Corpus and Method

This study is based on a corpus of 147 Mandate Palestine sex offence court cases. The civil court system that was established in Palestine after the official pronouncement of the Mandate in 1922 held orderly documented proceedings from its inception. Unfortunately, much of the earlier documentation does not survive today. The earliest court file in my corpus is from 1933 (in comparison, newspaper articles on sex offences date back as far as the Ottoman era). As Palestine's British administrators were avid recyclers of paper, it is quite possible that the pages of early files were re-used. Court transcripts were often typed on the blank sides of older documents such as administrative reports or other court files. On a few occasions I found indictments from the 1930s on the reverse sides of pages in a 1940s-era file. After the State of Israel was established in 1948, most existing Mandate court files did not survive the transfer to the

[43] Davis, 15–16.

new administration, apparently through disorder and neglect. However, I was able to locate files pertinent to my study at the Israel Archives, most of them from the Haifa District Court. Most of these materials had not yet been catalogued and were being made available to researchers for the first time.

The files of criminal cases heard in the Haifa court between 1939 and 1948 are largely intact and provide a comprehensive and systematic picture of the Haifa district during that period. The statements and testimony in these files, given by diverse social actors, form a valuable archival register for the study of plausibility. These materials reflect both the hegemonic, regulatory and labelling perspective of the rulers and the perspective of those who were tried, examined and labelled, containing the voices not only of the judiciary but also those of the accused, victims and witnesses.

The sex offence cases I discuss in this book were typically initiated by complaint to the police, who then conducted an investigation. The charges and the resulting investigatory materials were brought before a local magistrate who held a preliminary inquiry and decided whether a case should be tried at the district level.[44] Offences punishable by more than three years' imprisonment (most sex offences[45]) were sent on for trial in the district courts, and offences meriting lesser punishment were tried by the magistrate.[46] The witnesses in these cases thus gave a triple account: to the police, to the magistrate and to the district court. Some of the criminal files examined for this book contain materials from each procedural stage (the statements to the police were submitted at the preliminary investigation, the records of the latter were frequently submitted at trial and attached to the district court file, and the transcript of the district court proceeding was customarily attached to appeals to the Supreme Court). Statements made during the course of a police investigation, a preliminary inquiry or a trial were recorded by agents of social authority, whether police investigators, magistrates or judges, and reflect hegemonic conventions in terms of content, format and style. In addition, the different speakers (e.g. suspects, witnesses, lawyers or judges) might tailor their stories in accordance with their own interests. Their statements therefore should not be taken at face value but should be read carefully. Nevertheless, differences between speakers, individual modes of expression and idiosyncrasies are on vivid display, and it is clear that these texts reflect not just the

[44] An Ordinance to Regulate the Procedure in Criminal Cases within the Jurisdiction of the Court of Criminal Assize or of the District Court, Art. 3 (1924), An Ordinance to Regulate the Procedure in Criminal Cases within the Jurisdiction of the Court of Criminal Assize or of the District Court [1 September 1924], § 13.

[45] Rape and sodomy (fifteen years maximum imprisonment), rape by deception (ten years), attempted rape (seven years), illicit relation with unmarried girl (five years) and indecent act with force or upon a child (five years).

[46] An Ordinance Relating to the Constitution and Jurisdiction of Certain Courts in Palestine [1 September 1924], § 11(3). Offences punishable by death (a penalty that did not apply to any sex offence) were under the jurisdiction of the Court of Criminal Assizes, and the Supreme Court, as a High Court for Justice, could direct criminal cases to the Assizes. Ibid., § 10.

hegemonic authoritative perspective but also an array of social meanings and interpretations. Reflected in the primary sources are the perceptions of those from 'above' (the legislators and holders of judicial office) and those from 'below' (members of the local population), providing insight into the way each group viewed the other. In addition to presenting perspectives from 'above' and from 'below', the court files provide readers with an opportunity to reconstruct the voices of participants of different genders, ethnic communities, nationalities and social statuses.

The little scholarly work focused on sex offences in Mandate Palestine (most of it concerned with male-on-male sex) has so far completely failed to address the viewpoints of Arab subjects. Since most of the accused and many of the witnesses in the cases I examined were Arabs,[47] this book offers an opportunity to redress this neglect by reconstructing their voices. Beyond this particular contribution, examining plausibility in the context of these court files promotes more general understanding of the operation of proof and of persuasion 'in action'.

Additional sources used in this research included files from the Haganah Archives, the Central Zionist Archives, autobiographies and, most significantly, contemporary press accounts. While the Hebrew press often referred to sexual offences, the subject was not discussed in the contemporary Arab press.

## Book Outline

The first chapter of this study lays out the legal background relating to proof of sexual offences in Mandate Palestine. It describes preceding Ottoman Law and the British ordinances that gradually restructured the definitions and legal treatment of sexual offences as well as the relevant British legislation in the area of criminal evidence.

Subsequent chapters explore the notion of plausibility in relation to Mandate-era legal regulation of sexual conduct. The complex interaction between the elements that constitute plausibility provides the answers to questions like the following: What made a certain account a wrong story to tell? What depictions of sexual offences made sense? What were the prototypical narratives and who were the stock characters? How were stories about sex offences told outside the court? Were they different from those told inside? What role did emotional expression play in the narration of sexual offences? Did certain emotions need to be restrained and others expressed to convey a plausible story? Does it matter who told a story or to whom or about whom the story was told? Were the constitutive elements of plausibility embedded in

[47] According to statistical reports of the Mandate authorities, in the first half of 1943 all those who were tried in the District Court for sex offences were Muslims. In the Magistrate courts, of 102 persons convicted and sentenced, 21 were Jews, 70 were Muslims and 11 were Christians. *General Monthly Bulletin of Current Statistics*, Vol. VIII No. 5–10 1943, ISA/M/5302/9.

formal evidentiary mechanisms? The answers to these questions involve legal considerations, cultural narratives, the mediation of lawyers with their distinct occupational narratives and references to the identities of the participants in the discourse.

Plausibility hinges on the compatibility of a narrative with culturally rooted prototypical perceptions of how the world operates. Cultural narratives underlying the process of proof make some factual accounts the wrong stories to tell and other storylines seem right. Chapter 2 examines the cultural narratives underlying the process of proof through the lens of male-on-male sexual offences. The British criminalized both forceful and consensual sex between males. Analysis of the charges and testimonies in the cases that were tried in Palestine courts exposes recurring narratives of male sex and sheds light on socio-cultural perceptions of male sexuality. It reveals that despite the allegedly novel distinction drawn by the British between forced sodomy and consensual sex, the same prototypical narrative of an older and more affluent man penetrating a younger and poorer one underpinned court cases brought for both offences. Furthermore, notwithstanding the ambition of the British to fight the depraved morals of their 'Eastern' subjects, analysis of plausible narratives shows that their perception of male sex was more similar to local perceptions than they cared to admit. The plausible scenario for both locals and the British included a distinction between penetrating and penetrated partners and the association of these sexual roles with social status.

Plausibility cannot be detached from the identity of the witness who makes a factual claim, the issue taken up in Chapter 3. Judges routinely assess witnesses' credibility without making a distinction between individual criteria (such as skills of perception, interest in the result of the case, record of fraud and perjury, conflicting evidence, etc.) and the characteristics of the social category to which the witness belongs (gender, socio-economic status, occupation, ethnicity, race, etc.). In identifying a witness as a member of a certain social category the latter attributes also delineate the plausible roles, forms and content of interactions and the lines of action available to that witness. A witness's societal attributes help constitute the plausibility of his or her testimony. Inherent in such social constructions are potential stereotypes and bias that might colour the assessment of credibility. Chapter 3 explores the treatment of the child witness in Mandate sex offence cases to demonstrate how such constructions can tint the plausibility and consequently undermine the credibility of the very individuals legislation aimed to protect. The British colonial authorities explicitly purported to protect children from sexual assault. Children were competent witnesses. The oath requirement was relaxed with respect to children, so they were permitted to tell their stories even when they did not understand the meaning of oath-taking. Nonetheless, analysis of the evidentiary and substantive mechanisms in action reveals lingering suspicion towards the testimony of children. This chapter highlights three areas in which this suspicion surfaced: the preconditions of oath-taking, perjury charges against children and inquiry into the sexual past of child complainants, and it examines how the image of a vulnerable, innocent and violated child coexisted with the image of a fabricating, unreliable and seductive being. It demonstrates how, through evidentiary mechanisms, narratives articulated by child witnesses were constructed as less plausible.

The 'rightness' or 'wrongness' of a story turned not only on the identity of the narrator, but also on that of the story's audience. The study of plausibility inquires into the reason a story is told, by whom and to whom. A story tailored by lawyers to influence fact finders concerned with an alleged crime may be different from a newspaper story about the same crime. Chapters 4–6 explore the link between plausibility and ethnic and national identity in the context of narrator–listener interactions. These chapters not only explore a myriad of 'above' and 'below' perspectives on ethnic identity and sexual offences but also consider how the different social players viewed each other. Chapter 4 outlines stories of sex offences as told by British judges, Arab lawyers and the Hebrew press. The British strategy in criminal proceedings was to downplay the significance of participants' ethnic origin. Nevertheless, occasional derogatory remarks sometimes slipped into the British facade of neutrality and betrayed prejudice against Palestinian natives. The Arab press mostly ignored the subject of sexual crimes. In the courts, however, Arab defendants and defence witnesses, unlike witnesses for the prosecution, used ethnic labels. Arab defence lawyers sometimes tried to sway British judges by portraying the ethnicity of their clients as a mitigating circumstance (thus trying to manipulate possible prejudices of the judges).

The Hebrew press often reported on Arab sex offenders and seems to have fluctuated between avoiding sensational coverage of inter-ethnic sexual assaults, so as not to inflame political tensions, and portraying Arabs as sexually aggressive, especially dangerous to young boys or young female Jewish immigrants. Press accounts reinforced the plausibility that sex offences had a clear ethnic character. These accounts marked boundaries between the Jewish and Arab communities and reinforced a separation that was not only symbolic but also physical.

The manner in which a story is told also has a bearing on its plausibility. The emotions that accompany stories enfold socially constructed knowledge and can enhance or detract from their factual plausibility. Silence and other non-verbal expression can also send messages and convey emotions. Preceding the question of what is a wrong or a right story to tell is the question of whether a story should even be told at all and, if so, to whom. Chapter 5 focuses on the Jewish community and tracks untold stories about sex offences, stories that were never uttered or that were conveyed through actions rather than words. In examining how muted or non-verbal expression conveys emotions intrinsic to 'plausible' plots, I consider two contexts: the making of sexual offence complaints and acts of revenge. Shame is salient in the former context, anger in the latter.

Compared to Arabs, Jewish victims were less forthcoming with complaints about sexual assault, most noticeably within their own community. In examining why rape was a 'wrong' story for Jewish victims to tell authorities, Chapter 5 describes how silence constructed the shame that befell such victims and how this silence fortified ethnic borders. This chapter further scrutinizes a few yet horrifying acts of revenge carried out by representatives of the Jewish community against Arabs suspected of raping Jewish women. Acts expressing extreme anger sent a powerful symbolic message defining the meaning of inter-ethnic rape and were aimed at reinforcing the boundaries between the Jewish and Arab communities. Non-verbal acts, this chapter demonstrates, were significant rhetorical tools expressing emotions that were integral to 'plausible' stories about sexual assaults. Without using words or any official channels, those acts sent a powerful message from 'below'.

The rules of evidence delineate a formal method of proof. Chapter 6 takes up the rule of corroboration to illustrate the embeddedness of social perceptions of plausible scenarios in formal evidentiary standards. When proving sex offences in Mandate Palestine, it was not enough for complainants to be believable or credible; their testimony had to be supported by corroborating evidence. Underlying the demand for corroboration were social notions of plausible and implausible scenarios of sexual assaults. The demand for corroboration was not optional, triggered when an individual's credibility was in doubt; it applied to every complainant in every case of sexual assault, down to the most believable. Inherent in the rule of corroboration was the presumption that certain categories of witnesses were untrustworthy (females and children, especially 'natives'). Chapter 6 recounts how this evidentiary rule operated in constructing social and cultural credibility. The rule of corroboration reflected existing attitudes that many sexual assault complaints were implausible, and it also perpetuated those attitudes, by rendering convictions based on the testimony of witnesses from suspicious social categories very hard to obtain. In addition, the rule of corroboration was also a rhetorical device that allowed the judiciary to distinguish itself from the social categories that should not be believed or trusted.

Finally, Chapter 7 traces the boundaries of the plausible by invoking the implausible. It examines counter-narratives that the judiciary readily dismissed, focusing in particular on a 1933 rape case and reconstructing the hidden transcripts alluded to by Arab defence attorneys who challenged British superiority through substantive, evidentiary and procedural claims, neatly tailored in accordance with the conventions of common law. Beneath the facade of a criminal trial ran an undercurrent of stories about national identity that were utterly irrelevant to the judicial issues at hand. The chapter demonstrates that the concept of plausibility is relevant not only to the content of factual accounts but also to beliefs about the essence of the justice system.

In addition to the 'above' perspective of the judges and the 'below' perspective of the defendants, victims and other members of their social world, this chapter highlights the position of Arab lawyers as cultural intermediaries who sublimated tones of resistance into conventional common-law arguments. Those lawyers, located between the poles of 'above' and 'below', were acquainted with both worlds and could employ their skills as cultural translators to further their own aims.

*Plausible Crime Stories* employs plausibility as an analytic tool for studying the law 'in action' and, more specifically, the socially constructed character of the process of proof. The plausible story is an outcome of the interplay between law and culture, and it is predicated on communal perceptions of the legal system and legal proceedings as well as on accepted standards of normality and deviance, gender, morality, nationality, ethnicity, age, religion and other cultural institutions. Through the study of primary sources, the plausible story emerges as a missing link in the social study of law, since it provides important insights into the social embeddedness of proof and the constitution of evidentiary meaning in the courtroom.

# 1

# Legal Background

The British completed their military occupation of Palestine in 1918, during the waning days of the First World War. When the European powers divided the Middle East among themselves in post-war agreements, Britain took possession of Palestine (including what was later sectioned off as Transjordan) and Iraq, which were not defined as colonies but as 'mandates', supervised by the League of Nations.[1] Although the stated goal of the mandate system was eventual self-rule, the British maintained military, political, legal and administrative control of Palestine until 1948; from 1921 on, responsibility for its governance lay with the Colonial Office.[2] The two formal legal instruments constituting British rule, the League of Nations Mandate for Palestine and the British Palestine Order in Council, were promulgated in 1922.[3] The British transformed the territory's existing Ottoman legal system into a semblance of the common-law model, resulting in Anglicization qualified by Islamic and French elements.[4] Article 46 of the Palestine Order in Council limited the application of English common law and provided that it 'be in force so far only as the circumstances of Palestine and its inhabitants and the limits of His Majesty's jurisdiction permit and subject to such qualification as local circumstances render necessary'. The British refrained from implementing the jury trial, a key element of the English system, whose adoption would have entrusted local subjects with the power to influence judicial decisions. In addition, the evidence law they adopted did not directly apply common-law rules or follow the Indian Evidence Act of 1872 but, instead, retained some Ottoman arrangements.

The structure of the Ottoman court system was largely perpetuated, including the millet system, which endowed the religious courts with jurisdiction over matters of personal status (most notably, marriage and divorce).[5]

[1] Laura Robson, *Colonialism and Christianity in Mandate Palestine* (Austin: University of Texas Press 2011), 6. About the legal architecture of this new mode of sovereignty see Natasha Wheatley, 'Mandatory Interpretation: Legal Hermeneutics and the New International Order in Arab and Jewish Petitions to the League of Nations', *Past & Present* 227, no. 1 (2015): 209–12.

[2] John Strawson, *Partitioning Palestine: Legal Fundamentalism in the Palestinian-Israeli Conflict* (London: Pluto Press, 2010), 42.

[3] Ibid., chapter 2.

[4] Assaf Likhovski, *Law and Identity in Mandate Palestine*, ed. Thomas A. Green and Hendrik Hartog, Studies in Legal History (Chapel Hill: University of North Carolina Press, 2006), 23.

[5] On the structure and jurisdiction of the court system, see Part V of the Palestine Order in Council.

Preservation of precolonial legal structures was consistent with an imperial strategy of non-interference with the status quo as a means of forestalling local resentment and disobedience.[6] Two tiers of secular courts heard civil and criminal matters. Lower courts had jurisdiction over petty criminal and civil cases, and district courts handled more serious criminal and civil matters and heard appeals of lower court decisions. The Supreme Court in Jerusalem heard appeals taken from the districts, sitting in a tribunal that initially included at least two senior British judges, later reduced to one.[7] Capital crimes (no sexual offence was punishable by death) were under the jurisdiction of the Court of Criminal Assize. Certain judgments of the Supreme Court in civil matters could be reviewed by the Privy Council in London.

## Legal Background

When the British occupied Palestine in 1918, they found the territory governed by a legal system substantially different from their own. As part of the *Tanzimat* administrative reforms initiated in the middle of the nineteenth century, the Ottoman Empire had adopted modern legislation (a Penal Code, a Commercial Code and Codes of Civil and Criminal Procedure) based on the *Code Napoléon*.[8] This system was applied throughout the empire. The *Tanzimat* reforms aimed to centralize administration through modern standardized bureaucracy. Changes to criminal law echoed the principles of centralized law enforcement. An activist 'nanny state' took it upon itself to prosecute and punish perpetrators and control interactions between offenders and victims.[9] A penal code was introduced in 1840 and revised twice, in 1851 and 1858.[10] The 1858 Ottoman Penal Code (hereafter OPC) was largely a translation of the French code, yet it retained some Muslim principles.[11] Revised twice (in 1911 and 1914), it remained in effect until 1918.

Most sexual offences were grouped in Part III of the OPC, which, as its title states, 'sets forth the punishment for persons who violate honour'.[12] Honour, the key concept underlying this part of the OPC, focuses attention on the violation of social norms rather than the physical or emotional injury caused to the victim. The violation here was framed in terms of the damage done to the

[6] Robson, 48.

[7] An Ordinance Relating to the Constitution and Jurisdiction of Certain Courts in Palestine, Art. 3 (1924, revised 1935).

[8] Norman Bentwich, 'The New Criminal Code for Palestine', *Journal of Comparative Legislation and International Law* 20, no. 1 (1938): 71. The Islam-inspired Ottoman civil code, the *Mejelle*, which set evidentiary rules for civil matters, however, was influenced by Islamic principles. Omri Paz, 'Crime, Criminals, and the Ottoman State: Anatolia between the Late 1830s and the Late 1860s' (Ph.D. diss., Tel Aviv University, 2010), 67.

[9] Paz, 67. [10] Ibid., 18.

[11] Payment of blood money to the victim's kin (*Diyet*) was one such principle. Bentwich, 71.

[12] All references in the text to the OPC are to John A. Strarchey Bucknill and Haig Apisoghom S. Utidjian's English translation of the last revised version.

victim's honour, but it may also have implied a stain on the offender's honour, caused by transgression of the social code of honour. Part III spells out sanctions for sexual assaults, and yet it uses expurgated language; words such as 'rape', 'sex' and 'intercourse' do not appear, the pertinent clauses referring simply to 'abominable acts' without specifying what they consist of. Individual clauses prohibit 'abominable acts' with minors younger than fifteen (Art. 197), an 'abominable act' committed or attempted by force (Art. 198), an 'abominable act' committed against children by instructors, guardians or their employees (Art. 199), an 'abominable act' with an unmarried girl or deprivation of virginity (Art. 200), exposure of young persons to obscenities and adultery (Art. 201)[13] and commission of an 'abominable act' in public (Art. 202).[14] Other clauses relating to sex or reproduction are article 139, which, inter alia, prohibits the printing and publication of 'indecent pictures or images', articles 192 and 193, which bar abortions, and article 206, which specifies different types of abductions, including abduction of a girl or married woman subsequently subjected to an 'abominable act'.

The British presented themselves as the protectors of women and children in the land entrusted to their care by the League of Nations mandate, although their aspiration to enact reforms to safeguard these groups was consciously constrained by consideration of local norms and customs.[15] The British regulated matters such as child labour and child marriage[16] and also expressed their ideology in their criminal legislation. Part of their 'civilizing' mission was to institute a new regime to regulate sexuality, distinguished from the Ottoman one in its reflection of British values, as manifested in its legal terminology and categories pertaining to sex offences. Whereas the Ottomans had categorized sex offenders as 'persons who violate honour',[17] the British framed them as perpetrators of 'offences against women and children and against decency'[18] and, later, of 'offences against morality'.[19]

The British administration deemed the Ottoman criminal law outdated and unsatisfactory. In the words of Norman Bentwich, Mandate Palestine's first attorney-general, 'the Ottoman Code was not a suitable instrument of

[13] The article distinguishes between an adulterous woman, her partner and an adulterous husband. For a married woman, any extra-marital sexual relationship constituted an offence. The punishment for her partner was less severe if he himself was a married man (the article does not discuss a wife's extra-marital sex with another woman). Under this article, a husband committed adultery only if he had extra-marital sex with a woman in the residence he and his wife shared (sex with another man, therefore, did not establish an offence of adultery).

[14] In addition to the general prohibition, the last article specifies two types of illicit conduct that seem culturally embedded: a man's entry into a woman's residence wearing female attire, and forcing a woman to dance in open places such as vineyards and gardens or allowing her to do so voluntarily.

[15] Likhovski, 85–86. [16] Ibid., 13, chapter 4.

[17] Part III of the OPC '[s]ets forth the punishment for persons who violate honour'.

[18] Criminal Law Amendment Ordinance No. 2 1927 (hereinafter: CLAO).

[19] Title of Chapter XVII of the Criminal Code Ordinance 1936 (hereafter CCO). The CCO was published in September 1936 and went into effect in February 1937. Bentwich.

justice'.[20] Specifically referring to sexual offences, the High Commissioner, Herbert Samuel, stated that 'the defects of the existing [Ottoman] law are glaring and uncontroversial'.[21] The British prided themselves on bestowing on the inhabitants of the country the precious gift of British law.[22] Yet it was only in 1936 that the Mandate government promulgated comprehensive criminal law. Up to that point, the British had modified the substantive law, amending the Ottoman criminal law through a series of ordinances addressing particular issues of concern. Sexual offences were among the first issues targeted by these ordinances.

In 1927 the British fashioned many prohibitions related to prostitution and brothels, defined categories of more and less severe sexual assaults (rape and forcible and non-forcible indecent acts) and distinguished between 'rape' and 'sodomy'.[23] Instead of the cleansed term 'abominable act', the British used the words 'intercourse', 'rape' and 'sodomy'. Rape was deemed a form of 'unlawful sexual intercourse'. This phrasing portrayed rape as a sexual act and emphasized its unlawfulness rather than its violation of honour, thus hinting that some instances of forcible sexual intercourse might not be regarded as unlawful and therefore constitute criminal offences. Some of the same elements are present in both the Ottoman Penal Code and the British amendment, for example, the prohibition of sexual contact with children (which constituted an offence notwithstanding consent or lack of physical force),[24] children's sexual exploitation by guardians,[25] sexual contact with an unmarried girl[26] and obtaining sex by deception.[27]

[20] Ibid., 71. Bentwich was the legal secretary to the British military administration in Palestine in 1918, and when the mandatory government was established in 1922 he became Palestine's first attorney-general, serving until 1929. Walter Zander, rev. Robert Brown, 'Bentwich, Norman De Mattos (1883–1971)', *Oxford Dictionary of National Biography* (2004), www.oxforddnb.com /view/article/30811.

[21] Secret letter dated 1 April 1925, to L. S. Amery, Secretary of State for the Colonies, TNA: CO 733/92, p. 3.

[22] In the words of Sir William Fitzgerald, the last British chief justice of Palestine: 'Britain's greatest contribution to the science of the government of man is British law and British legal procedure. . . . I do not hesitate to mention that the one thing they shall forever be grateful for, namely, that we have given to them our ideas of British law.' Cited by Martin Bunton, 'Inventing the Status Quo: Ottoman Land-Law During the Palestine Mandate, 1917–1936', *The International History Review* 21, no. 1 (1999): 32.

[23] Except for the numbering (89 instead of 3) the phrasing of the sections pertaining to sex offences was not modified when CLAO was amended by Criminal Law Amendment Ordinance No. 30 1934 (also referred hereinafter as CLAO). § 89(a) & (b) of CLAO.

[24] OPC Art. 197 relates to '[w]hoever does the abominable act to a child who has not completed the age of fifteen years', § 89(c)of the CLAO targets any person who 'has unlawful sexual intercourse or commits an act of sodomy with a child under the age of sixteen years'.

[25] Art. 199 of the OPC targets the 'the instructors or guardians of the victims over whom they have authority or on the part of their salaried servants' who commit an 'abominable act'. § 92 of the CLAO prohibits an illicit relationship with an unmarried girl aged sixteen to twenty-one, who is a man's 'descendant or the descendant of his wife, or his ward, or has been entrusted to him for the purpose of education or supervision'.

[26] Art. 199 of the OPC (which specifies the use of force) and the consensual sex prohibited by the above-mentioned § 92 of the CLA.

[27] Art. 200 of the OPC targeted the tempting of a virgin by false marriage promises, and § 90 of the CLA established rape where the consent of the woman was obtained through deception, threats or exploitation of her mental state.

The British had expressed concerns about the amendment of the Ottoman norms. In November 1925, the High Commissioner appointed a committee to consider proposed amendments to existing Ottoman sexual offences and further measures to implement international conventions against the trafficking of women and children.[28] The committee, which was headed by Thomas Wagstaffe Haycraft, the Chief Justice of Palestine (1921–1927), included such British officials as Colonel Arthur Stephen Mavrogordato, Chief Commander of the Palestine Police,[29] Colonel G. W. Heron, Director of the administration health department,[30] Humphrey Bowman, Director of Education in Palestine,[31] and Margaret Nixon, Government Welfare Inspector.[32] It also included two local members: Chicago-born Martha Spafford Vester, the founder of an orphanage that would later become a children's hospital,[33] and Dr Helena Kagan, the Jewish head of the paediatrics department at the Rothschild-Hadassah hospital in Jerusalem.[34] There were no Arab committee members. The committee's report expresses explicit concern about interfering with existing norms through criminal legislation. The proposed legislation was considered possibly 'so advanced as to be difficult to put into practice satisfactorily, even if administered by agents of exceptional quality'. The report further expresses concern that the regulation of prostitution contradicted the goal of suppressing brothels. Nevertheless, the committee supported amendment of the OPC.

A few months earlier, in a detailed memorandum, Sir Gerard Leslie Makins Clauson, a civil servant at the Colonial Office, had pointed to some possible paradoxical outcomes of the proposed amendment:[35]

> It is proposed to introduce into Palestine the rigid laws regarding ordinary copulation which apply in this country with additional elaboration. At the same time, it is not proposed to make sodomy an offence unless committed with a person under the age of 16 or unwilling. The natural assumption is that if copulation is so much discouraged sodomy will proportionately flourish.
>
> It is more for the High commissioner than for us to say whether sodomy is such a national institution that it must be permitted to continue, but personally I should have thought that the proper course was to make it illegal & gradually to wean the population to less unnatural practices. If this step is considered too drastic then clearly what for the want of a better word may be described as 'male

28 A report from December 1925, submitted by the committee members to the High Commissioner. TNA: CO 733–113.

29 http://cosmos.ucc.ie/cs1064/jabowen/IPSC/php/authors.php?auid=23100.

30 Nick Reynold, *Britain's Unfulfilled Mandate for Palestine* (Lanham, MD: Lexington Books, 2014), 81.

31 'Humphrey Bowman Collection' (PDF). *Middle East Centre*. St Antony's College, Oxford, www.sant.ox.ac.uk/mec/MEChandlists/Bowman-Collection.pdf.

32 Likhovski, 218. 33 www.spaffordcenter.org/history.

34 http://jwa.org/encyclopedia/article/kagan-helena.

35 Memorandum dated 31 May 1925, TNA: CO 733–113.

brothels' must be subject to the same disabilities as the ordinary variety, or the disgruntled brothel keepers will go into a still more unsavoury line of business.

Incidentally bestiality is not even touched upon, though in certain classes of Moslem society (particularly the nomadic tribes) it is almost as much a national institution as sodomy. It may have been left out, because it would be practically impossible to suppress it. This is probably the case.

Regulating 'ordinary copulation', namely, heterosexual sex, through restrictions on prostitution or sex with children, Clausen fears, might result in the flourishing of sodomy, which was not criminalized by the British at this stage unless committed with children younger than sixteen. A scholar of Turkish philological studies,[36] Clausen leaves it to Palestine's High Commissioner to determine whether sex between men is a local 'national institution' that ought not be interfered with. Although he favours uprooting sodomy, he advises caution and gradual change. The local population has to be 'weaned' to 'less unnatural' sexual practices, a choice of words redolent of colonial distinctions, as it implies the local population's infantile addiction to corrupt physical pleasures and uncontrollable urges, completely opposed to British rationality, maturity, restraint and superiority. Implicit in Clauson's words is the identification of sodomy with the Muslim population.

Consensual male sex and bestiality were criminalized a decade later in the 1936 Criminal Code, but the road travelled by the Code before it reached Palestine was full of twists and turns. The bill was formed after the Code chosen for the East African colonies and protectorates, which, in turn, was derived from the Queensland Criminal Code Act, 1899. The Queensland Code was adopted by Northern Nigeria in 1904 and in 1916 was applied to the rest of country under British rule. This version became the basis for the East African Code. A draft version of the East African Code was endorsed in Cyprus (a Crown Colony in which the Ottoman Code had been replaced by an English model) in 1928. The Cypriot version of the Code was followed in Palestine[37] but was amended 'to bring it into conformity with' local 'conditions and requirements'.[38]

Michael McDonnell (1882–1956), the Chief Justice of Palestine between 1927 and 1936, consulted with fellow judges of the Supreme Court and District Courts and one experienced judge of the lower instance on the proposed draft of a comprehensive Code.[39] McDonnell compiled the comments of his fellow

[36] Clifford Edmund Bosworth, 'Gerard Leslie Makins Clauson', in *A Century of British Orientalists 1902–2001*, ed. Clifford Edmund Bosworth (Oxford: Oxford University Press, 2001), 90–93.

[37] Bentwich, 72; Yoram Shachar, 'The Origins of the Criminal Code, 1936', *Iyunei Mishpat* 7 (1979): 75.

[38] A letter dated 1 June 1929 from the High Commissioner to the Secretary of State. ISA/RG 2/M/265/7.

[39] In a letter dated 7 March 1929, Chief Justice McDonnell conveys the remarks made by the British judges. He mentions that he invited Palestinian judges to provide comments, but they had not delivered them as yet. ISA/RG 2/M/265/7.

jurists and delivered them to the High Commissioner for his consideration. He suggested preserving the provisions of the Criminal Law Amendment, 1927, subject to a few changes; for instance, he recommended against importing the Cypriot offence of bestiality. McDonnell reasoned that '[t]his constitutes a new offence in Palestine. Bestiality, as far as I am aware, is not prevalent in this country, and to insert it in the Code might lead to blackmailing charges.' As to the enactment of a prohibition against sodomy, McDonnell described the conflicting attitudes of his fellow judges:[40]

> The clause as it stands assimilates the law to that of England. Judge Kermack states that he thinks the chance of making false charges given by this clause is probably greater than the good that might be done by it.
>
> Judge Copland, on the other hand, considers that it is time that something should be done to stop the offence of sodomy which is appallingly rife, so he states, in his District amongst all classes. He writes that he has tried 40 cases of this offence or attempt to commit it last year. Others with longer experience than I have of the East will say whether there is a danger of legislating in advance of public opinion.[41]

McDonnell postulates that a better balance between progressive British legislation and local norms might be suggested by others with longer experience of 'the East'. His choice of the word 'East' insinuates not only an array of ideas about the Orient, 'its sensuality, its tendency to despotism, its aberrant mentality, its habits of inaccuracy, its backwardness',[42] but also a hierarchical distinction between the British and their Palestinian subjects. The judges' contradictory attitudes toward the regulation of sodomy reveal manifold tensions regarding the inexplicable and shadowy 'East', seen as a land of uncontrolled sexuality expressed in 'appallingly rife' deviancy and a place whose occupants – deceitful, extortion-minded and of undeveloped mentality – were prone to make illicit use of the precious gift of British law. The redefinition of sexual offences allowed the British to present themselves as the protectors of women and children and the bearers of high moral values, a manoeuvre of substantial declaratory value, both for British and international public opinion and for the local community.[43]

In short, the British made explicit declarations about revolutionizing the regulation of sexual offences and about the need to take local norms and

[40] McDonnell's letter to the High Commissioner dated 7 March 1929, p. 3, ISA/RG 2/M/265/7. The letter contains remarks regarding the suggested criminal code. Islamic texts regarded consensual homosexual practices as transgressive, but it was debatable whether they were punishable under Ottoman law. The OPC, however, criminalized sexual violence and the abuse of minors. Dror Zeevi, 'Changes in Legal-Sexual Discourses: Sex Crimes in the Ottoman Empire', *Continuity and Change* 16, no. 2 (2001): 226.

[41] McDonnell's letter, p. 12. In his memoirs, Judge Kermack, who was also consulted, cited his frustration at not being appointed to the District Court as the reason for his decision to leave Palestine in 1930. Bunton, 38.

[42] Edward W. Said, *Orientalism* (New York: Vintage Books, 1979), 205.

[43] On the British use of progressive legislation for international, domestic and local political purposes, see Likhovski, chapter 4.

conditions into account. The two most significant changes to substantive law were the criminalization of consensual sex between males[44] and the repeal of the gender-neutral commission of an 'abominable act'.[45] Instead, the British introduced the two separate and distinct offences of 'sodomy' (committed with 'any person') and rape (committed on a female).[46] Regardless of recurring policy statements about reluctance to interfere with local norms and customs, the new legislation seems to have followed standard English and colonial patterns. The legal ban on homosexuality was a long-standing British norm,[47] and same-sex sexual activity, consensual or not, was criminalized across the colonies of the British Empire.[48] Nonetheless, a novel feature that was introduced in colonial Cyprus and Palestine was the distinction between forceful and consensual sex between males, the former carrying a heavier punishment than the latter, as I discuss in detail in the next chapter.[49] In contemporary England there was no distinction between consensual adult sex and forced male sex or sex with children. All these acts were covered by a single offence, sodomy, and carried the same punishment.

## Evidence

Historiography of the British Empire has emphasized the grafting of substantive rather than procedural norms onto local legal systems.[50] Yet the criminal law prohibitions present only part of the picture, and one also needs to take into consideration both the rules of evidence and procedure that underlie proof of offences and the level of enforcement by the authorities. Evidentiary standards that are extremely hard to meet and lack of enforcement may render penal sections theoretical constructs – existing on the books but not in action.

44 § 152(2)(c) of the CCO.

45 Article 198 of the OPC reads as follows: 'If a man does the abominable act to a person, that is to say violates his honour, by force he is placed in kyurek temporarily.' Küreks were the Ottoman penal hard labour camps. The main purpose of this phrasing may have been to avoid the discussion of same-sex relations; see Dror Zeevi, *Producing Desire: Changing Sexual Discourse in the Ottoman Middle East, 1500–1900* (Berkeley: University of California Press, 2006), 73.

46 Section 2 of the CLAO repealed articles 197–200 and 202 of the OPC; the remaining articles continued to coexist until the enactment of the 1936 CCO.

47 Same-sex sexual activity was outlawed long before the Victorian Criminal Law Amendment Act, 1885, which set forth various categories of sex offences. The roots of the prohibition date back to a 1533 Henrician statute adopted around the eighteenth century to criminalize homosexual activity. Harry G. Cocks, *Nameless Offences: Homosexual Desire in the Nineteenth Century* (London: I. B. Tauris, 2003), 17.

48 Michael Kirby, 'The Sodomy Offence: England's Least Lovely Criminal Law Export?', *Journal of Commonwealth Criminal Law* 1, no. 1 (2011): 28.

49 §§ 152(1) & (2) CCO, §§ 157, 158, 160 of The Cyprus Criminal Code Order in Council, 1928. The terminology and punishments in the Cypriot provisions are different from the Palestinian, but the statutory distinction and the structure of the prohibitions are similar.

50 An outstanding exception is the work of Binyamin Blum. Binyamin Blum, 'Evidence Rules and Colonial Difference(s): Reexamining the Complexities and Lessons of Legal Grafting', in *Paper presented at the Mandate Law Research Group* (Berg Institution of Law and History, Tel Aviv University, 2011), 4.

Criminal procedure and evidence in Palestine had been controlled by the 1858 Code of Criminal Procedure, replicated from the French code.[51] The *Mejelle,* the Ottoman code of obligations, governed civil matters.[52] By 1918, criminal cases in the Ottoman Empire were not subject to the two-eyewitness requirement[53] and did not require corroboration. To weed out unreliable witnesses, the Ottomans relied heavily on the concept of competency.[54]

Despite the condescending approach of the British towards Ottoman law, they did not forsake it altogether. Sensitivity to local distinctiveness and idiosyncrasies and reverence for the status quo were explicit principles of British legislation in Mandate Palestine. The British kept in mind that local Muslim inhabitants might be offended should they discard the *Mejelle,* which was based on Islamic principles.[55] Unless explicitly repealed, Ottoman legislation (both civil and criminal) remained in effect.[56] However, in comparison with 'substantive' norms, procedure and evidence are typically perceived as more technical and neutral in nature, and thus relatively easier to modify and replace. Amending the law of evidence, in particular, was regarded by the British as necessary and urgent for the administration of justice.[57] They gradually replaced Ottoman legislation with a series of ordinances pertaining to procedure and evidence.[58] Although the *Mejelle* did not control criminal matters, its principles were sometimes referred to in the criminal context. The Evidence Ordinance controlled both civil and criminal proceedings, which may account for some confusion. The Evidence Ordinance did not set out to replace the entire Ottoman statutory arrangement and contained only

[51] Richard Volger, *A World View of Criminal Justice* (Aldershot, UK: Ashgate, 2005), 116.

[52] Although the *Mejelle* was based on Islamic law, it was still part of an effort to craft a modern and centralized system of law, and it sometimes diverged from Islamic principles. For example, it considered the testimony of non-Muslims acceptable. Blum, 10–11.

[53] L. Sebba, 'The Requirement of Corroboration in Sex Offences', *Israel Law Review* 3 (1968): 75.

[54] Article 146 of the Ottoman Criminal Procedure Code provided that '[t]he accused person's ascendants, descendants, brothers, sisters, collaterals in the same degree, wife or husband, even when divorced, cannot be called or heard as witnesses, but the admission of their evidence is not a ground for quashing the case when neither the prosecutor, the civil claimant or the accused have taken objection to the evidence being heard'. The English translation of this article appears in S. G. Kermack, *A Handbook of the Law of Criminal Procedure in Palestine* (Jerusalem: Tarbuth, 1928), 131.

[55] Letter from High Commissioner Herbert Samuel to Duke of Devonshire, 28 February 1923. ISA/RG 2/M/8/17: 'the matter is one requiring great care and deliberation because of the strong feeling of the Moslem population for the maintenance of the Rules of Evidence in the Ottoman Civil Code which are based upon the Moslem Religious Law'.

[56] Article 46 of the Palestine Order in Council, 1922 stipulated that the Ottoman Law existing on 1 November 1914 should remain in force until replaced by other legislation.

[57] Blum, 13.

[58] Criminal Procedure (Arrest and Searches) Ordinance (No. 4 of 1924, No. 34 of 1927); Criminal Procedure (Evidence) Ordinance (No. 33 of 1927, No. 30 of 1934); Criminal Procedure (Release on Bail) Ordinance (No. 35 of 1927); Criminal Procedure (Trial upon Information) Ordinance (No. 22 of 1924, Sec. 5 of No. 29 of 1926, No. 37 of 1929, No. 30 of 1934) and Evidence Ordinance (No. 11 of 1922, No. 13 of 1924, No. 28 of 1924, No. 17 of 1928, No. 19 of 1928).

13 articles (a far cry from the exhaustive 167-article Indian Evidence Act of 1872).[59] It expanded judicial discretion and released judges from Ottoman constraints. The Ottoman criminal procedure recognized a wide array of incompetent witnesses (it excluded parents, children, ascendants and descendants, siblings, relations-in-law of the same degree, spouses, former spouses and criminal defendants).[60] The Evidence Ordinance diverged from the Ottoman procedure by declaring that 'all persons are competent to give evidence in all cases' (art. 3). Yet the Ordinance maintained two exceptions to this rule – parents and (later) children were declared incompetent to testify against each other as were spouses. Spousal incompetence was curtailed by an additional rule, which allowed adverse testimony in cases of adultery and 'bodily injury or violence' inflicted on one spouse by the other.[61] This exception is clearly relevant to cases of forcible rape or sodomy involving the 'use of force or threats of death or severe bodily harm'.[62] Yet, under the British law, rape or sodomy might also occur in the absence of force: if the victim was unconscious, incapable of resisting or underage.[63] Some statutory sexual offences did not include an element of bodily injury or violence, for example, sexual contact 'against the order of nature',[64] 'carnal knowledge of an animal',[65] rape by deception,[66] an illicit relation with an unmarried girl[67] and intercourse by husband with a wife under fifteen years.[68]

Despite the potential barrier of incompetency, cases of non-forcible sexual offences in which a daughter testified against her father or a wife against her husband were heard by the courts of Mandate Palestine. I was able to find only one case of alleged forceful rape and sodomy in which the defence explicitly objected to the testimony of the victim by claiming that marriage to the accused rendered her an incompetent witness. In this case, the Supreme Court held under article 5(1) of the Evidence Ordinance that spouses were incompetent to testify against each other except in cases of adultery and when one spouse inflicted 'bodily injury or violence' on the other spouse and, therefore, that a wife could testify against her husband in a case of forcible rape.[69]

Under the Ottoman Code of Criminal Procedure, a conviction could rest on the testimony of a single witness.[70] The British Evidence Ordinance diverged

[59] Blum, 16. [60] Supra note 54. [61] Article 5(1) of the Evidence Ordinance.

[62] Section 152(1)(a) & (b) of the Criminal Code Ordinance 1936 and its earlier versions as they appear in CLAO.

[63] Section 152(1)(a), (b) & (c) of the Criminal Code Ordinance 1936.

[64] Section 152(2)(a) & (c) of the Criminal Code Ordinance 1936.

[65] Section 152(2)(b) of the Criminal Code Ordinance 1936.

[66] Section 153 of the Criminal Code Ordinance 1936.

[67] Section 155 of the Criminal Code Ordinance 1936.

[68] Section 156 of the Criminal Code Ordinance 1936.

[69] Cr.A 36/33, *George Georgiades and Others* v. *The Attorney General* (1933), reported in *Palestine Post* (29 May 1933, p. 4); for the District Court case see Henry Cattan's file. ISA/RG 66/M/188/33 (original docket #; Cr.C 44/33).

[70] Blum, 36.

from this precedent by introducing a new concept: corroboration. In cases of sexual offence, the complainant's testimony, credible as it may have been, did not suffice for conviction, and additional incriminating evidence was mandatory. In Chapter 6 I consider how this demand often rendered conviction in sexual assault cases impossible.

When we try to figure out what makes a story plausible, our attention is naturally drawn to substantive legislation. Each statutory prohibition tells a story of distinctive type of criminal behaviour. I argue in this book that, for the purpose of investigating the social constitution of plausibility, we should pay close attention not only to substantive elements of criminal offences but also to evidentiary and procedural mechanisms. The law of evidence is a significant site for the study of the constitution of plausibility. Narratives about offences are not only laid out in testimonies but are also embedded in evidentiary and procedural arrangements. Chapter 6, which focuses on corroboration, and Chapter 3, which considers oath preconditions and forensic evidence of children's sexual past, explore the interfaces of plausibility, evidence and procedure.

A study of evidence and procedure highlights the subtle ways in which cultural perceptions of plausibility permeate what seem at first glance to be neutral and technical rules, and it lays bare the extent to which the socially constructed nature of evidentiary rules is often well disguised. Such an analysis can shed light on the disconnect between the declared goals of the law on the books (e.g. the stated British intent to regulate sexuality and protect women and children) and the law in action (e.g. Mandate judges' deep suspicion of locals' complaints of sexual assault, as embodied in the practice of corroboration). With this focus in mind, and having surveyed the background of both substantive and evidentiary arrangements, we can now embark on our journey into cases of sexual offences in Mandate Palestine, and on our exploration of what makes one story plausible and another implausible.

# 2

# Cultural Narratives Underlying Proof: Male-to-Male Offences

Sixteen-year-old Acre resident Mustafa Naif, suspected of having sex with another man, stated before the police investigator on 30 June 1943, 'I know Mustafa Zahran and [he] is my friend and mate, I used to love him and he used to love me, and that this man had a sexual intercourse with me twice with my consent and free will, because he loves me and I love him.'[1] A story of mutual love was definitely a 'wrong' story for a man suspected of 'unnatural offences', namely, consensual male sex, to tell the Mandate authorities. Such a story constituted an admission of culpability in a crime punishable by a ten-year prison term.[2] The story was also 'wrong' because it was a culturally implausible account of a relationship between men. It is no wonder that Mustafa Naif subsequently recanted his romantic version and denied knowing Mustafa Zahran or having anything to do with him. His denial might be interpreted as yet another manifestation of his love for his friend, who was acquitted as a result of the contradictory statements. Mustafa Naif himself was convicted of perjury.

Mutual passion and enjoyment of male sex was another 'wrong' story to tell the British authorities in Mandate Palestine. This was the lesson learned by Carlo Rykante, a sergeant from the Italian Division.[3] He was caught by British soldiers, pants down, with eighteen-year-old Mohammad, in the local military camp stables. At the preliminary examination, with no trace of embarrassment, he described their mutual sexual attraction and the details of the passionate encounter that ensued. Later, testifying as a prosecution witness in Mohammad's trial (Carlo was not charged), he told the disbelieving judges that he and Mohammad were just having a 'friendly chat'. By then Carlo had become conscious of the British expectation that male sex, forbidden and shameful, should be hidden and denied.

The revised narratives that unfolded in the courtroom in these two cases, however, do not merely reflect internalization of British denigration of male sex. If narratives of love or mutual, egalitarian relationships did not impress the British, they also did not entirely adhere to local perceptions of male sex. The British, who had explicitly set out to overthrow the Ottoman norms that previously governed male sex in Palestine, utilized criminalization and the

[1] ISA/RG 30/Law 2029 (original docket # Cr.C 222/43). [2] §152(2) CCO.
[3] ISA/RG 30/Law 2046 (original docket # Cr.C 211/45).

stereotypes surrounding male sex in the 'East' to distinguish themselves from their subjects and bolster their superiority.[4] Nonetheless, examination of Mandate legislation and court cases reveals a significant intersection between colonial law and local culture.

## Theoretical Setting

The history of male sex in Mandate Palestine has gone largely unexplored,[5] aside from Ofri Ilany's analysis of the Hebrew press's characterization of homosexuality as oriental vice.[6] Ilany assumes that the paucity of scholarship reflects the fact that many practitioners did not define themselves as 'homosexuals' and that male sex went largely undocumented because of its clandestine nature. Although he aims to give voice to practitioners of male sex in Mandate Palestine, his materials yield mostly judgemental views. He presents the perspectives of only three 'insiders', Jewish literary writers (De Haan, Zweig and Langer) who he claims had internalized European Orientalist concepts. Beyond Ilany's research, male sex in Mandate Palestine has received only incidental scholarly attention. For example, in his work on colonialism and homosexuality, Robert Aldrich mentions Orthodox Jewish Dutch author Jacob De Haan's relationships with Arab boys and refers to British troops procuring male sex;[7] Liat Kozma briefly considers male sex in her work on the discourse of sexology in the Jewish settler community in Palestine;[8] and Tammy Razi touches on the subject in her study of the life of Jewish street children in Mandate Tel Aviv.[9] Occasional references to homosexual

[4] For examples of Western condescension towards the Islamic world through reference to the 'depravity' of male sex, see Stephen O. Murray, 'Some Nineteenth-Century Reports of Islamic Homosexuals', in *Islamic Homosexualities: Culture, History, and Literature*, ed. Stephen O. Murray and Will Roscoe (New York: New York University Press, 1997).

[5] The last three decades have seen the emergence of scholarship on the history of homosexuality in other times and places in the Islamic world; see, for example, Stephen O. Murray and Will Roscoe, eds., *Islamic Homosexualities: Culture, History, and Literature* (New York: New York University Press, 1997); Afsaneh Najmabadi, *Women with Mustaches and Men without Beards: Gender and Sexual Anxieties of Iranian Modernity* (Berkeley: University of California Press, 2005); Dror Zeevi, *Producing Desire: Changing Sexual Discourse in the Ottoman Middle East, 1500–1900* (Berkeley: University of California Press, 2006); Hassan El Menyawi, 'The Great Reversal: How Muslim Nations Went from Tolerating Same-Sex Practices to Repressing LGB People 1750-2010' (2014 working paper in the author's possession).

[6] Ofri Ilany, 'A Fine Bequest from Our Neighbors', in *Another Sex: Selected Essays in Israeli* Queer *and LGBT Studies* [in Hebrew], ed. Aeyal Gross, Amalia Ziv and Raz Yosef (Tel Aviv: Resling, 2016). For an English discussion of issues raised in this article, see Ofri Ilany, 'An Oriental Vice: Representations of Sodomy in Early Zionist Discourse', in *National Politics and Sexuality in Transregional Perspective: The Homophobic Argument*, ed. Achim Rohde, Christina von Braun and Stefanie Schüler-Springorum (Abingdon: Routledge, 2017).

[7] Robert Aldrich, *Colonialism and Homosexuality* (London: Routledge, 2003), 84–85.

[8] Liat Kozma, 'Sexology in the Yishuv: The Rise and Decline of Sexual Consultation in Tel Aviv, 1930–39', *International Journal of Middle East Studies* 42 (2010):231–49.

[9] Tammy Razi, *Forsaken Children: The Backyard of Mandate Tel-Aviv* [in Hebrew] (Tel Aviv: Am Oved, 2009), 116.

relationships between Britons and Arabs or Jews and Arabs are found in memoirs and some intelligence reports.[10]

Comparative studies of the criminalization of male sex across the British Empire necessarily explore the perspective of the colonizers, the imperial gaze.[11] Other historical scholarship scrutinizes the application of criminal prohibitions in specific colonial contexts. Understanding the local statutory arrangements in their social and cultural context entails the study not only of the perspective of the colonizers but also that of their subjects. What were the local attitudes toward sex between men? How did colonial subjects perceive the criminal prohibitions imposed on them? Did they resist this sexual regulation, internalize it or overtly react to it in any sense? The foci and findings of such research vary across colonial territories, depending on local culture and available archival materials. What remains constant is that traces of subaltern voices are often scarce and elusive. Suzanne LaFont, who studies the interweaving of elite and Afro-Jamaican sexual mores, was unable to find colonial-era descriptions of sodomy between slaves in Jamaica.[12] Anjali Arondeker points to the paucity of legal sodomy adjudications in the archives of colonial India and explores other evidentiary sources. Forensics, juridical rhetoric surrounding the crime, and intersecting debates allow her to examine the local legal translation of native sexuality.[13] She further juxtaposes the Western reading of the *hijra* (transgender eunuch) as a 'third sex' with a reading that avoids such gendered reifications. She studies hijras not only from the standpoint of their sexuality but also from that of their relation to state and economy.[14] Jessica Hinchy also uses the example of the hijra to illustrate how the regulation of native sexuality intersected with broader colonial agendas and projects.[15] Furthermore, she points to practices of resistance and evasion by hijras across colonial India, who made the most of the uneven enforcement of the regulation against them. Christine Stewart examines the application of colonial Australian law criminalizing consensual sex between men in Papua New Guinea. Relying on several cases that were heard in the years preceding PNG's independence in 1975, she points to the tension between

[10] Ilany, 'An Oriental Vice'.

[11] Douglas E. Sanders, '377 and the Unnatural Afterlife of British Colonialism in Asia', *Asian Journal of Comparative Law* 4 (2009): 1–19; Alok Gupta and Scott Long, 'This Alien Legacy: The Origins of "Sodomy" Laws in British Colonialism' (New York: Human Rights Watch, 2008), www.hrw.org/sites/default/files/reports/lgbt1208_web.pdf; Enze Han and Joseph O'Mahoney, 'British Colonialism and the Criminalization of Homosexuality', *Cambridge Review of International Affairs* 27 (2014): 268–288.

[12] Suzanne LaFont, 'Very Straight Sex: The Development of Sexual Mores in Jamaica', *Journal of Colonialism and Colonial History* (2001): 49.

[13] Anjali R. Arondekar, *For the Record: On Sexuality and the Colonial Archive in India* (Durham, NC: Duke University Press, 2009).

[14] Ibid., 90–91.

[15] Jessica Hinchy, 'Obscenity, Moral Contagion and Masculinity: Hijras in Public Space in Colonial North India', *Asian Studies Review* 38 (2014):274–94.

the austerity of colonial law and local customs and opinions pertaining to sex between men.[16] She also points to the pertinence of sexual roles and race to the local application of law.[17] In this book I argue that the study of the process of proof provides nuanced insight into the perceptions and agendas behind the colonial prosecution of sex offences. It allows us to discern not only the tensions but also the points of compatibility and interaction between the colonial apparatus and subaltern voices.

## British Attitude towards Male Sex

The criminalization of male sex, dictated from 'above' by the colonial rulers, was not the only novelty the British introduced in Palestine. Another innovation was the distinction between forced male sex ('sodomy') and consensual male sex ('unnatural offences' or activities 'against the order of nature'). In England there was no similar distinction between forceful and consensual sexual acts or between adult and minor partners.[18] Not until 1994 was male rape explicitly and distinctly acknowledged in English criminal legislation.[19] In Palestine, the British had addressed it almost sixty years earlier. The legal prohibition on anal sex recognized two scenarios. One, defined under section 152(1) of the Criminal Code Ordinance (CCO), was sodomy committed on a person against his will by the use of force or threats of death or severe bodily harm, on a person who was unconscious or unable to resist, or with a child under the age of sixteen, regardless of consent or the absence of force.[20] The other scenario involved sex between

16 Her claim that the issue of ritual homosexuality was not raised in any of the cases seems somewhat mislaid, as none of the cases involved such an occurrence, and she acknowledges that the court, at least in one case, considered whether sodomy violated local custom. Christine Stewart, 'Men Behaving Badly: Sodomy Cases in the Colonial Courts of Papua New Guinea', *Journal of Pacific History* 43 (2008): 88, 83.

17 Ibid., 92.

18 The prohibition was statutory by nature, and its 'common law' aspect related to a tradition of interpretation. Harry G. Cocks, *Nameless Offences: Homosexual Desire in the Nineteenth Century* (London: I. B. Tauris, 2003), 17; A. D. Harvey, 'Prosecutions for Sodomy in England at the Beginning of the Nineteenth Century', *The Historical Journal* 21, no. 4 (1978): 941; Janet E. Halley, 'Reasoning About Sodomy: Act and Identity in and after Bowers v. Hardwick', *Virginia Law Review* 79, no. 7 (1993): 1759.

19 Section 142 of the Criminal Justice and Public Order Act 1994. In an ironic twist of fate, the legal framework England adopted in 1994 was conspicuously similar to the Ottoman rule colonial authorities had despised and steered away from in Mandate Palestine in 1927. This is not to say that the nineteenth-century Ottoman arrangement and the late twentieth-century English provisions regulated sexuality in the same way. The resemblance only demonstrates that the statutory provisions are a fraction of the broader picture and that their meaning is constructed through their interaction with the wider social environment.

20 Section 152(1) set forth that 'any person who . . . (b) commits an act of sodomy with any person against his will by the use of force or threats of death or severe bodily harm, or when he is in a state of unconsciousness or otherwise incapable of resisting; or (c) has unlawful sexual intercourse or commits an act of sodomy with a child under the age of sixteen years' was guilty of a felony punishable by fourteen years' imprisonment.

consenting adult males, titled 'offences against nature' under section 152(2) of the CCO.

Judicial decisions deplored the prevalence of sodomy in Palestine, sometimes while lamenting English procedural and evidentiary conventions that prevented conviction. When acquitting a man accused of sodomizing a ten-year-old boy, Judge Weldon, president of the Haifa District Court, stated, 'I wish to say quite frankly that under application of English law to this country nearly all such offences as the present one cannot be proved; they are all too common in this country and unfortunately it is almost always impossible to bring to book the offender.'[21] In another case, in which the accused lured thirteen-year-old boys into having sex with him, the court expressed sorrow for being unable to order flogging as punishment.[22]

As discussed in Chapter 1, the British rhetoric surrounding the introduction of the criminal prohibitions of 'sodomy' and 'unnatural offences' represented the local inhabitants as morally depraved, addicted to physical pleasure and uncontrollable urges. It is noteworthy that despite their alleged commitment to legislation tailored to local conditions, the British portrayed their Palestinian subjects in broad brushstrokes as an 'Eastern' people, without addressing their particular circumstances. Indeed, the wordings of the sodomy clauses in Mandate Palestine were modelled after a standard colonial formula that did not target local concerns. Rather, they reflected concerns about colonial subjects in general, whether in Queensland, Nigeria or Palestine. While sometimes willing to accommodate the ethno-cultural diversity of Palestine's inhabitants – for example, when applying a standard of 'reasonableness' for provocation in a murder case[23] – the British approached sodomy with the explicit intention of eradicating local custom.

## The Plausibility of Non-consensual Male Sex

Rape is often regarded as a gendered crime, with mostly female victims.[24] The data for Mandate Palestine reveal a different reality. Of the 147 cases in my research corpus, 72 involved offences committed by males on males, 64 of which involved sodomy, indecent acts or attempted indecent acts, or perjury pertaining to such allegations,[25] and 8 of which involved offences 'against the order of nature'.[26]

21 ISA/RG 30/Law 2032 (original docket # Cr.C 50/44).

22 'It is with great regret that there is no provision in the laws of this country for the infliction of flogging for such bestial offences.' ISA/RG 30/Law 2043 (original docket # Cr.C 92/45).

23 Yoram Shachar, 'The Reasonable Person and Criminal Law' [in Hebrew], *Hapraklit* 39, no. 1 (1989): 82–83.

24 Claire Cohen, *Male Rape Is a Feminist Issue: Feminism, Governmentality and Male Rape* (Basingstoke: Palgrave Macmillan, 2014), 3.

25 Of eight defendants in perjury cases, five were males and three were females.

26 The eight cases stemmed from seven incidents (in one case, the partners were indicted separately) (Cr.C 140/43 & Cr.C 141/43).

The definition of sodomy as delineated by the CCO included three situations: (1) forcible male rape (through actual force or threats of death or severe bodily harm); (2) sodomy with a person who was unconscious or otherwise incapable of resisting; and (3) sodomy with a child under sixteen. The underlying assumption in the latter two situations was lack of capacity to give real consent.

Although the British rulers of Palestine distinguished non-consensual male sex (sodomy) from consensual acts (offences against the order of nature), force was often irrelevant when prosecuting 'sodomy'. The analysis of available court cases reveals that of the three situations constituting 'sodomy', prosecutions most often targeted sexual contact with children, in which proof of force was not necessary. Notably, of fifty-five sexual assaults (excepting consensual cases of the total count, and eliminating multiple perjury charges pertaining to the same circumstances), most concerned children younger than sixteen (forty-four cases). Seven other cases involved minor victims (younger than eighteen), and of the four remaining cases, one concerned a twenty-three-year-old British soldier who was allegedly assaulted by a fellow soldier, one involved a twenty-year-old, and two victims were of unknown age. The pattern of prosecution coalesced around sexual assaults of minors.

One explanation for the high proportion of minor victims is their obvious vulnerability. It may also be the case that the authorities were more interested in protecting children than in regulating sexual relations between adults, notwithstanding the formal criminal prohibitions against both forceful and consensual sexual acts between adult males. But the focus on one 'scenario' of male rape may also reflect the implausibility of a story in which an adult male protagonist is the victim of rape.[27] Rendering the element of force negligible in most court cases of male rape (as most involved minors) had the potential to strengthen the myth that men could not be overcome by physical force and, thus, raped. This could then imply that men who complained of having been raped had brought it on themselves and were somehow at fault. Even boys could be blamed for not preventing the perpetrator from committing the act. Such argumentation is found in Judge Curry's acquittal of the accused in a sodomy case in which, despite medical evidence of a tear in the anal canal of the complainant, he found the story of rape implausible:

> I am very far from satisfied that accused committed the act of sodomy without the consent of the complainant. Accused is not particularly powerfully built and the complainant is a boy of some 15–16 years of age who could quite easily prevent the accused from committing the act had he so wished. It is to be noted that there were no other marks of violence on the complainant other than the

[27] For a review of literature on the subject of male rape, see Jessica A. Turchik and Katie M. Edwards, 'Myths About Male Rape: A Literature Review', *Psychology of Men & Masculinity* 13, no. 2 (2012).

evidence of the actual act of sodomy. I disbelieve the Prosecution Witness that the boy was screaming for help.[28]

Early forensic literature expressed explicit doubts about whether rape of an adult either male or female could even occur. Samuel Farr put the question in just such terms, asking '[w]hether a rape, strictly so called, be possible?'[29] He claimed that unless 'great force [is] exercised over a woman to violate her chastity', then 'the consummation of a rape ... without any consent or permission of the woman seems to be impossible'.[30] In regard to sodomy, Alfred Swaine Taylor opined that unless the victim is insensible, 'it is not possible to conceive that this offence should be perpetrated on an adult of either sex against his or her will; the slightest resistance would suffice to prevent its perpetration'.[31] The disappearance of such statements from, or their softening in, twentieth-century forensic literature does not necessarily imply that the underlying myths about the impossibility of rape in general and of men in particular had vanished. Complainants continued to be suspected of giving their consent to carnal relations throughout the twentieth century.

The 'plausible' victim of a 'real' rape is a female who is characterized in terms of conformity to patriarchal norms of a 'good' woman.[32] In contrast, 'bad girls', less compliant with gender norms, 'ask for it'. In the same vein, gendered rape myths construct the ideal male victim vis-à-vis his conformity to masculine gender roles, thus similarly bolstering the patriarchal model.[33] Concentrating on minor victims does not disrupt this model. An adult male who adheres to gender norms can and does defend himself and therefore cannot be raped.[34] The narratives of adult males who are nevertheless attacked are underscored by other rape myths: that only gay men are victims of rape; that homosexual and bisexual individuals are deviant and therefore deserve to be raped; or that a man who was raped must have wanted it.[35] Even young boys, who might be expected to lack the strength to fight off their attackers, are susceptible to such interpretations, as the example above demonstrates. Unsurprisingly, then, beyond the standard impediments to proving sexual assault (general distrust of local witnesses and the evidentiary barrier embodied in the demand for corroboration, especially high when children were concerned), male complainants in Mandate Palestine were met with heightened suspicion that focused on their sexual tendencies and history. This suspicion was rooted in cultural scripts that existed outside the courtroom and in formal definitions of the substantive criminal norm.

28 ISA/RG 30/Law 2038 (original docket # Cr.C 286/44).

29 Samuel Farr, *Elements of Medical Jurisprudence*, 1st ed. (London: T. Becket, Pall-Mall, 1788), 41.

30 Ibid., 41–42.

31 Alfred Swaine Taylor, *A Manual of Medical Jurisprudence*, 9th ed. (London: J & A Churchill, 1874), 677.

32 Cohen, 39. 33 Ibid., 40. 34 Turchik and Edwards, 212. 35 Ibid.

Alleged male victims were routinely examined for signs of rectal penetration and bodily injuries. The medical examinations were underpinned by British and local beliefs about men's 'rapability'. Medical-forensic evidence was highly valued by the judiciary as factual and objective and was seen as emblematic of the British imposition of progress on an undeveloped country.[36] A medical report supporting a claim of sexual assault was therefore a trump card. It could not, however, be detached from socio-cultural perceptions of male-on-male sex and could become a double-edged sword. Medico-legal reports, for instance, customarily indicated whether a child victim was a 'habitual sodomist' or a 'passive subject'. Dr Ahmed Kamel followed this form in his report on twelve-year-old Moshe, who had reported being sodomized by two men. In addition to redness indicative of penetration, the physician found that the 'anus is funnel shaped and its opening is wider than expected for his age. These are signs which indicate an habitual sodomist.'[37] In the trial of a man accused of sodomy of a thirteen-year-old boy, Dr Kamel testified, 'I should think the boy had been used more than once for this purpose, as he had a funnel shaped rectum.'[38]

Dr Ali Akila, who examined Deeb, an eleven-year-old victim of sodomy, testified before the magistrate about the fissures and scratches found on the boy's body. He also added that the boy had a funnel-shaped anal canal, indicating that 'he was used much before'.[39] Reports sometimes indicated the absence of such evidence. For example, Dr Torian, who examined Mahmoud, a seven-year-old who was brutally attacked, described bruises and tears and also remarked that 'the Anal Canal was normal not a funnel shape. I mean that the boy was not previously acted on.'[40]

Why should the medical evidence have delved into the sexual past of very young children, when the consent of those younger than sixteen was immaterial to proof of sodomy? The evidentiary value of a boy's sexual past was probably analogous to that attached to a girl's virginity: the accused might not be held responsible if penetration could be shown to have occurred prior to the episode described in the charges. When virginity or its male equivalent was not at issue, the sexual past and consent of a boy younger than sixteen were irrelevant to charges of sodomy. Nevertheless, the portrayal of the child as a 'habitual sodomist' created an impression of moral depravity, which could damage the complainant's credibility. A victim who breached gender norms was blameable.

36 Orna Alyagon Darr, 'Relocated Doctrine: The Travel of the English Doctrine of Corroboration in Sex Offense Cases to Mandate Palestine', *Yale Journal of Law & the Humanities* 26, no. 2 (2014): 199.

37 ISA/RG 30/Law 2009 (original docket # Cr.C 168/40).

38 ISA/RG 30/Law 2010 (original docket # Cr.C 195/40).

39 ISA/RG 30/Law 2015 (original docket # Cr.C 66/42).

40 ISA/RG 30/Law 2030 (original docket # Cr.C 252/43).

Forensic examinations to document signs of sodomy had roots in nineteenth-century England. In 1870 Ernest Boulton and William Park, who went around London wearing women's clothing and flaunting their feminine-style sexuality, were arrested on sodomy charges and subjected to medical examination that revealed both men had dilated anuses (Park was also diagnosed with syphilitic sores).[41] In his 1874 edition of *A Manual of Medical Jurisprudence*, Alfred Swaine Taylor used the term 'funnel shaped' to describe anal deformation caused by sodomy.[42] Such forensic evidence was not in itself sufficient to prove the act of sodomy, and Boulton and Park were acquitted. Insufficient to convict, such evidence could also lead to dismissal of a case if it was interpreted as casting suspicion on a complainant's story. For example, in 1897, a Devon grand jury rejected a case in which the complainant, a twelve-year-old boy, was found by a physician to have practised sodomy for some time, as evidenced by two small fissures inside a dilated anus.[43] Similar medical examinations were conducted in colonial India. The examination of Khairati, a defendant in an 1884 precedential case, discovered he had 'the characteristic make of a habitual catamite – the distortion of the orifice of the anus into a shape of a trumpet – and also be affected with syphilis in the same region in a manner which distinctly points to unnatural intercourse within the last few months'.[44] Khairati was convicted by the session judge, who opined that, although none of the circumstances (the defendant's dilated anus, syphilis, use of women's clothes) individually sufficed for conviction, cumulatively they left no doubt he had engaged in sodomy. His conviction was overturned by the Allahabad High Court for lack of particulars of the offence.[45] Forensic evidence of a 'funnel-shaped' anus began to be used in colonial India at the end of the nineteenth century.[46] Although forensic examination of the anus originated in England, not all English forensic experts agreed it could demonstrate sodomy. Sir Sydney Alfred Smith, the author of the textbook *Forensic Medicine* (the first of numerous editions appeared in 1925), stated that '*Habitual Sodomy* leads to permanent changes in the condition of the anus, especially if the person commences this practice whilst young.'[47] He further added that, although '[m]any writers have thrown doubt on constant sodomy producing these changes',[48] he disagreed with them on the basis of his experience in 'the East'. Before being appointed Regius Chair of Forensic Medicine at Edinburgh

41 Michael Diamond, *Victorian Sensation, or, the Spectacular, the Shocking, and the Scandalous in Nineteenth-Century Britain* (London: Anthem Press, 2004), 121–122.

42 Taylor, 678; Victoria Bates, *Sexual Forensics in Victorian and Edwardian England: Age, Crime and Consent in the Courts* (Basingstoke: Palgrave Macmillan, 2016), 44.

43 Ibid., 88.

44 Cited by Anjali Arondekar, 'Without a Trace: Sexuality and the Colonial Archive', *Journal of the History of Sexuality* 14, no. 1–2 (2005): 21.

45 Ibid. 46 Gupta and Long.

47 Sidney Smith, *Forensic Medicine: A Text-Book for Students and Practitioners*, 8th ed. (London: J & A Churchill, 1945), 313.

48 Ibid., 314.

University in 1928, Smith served for eleven years (1917–1928) as the principal medico-legal expert to the Egyptian government, holding a lectureship in forensic medicine at the School of Medicine in Qasr al-aini, Cairo.[49] Smith reports that, 'on making an examination of fifty professional sodomists (in the East) especially for this, I found the condition in the majority of them'.[50]

From the criminal files in my corpus, it is evident that in Mandate Palestine medical examinations became a routine procedure in cases of sodomy and unnatural offences. Medical experts' reference to an alleged victim as a 'habitual sodomist' constructed him as a person with little if any right to refuse sexual advances.[51] The defining characteristic of an act of sodomy was lack of consent. Conviction for consensual acts carried lesser maximum penalties (ten years as opposed to fourteen years for sodomy).[52] Nevertheless, the formal distinction between forceful and consensual acts was blurred, as the element of force was undermined in most sodomy cases, because the victim was a minor (regarding whom no use of force had to be proved) or he had brought the offence on himself by not resisting or through sexual habits that 'invited' penetration.

The medical opinions incorporated a widespread theme of Islamic folklore: a boy known to have been sodomized was regarded as 'fair game for others'.[53] Interspersed in the testimony of the medical experts were vernacular terms such as 'used' or 'habitual sodomist', the latter term pointing to a behavioral pattern more than to medical pathology. The reference to a victim's possible past sexual corruption is consistent with cultural and social doubts about male rapability.

## The Plausibility of Consensual Male Sex (Offences against the Order of Nature)

The offence of 'sodomy', as it was defined in Palestine, drew a sharp line between the perpetrator and the victim, on whom the act had to be committed 'against his will by the use of force or threats of death or severe bodily harm, or when he is in a state of unconsciousness or otherwise incapable of resisting'. However, when consensual homosexuality became a crime, both partners were accomplices. Although the term 'homosexual' existed in contemporary

[49] Francis Camps, 'Smith, Sir Sydney Alfred (1883–1969)', *Oxford Dictionary of National Biography* (2004), https://doi.org/10.1093/ref:odnb/36159.

[50] Smith, 314. [51] Gupta and Long, 34.

[52] In practice, the punishment for consensual sex between males ranged from a bond for good behaviour to imprisonment for three months to four years. The punishment for sodomy ranged from two years' probation and bond to six strokes to imprisonment for a few months to seven years. It should be noted, however, that convictions for both offences usually involved prison terms of one to two years.

[53] Stephen O. Murray, 'The Will Not to Know', in *Islamic Homosexualities: Culture, History, and Literature*, ed. Stephen O. Murray and Will Roscoe (New York: New York University Press, 1997), 18.

medical and legal literature, many of those who engaged in homosexual practices did not apply the term to themselves, either being unfamiliar with it or not identifying with its implications.[54] None of the defendants or witnesses in the cases examined for this book used the term. Terms that attempt to translate the word 'homosexuality' into the Arabic language appear only in the second half of the twentieth century.[55] The word 'homosexual' does not appear in the British legislation, and the terminology 'against the order of nature' is actually a prohibition on anal sex with either a male or a female partner. In practice, however, the authorities routinely regarded the criminal norm as a ban on homosexuality, an interpretation that implied a complete identification of homosexuality with anal sex, 'as there was no homosexuality without anal sex, and there was no anal sex without homosexuality'.[56] While judges in colonial India made considerable efforts to extend the scope of the prohibition on sodomy to include oral acts,[57] the Palestine District Court cases consulted for this analysis discussed only incidents of anal sex.

The Mandate cases of 'offence against the order of nature' entailed typecasting the accused according to culturally accepted roles. The recurrent and most plausible pattern involved an older man who penetrated a teenage boy, sometimes (but not necessarily) in return for payment.[58] Such was the 1943 case involving two labourers at an army cavalry post, Abdel Hamid, a thirty-year-old Muslim originally from Egypt but then residing in Haifa, and Ali Mustafa, a Muslim teenager from Haifa.[59] Having been observed by a British soldier with their trousers down, about to engage in a sexual act, they were brought before the magistrate. Abdel Hamid was charged with an attempt to have carnal knowledge and Ali Mustafa with an attempt to permit carnal knowledge. Although the penalty under sections 152(2)(a) & (c) of the CCO was the same for a person who 'has carnal knowledge' of another and for a person who 'permits a male person to have carnal knowledge of him' (ten years' imprisonment), the British differentiated between activity and passivity, penetrating and being penetrated, as distinct offences. The formal legal

[54] Ilany, 'A Fine Bequest from Our Neighbors'; H. G. Cocks, 'Secrets, Crimes and Diseases, 1800–1914', in *A Gay History of Britain*, ed. Matt Cook (Oxford: Greenwood World Publishing, 2007), 135. Sydney Smith, a leading authority on forensic medicine at the time, commented that, although he employed the commonly used term 'sodomist', that term should really apply only to the 'active agent', the proper term for the 'passive agent' being 'catamite'. He further noted, that the term 'pederast' could be applied to either party. Smith, 314.

[55] Samar Habib, *Female Homosexuality in the Middle East: Histories and Representations* (New York: Routledge, 2007), 17–18; Brian Palmer, 'How Do You Say Gay in Arabic?', *Slate* (2012), www.slate.com/articles/life/explainer/2012/08/homosexuality_and_islam_how_do_you_say_gay_in_arabic_.html.

[56] Yuval Yonay and Dori Spivak, 'Constructing the Identity of Homosexuals in the Israeli Legal Discourse, 1948–1988', in *LGBT Rights in Israel*, ed. Alon Harel, Yaniv Lushinsky and Einav Morgenstern (Jerusalem: Hebrew University Press: Harry Sacher Institute, 2015).

[57] Gupta and Long.

[58] For similar motives in court cases that were heard in the courts of Papua New Guinea prior to its independence, see Stewart, 89–90, 92.

[59] ISA/RG 30/Law 2028 (original docket # Cr.C 157/43).

distinction resonates with the ancient pattern of age- and status-stratified male sex,[60] a premodern patriarchal notion that measured masculinity in terms of sexual roles demonstrated by activity or passivity. Penetration signified subjugation and humiliation of another, whether performed on a woman, a slave, a boy or a man.[61]

Even in a case in which the ages of the partners were relatively close (twenty and seventeen, respectively), the pattern remained the older penetrating the younger. Mohammad, the older accused in that case, explained that 'I asked him to act upon him as I heard that he is used. Whereas I am ignorant and unmarried I entered with him to the shelter in the ditch and acted upon him.'[62] The medical examination revealed that Hussein, the younger accused, was infected with syphilis in his rectum. While not much younger than Mohammad, Hussein seems to have come from the lower end of the social spectrum, a vulnerable and exploited boy. The manner in which Mohammad describes the event conforms to premodern images of same-sex relations. For him, having sex with Hussein was not a self-defining act of homosexual identity. As Mohammad was not yet married, the younger boy was merely a passing object for his sexual satisfaction. Mohammad described himself as 'ignorant', an expression that conveys awareness of distinct British sexual norms and submissiveness.

In light of Hussein's syphilis, the judges ordered his segregation from other prisoners in the jail. This order implies acknowledgement that the punishment meted out for forbidden male sex – imprisonment – was likely to result in similar acts during incarceration and that these acts would likely conform to the pattern of older and stronger men exploiting the younger and weaker.[63] Conviction and imprisonment, then, were concerned with symbolic demarcation of socially illegitimate acts perhaps even more than their actual prevention.

Like sodomy suspects, those suspected of 'unnatural offences' were routinely examined medically to determine whether they were 'habitual sodomists' or 'passive subjects'. This practice presupposed that, aside from the presence or absence of venereal diseases, practitioners of anal sex were medically distinguishable. In cases of consensual acts, both partners could be examined, as happened to Abdel Hamid and Ali Mustafa. Both were found to have funnel-shaped anal canals, which was suggestive, according to expert opinion, 'of [one] being a passive subject' (Ali Mustafa) and the other 'being a passive perversity' (Abdel Hamid).

60 Yaron Ben-Naeh, 'Moshko the Jew and His Gay Friends: Same-Sex Sexual Relations in Ottoman Jewish Society', *Journal of Early Modern History* 9, no. 1–2 (2005): 90.

61 Ibid., 81.

62 ISA/RG 30/Law 2030 (original docket # Cr.C 230/43).

63 De facto British recognition of sexual activity behind prison walls is attested by the practice in Jerusalem's central prison of locking up European detainees separately from Arab prisoners, in a caged cell under constant supervision, to prevent Arabs from sodomizing them. Joshua Kaspi, 'Prisons in Mandate Palestine' [in Hebrew], *Kathedra* 32 (1984): 141, 146.

Medical examinations were also used to determine age. Despite suspicions that they were sodomists, despite having literally been caught with their pants down, and despite the legal prohibition on consensual homosexual relations, both Abdel Hamid and Ali Mustafa escaped legal sanction. An X-ray revealed that Ali Mustafa might have been younger than sixteen. This possibility had double legal consequences. First, it rendered Ali Mustafa a victim rather than an offender, and the magistrate dismissed the charges against him. Second, Abdel Hamid was charged with the more serious offence of attempted sodomy, as consent was irrelevant when a partner was younger than sixteen. Nevertheless, the district court discharged him, finding no hard evidence that Ali Mustafa was under age and thus that there was no case for Abdel Hamid to answer. Theoretically, Abdel Hamid could have been made to answer the lesser charge of attempting to have carnal knowledge. One can surmise that this path was not taken because the alleged victim, Ali Mustafa, was a 'habitual sodomist' and because the judicial system was more lenient when consent was not at issue.

In England, homosexuality charges were sometimes a practical substitute for more severe sexual charges that could not be proved.[64] Perhaps in Palestine too, the lesser offence 'against the order of nature' was used for cases of suspected forceful sodomy that were difficult to prosecute as such because of evidentiary difficulties, for instance, insufficient evidence to prove the use of force,[65] or some moral vice of the penetrated party (such as his being a 'habitual sodomist' or a prostitute) that might have undermined his claim of being violated.

The substantive statutory arrangement differentiated between having and permitting others to have 'carnal knowledge', thus clearly distinguishing between the roles of penetrator and penetrated. Such distinction had deep roots in Islamic culture as well as in the Arabic language, which has no general term for 'homosexual' but, rather, specific terms for active and passive sexual roles.[66] Although both male partners to an act of 'carnal knowledge' could be charged, the specific charges differed according to role. Elias, a twenty-year-old Christian from Haifa, and Mohammad, a twenty-nine-year-old Muslim from Jaffa, were listed on the same charge sheet, accused of engaging in consensual sex.[67] Elias, however, was charged with permitting Mohammad to have carnal knowledge of him against the order of nature, whereas Mohammad was charged with having carnal knowledge of Elias against the order of nature. The event precipitating the charge occurred in Jissir Mejami, where

[64] Cocks, *Nameless Offences*, 33.

[65] One example is a 1946 case, in which the medical report pointed to penetration but did not find injuries compatible with the victim's story. The accused was therefore charged with the lesser offence of having carnal knowledge against the order of nature. Ultimately, the attorney-general stayed the proceedings. ISA/RG 30/Law 2055 (original docket # Cr.C 183/46).

[66] Other terms designated men drawn to boys, boys and men offering their anuses for penetration, male prostitute, and so on. Murray, 'The Will Not to Know', 28–32.

[67] ISA/RG 30/Law 2039 (original docket # Cr.C 227/43).

Mohammed was a cook in a restaurant. Originally from Jaffa, he had moved to Jissir Mejami, where his brother-in-law resided. Mohammad's restaurant served workmen from a nearby camp run by the works department. On the evening of 12 September 1943, after all the workers had left the restaurant, Mohammad remained in the kitchen drinking brandy, and Elias also remained there. Mohammad stated that Elias asked him for money and offered anal sex in return. Elias asserted that Mohammad closed the door, put a half-pound banknote in his (Elias's) pocket, dimmed the lights, and forced him to commit 'the abominable act'. Adel, the owner of another restaurant in Jissir Mejami, arrived and, hearing noises from inside the kitchen, peeked through a crack in the door. He saw Mohammad 'riding over' Elias, both of them naked below the waist. Adel called Abdul Karem, a foreman from the work camp, who was sleeping in a room near the restaurant. Through the crack in the door, Abdul Karem also saw what the two men inside were doing and sent for the police. Elias later told the police that the onlookers called, 'Come, oh good people, and see' but that Mohammad continued 'until he finished his act'. The police subsequently came and arrested him and Mohammad.

The statements and testimony of the accused and witnesses during the investigation and prosecution (first before the magistrate at the preliminary examination and later in the Haifa District Court) illustrate some of the recurring elements of 'offences against the order of nature' that were heard in the courts of Palestine. One is that the complaint came from an inadvertent witness. The authorities are never described as initiating an investigation but, rather, as responding to a complaint brought to them. Here, the first move was made by a restaurant owner who perhaps saw an opportunity to eliminate a business competitor. While the British explicitly expressed their ambitions to reform sexual behaviour in the colonies, the prosecution policy in Palestine, at least as reflected in the primary materials on which this book is based, seems to have been quite lax. Whereas in England sex between males was subjected to surveillance by various agencies, and was actively targeted by raids and crack-downs, in Palestine the authorities mainly responded to cases presented to them.[68] In England criminal prosecution was aimed at rooting out not just sodomy but a wider sub-culture. It may be that the homosexual sub-culture in Palestine was not perceived as threatening to British self-perceptions, perhaps because male on male sex was regarded as 'oriental' or as a trait of non-civilized culture or perhaps because the Palestinian sub-culture was more opaque to the British gaze than that in their own culture back home.

A second recurring element is the link, here drawn by the accused parties, between homosexuality and male prostitution. Mohammad claimed that Elias asked him for money and offered sex in return, whereas Elias claimed that

[68] On policing of homosexuality in contemporary England, see Matt Houlbrook, *Queer London: Perils and Pleasures in the Sexual Metropolis, 1918–1957* (Chicago: University of Chicago Press, 2005), chapter 2. On nineteenth-century policing in streets, pubs, molly houses, theatres, parks and urinals, see Cocks, 'Secrets, Crimes and Diseases, 1800–1914', 114–19, 151–52.

Mohammad put the money in his pocket and forced him to have sex, and he gave the banknote to the police investigator as evidence. In both versions, it was plausible that anal sex was something to be paid for. However, each defendant manipulated this convention for different purposes. For Mohammad, having sex with a prostitute was the lesser of two evils, preferable to more severe charges of forceful sodomy. Indeed, he told the inspector, 'I know this boy previously from Haifa and he is used since old time' (a statement supported by the medical examination, which found that Elias 'was used more than once'). Implicit in his statement was the assumption that it was plausible for him to have sex with a boy who was already 'used'. Elias described forced payment to negate the claim that he permitted Mohammad to penetrate him and thus to present himself as a victim rather than an accomplice (in vain, as he was eventually charged). The link between sodomy and prostitution meant that banknotes could be produced as evidence of the sodomitic act.

Payments figured in other suspects' narratives as well. Two Haifa residents, Mohammad, a thirty-year-old Muslim originally from Jaffa (Jebaliyeh), and Malik, an eighteen-year-old Arab Christian originally from Lebanon, were in the bomb shelter under the Central Hotel in Haifa when three other men entered and realized that they had intruded on the aftermath of a sexual act.[69] One of them said he heard Malik demand money from Mohammad, who refused to pay, claiming he had not ejaculated, a statement denied by Malik. Malik told the police investigator that Mohammad had offered him money for a 'ride', and when he responded, 'This is not my work', Mohammad sodomized him by force, beating him and threatening him with a knife. Malik also stated that one of the witnesses also asked him for a 'ride'. In his statement, Malik describes himself as a victim and presents Mohammad's offer to pay him as an indication of the latter's sole culpability (to no avail, as he was eventually charged with permitting Mohammad to have carnal knowledge of him). Mohammad told quite a different story. He stated that he had demanded Malik repay a debt he owed him and that Malik had refused, although he had a box rattling with money. Malik, he claimed, offered sex in lieu of the money. Mohammad alleged that he had refused this offer, saying he was too sick to engage in sex. Mohammad's version pointed to Malik as a willing and even an instigating party. His strategy was successful in that he was not charged with forceful sodomy but with the lesser offence of having carnal knowledge of Malik. Mohammad's insinuation that Malik was a prostitute was possibly fortified by the expert opinion that Malik was a 'habitual passive subject' and by Malik's own statement that one of the witnesses had asked him for a 'ride'.

In one exceptional 1943 case, Abdalla (who claimed to be sixteen although the police put his age at twenty) was charged not only with permitting a man to

[69] ISA/RG 30/Law 2028 (original docket # Cr.C 141/43) and ISA/RG 30/Law 2028 (original docket # Cr.C 140/43).

have carnal knowledge of him but also with keeping a brothel and living off the earnings of prostitutes.[70] Abdalla, according to testimony in the file, often wore a woman's robe and artificial breasts, made his face up with powder and rouge, and completed his feminine look by weaving a rose into his long hair. Abdalla's parents lived in Haifa, but he was accused of running a brothel in Acre, where he employed two Arab female prostitutes, Zeinab and Khadijeh, and two Jewish female prostitutes, Rachel and Rashel. The prostitutes testified that they had been recruited by Abdalla, who had told them much of his business was with the army. Upon entering Abdalla's shabby house around 11 p.m. on 19 April 1943, police constables, who had been called by an annoyed neighbour, found English soldiers dressing and counting money. The constables left 'to avoid collusion with the Army'. When they returned the following night, they found Abdalla and the four prostitutes with a mixed clientele of two English soldiers, one Greek soldier, one Arab soldier and two non-military Arab clients, one from Tiberias and the other from Acre. All but the soldiers, who refused to accompany the policemen, were taken to make statements at the police station. The information filed in the district court against Abdalla included a charge of permitting a male to have carnal knowledge of him, but the identity of his partner remained unspecified. Abdalla admitted to the police investigator that he worked as a prostitute:

> I have been for six years permitting men to have carnal knowledge of me. I am well-known to the public. I dress like a woman and put rouge and powder inside my house. I still permit men to have carnal knowledge of me like the sexual intercourse of a male to female from the rear. This is because I am poor and my right hand is disabled. I take money in consideration of that.

Abdalla pleaded guilty to the charges against him, and the only controversy focused on his age. The judges accepted his claim that he was sixteen years old, and, agreeing that it was useless to fine him or send him to prison, gave him a very light punishment, discharging him on his own recognizance with the admonition that he be of good behaviour for three years.

Prostitution, as this story indicates, was treated as a plausible mitigating storyline, a relevant factor in determining whether a sexual act was consensual.[71] While prostitution places male sex beyond the borders of the dignified, it is still an enduring social phenomenon. Male sex in exchange for money does not threaten the social order, kinship or even masculinity as much as consensual sex based on love or mutual passion does. The penetrator is still fulfilling the classical masculine sex role, and the one who is penetrated is

70 ISA/RG 30/Law 2028 (original docket # Cr.C 154/43).

71 A clear example of the use of prostitution to defend against charges of sodomy is found in a Papua New Guinea case involving two men accused of having sex with a male prostitute. The accused, who claimed to be the prostitute's victims, were given warnings and suspended sentences, while the fifteen-year-old prostitute was sentenced to nine months' imprisonment. Stewart, 85.

motivated by the money, not by attraction. The testimony in the trials points to a strong link between homosexuality and prostitution. Generally, the cases in my corpus reflect a perception that same-sex relations either were the result of power differences or involved monetary exchange. Money often exchanged hands, even when sex was not explicitly defined as a service rendered in return for pre-agreed payment. The penetrator would frequently pay the penetrated, if only a symbolic sum. This chapter opens with the seemingly romantic statement by Mustafa Naif that he engaged in sex with his friend, Mustafa Zahran, out of love. Nevertheless, Mohamad Sunji, an acquaintance of the couple, who claimed to have witnessed the sexual act, stated that, subsequent to its conclusion, Mustafa Zahran paid Mustafa Naif thirteen piastres, saying he had no more money to give him. In this description, the transfer of coins from the hand of the penetrator to the hand of the penetrated is a marker of inequality, a transaction acknowledging a joint understanding that the act was for the benefit of the penetrator.[72]

Romantic love between men was not recognized as a motivation for sex, either by the British or by locals. Male relationships were not equivalent to heterosexual relationships. I would stress, however, that the prevalence of such dispositions does not rule out the existence of long-lasting homosexual relationships or of exclusive homosexual identity. Recent literature suggests Middle Eastern culture was not devoid of exclusively homosexual relationships.[73]

It is noteworthy that witness narratives do not portray males who engaged in sex with each other as effeminate. Some penetrators who compared male sex to sex between male and female spoke of it as a practical substitute ('I had sexual intercourse with him like women',[74] 'I am . . . unmarried'[75]). Such statements imply that the masculinity of at least some penetrators remained intact and that sex with men was simply an act and not, to use the Foucauldian terminology, a signifier of a type of personhood.

Most of those who were penetrated portrayed themselves as weak and exploited but not as effeminate; they rarely compared their sexual role to that of a female. Abdalla, the prostitute from Acre, was exceptional in this respect. Abdalla dressed up as a woman, augmented his physique with artificial breasts, and discursively compared himself to a female, admitting he allowed his clients 'sexual intercourse of a male to female from the rear'. Yet even Abdalla explained his choices by reference to his poverty and disability and not in terms of an effeminate disposition. Another rare example surfaces in a 1931 murder case. The police believed that the accused murderer killed his adolescent former lover out of homosexual jealousy. According to one newspaper article, the murder happened after the boy had told the accused, 'I am not your

[72] See his evidence before the police investigator on 11 June 1943. ISA/RG 30/Law 2029 (original docket # Cr.C 221/43).
[73] Habib, 63. [74] ISA/RG 30/Law 2023 (original docket # Cr.C 481/42).
[75] ISA/RG 30/Law 2046 (original docket # Cr.C 211/45).

wife. I am free.'[76] Even as the boy specifically denied that his role in the relationship could be labelled feminine, he suggested a possible analogy between a penetrated male partner and a 'wife'.[77] In a framework of ubiquitous heteronormativity, in which gender categories are reduced to two, male and female, and are congruent with the sexual roles of penetrator and penetrated, being penetrated implies effeminacy.[78] In the descriptions heard in the Palestine courts, male sex roles were not automatically conflated with gender roles, and same-sex desire was not analogous (nor did it contrast) to a heterosexual sexual or romantic relationship.

Charges of 'offences against the order of nature' turned almost exclusively on plausible narratives of homosexual relations. Despite the language that forbade the commission of such offences with any 'person', prosecution for consensual anal sex with a female was relatively rare. One such case relates to relations that were not forced on but were hardly desired by the female partner. Rushdi, a twenty-five-year-old Muslim carpenter from Haifa, was charged with repeatedly having anal sex with his twenty-year-old wife, Fatmeh, to whom he had been married less than a year. When the reluctant Fatmeh finally refused, Rushdi beat her and she left him. Later, Fatmeh, divorced and pregnant, requested the charges against Rushdi be dropped. The magistrate referred the case to the attorney-general for consideration. Rushdi was apparently never tried by the district court, despite the ample evidence against him.[79] A narrative of 'unnatural offences' between a man and a woman did not match the stereotypical view of the offence and did not constitute a case that necessarily had to be pursued in court.

## Conclusion

Plausibility assumes a common cultural knowledge of how the world operates. Narratives that unfold during the process of proof and rely on such knowledge make good stories to tell, while those factual accounts that deviate from the accepted pattern of knowledge make for wrong stories. In their regulation of sex between males the British wished to construct new knowledge in the territory entrusted to their rule. Yet the examination of plausible narratives

[76] 'The Murderer from Sarefend Sentenced to 15 Years', *Davar*, 30 October 1931, p. 3.

[77] Interestingly, Jewish depictions of homosexual relationships characterized the practitioners as effeminate. For example, in his prison memoirs, Abba Achimeir, a Jewish revisionist, related the jealousy a Jewish prisoner displayed in regard to his Arab partner, whom Achimeir dubbed 'his wife'. Ilany, 'A Fine Bequest from Our Neighbors', n. 57. Another Jewish revisionist, Shmuelevitz, uses the term 'wife' in referring to a prisoner whose role was to serve as the sexual partner of another, more prominent, prisoner. Cited by Kaspi, 141, 165.

[78] Najmabadi, 16.

[79] ISA/RG 30/Law 2029 (original docket # Cr.C 211/43). Bestiality, another offence that was introduced by the British and included in the section of 'offences against nature', was also rarely prosecuted. During research for this book, I found only one such case, that of a labourer from Syria who was convicted after being caught in the act with a sheep. ISA/RG 30/Law 2027 (original docket # Cr.C 131/43).

in the process of proof reveals that their legislative innovation was not as revolutionary a change as it might initially seem. The penetrator/penetrated distinction it drew was congruent with local Arab traditions of age- and status-stratified male sex. Furthermore, the clear statutory distinction between non-consensual sodomy and consensual offences against nature (a distinction that was absent in contemporary English law) was not always sharply maintained in practice, as analysis of the stories told in court demonstrates. Consensual 'offences against the order of nature' were perceived as reflecting unequal power relations, and the prosecution of 'sodomy' focused mostly on 'blame-able' victims and on sex with children, a criminal prohibition that did not require proof of force. The criminalization of consensual acts was underscored by myths underlying forcible rape, thus constructing homosexuality not as an egalitarian, reciprocal, romantic, affectionate or mutually passionate relationship but as the result of power differentials and aggression.

Stigmatized as an oriental vice, sodomy was regarded not as an individual pathology but, rather, a cultural depravity. This view entailed 'casting' local Arabs in the role of the accused[80] (a role consistent with the Western Orientalist image of Arab sexuality) and constructed an implicit distinction between the British and their subjects, a distinction that presumably justified colonial authorities' regulation of sexual conduct. Yet the penetrator/penetrated binary had roots in both British and local Arab cultures. The view of homosexuality as a practice enforced by older on younger males was not foreign to the British.[81] The egalitarian 'gay' homosexuality of today did not exist during the British colonial era, and the term 'homosexual' was used neither by judges and legislators nor by defendants and witnesses.

The medicalized identification of the passive partner demonstrates that the formation of the homosexual 'personage' in the Foucauldian sense[82] was

[80] When British or other soldiers (like the Italian sergeant mentioned in this chapter) were involved in consensual sex with local men, they were not prosecuted. Three British soldiers who were accused of sexually assaulting a fellow soldier were eventually acquitted (convicted of assault rather than commission of an indecent act). ISA/RG 30/Law 2028 (original docket # Cr. C 154/43), ISA/RG 30/Law 2046 (original docket # Cr.C 211/45), ISA/RG 30/Law 2009 (original docket # Cr.C 173/40). David Tidhar, who served in the Palestine Police in the years 1921–1926 and rose to the rank of inspector in charge of three stations in Jerusalem, acknowledged that the British were reluctant to investigate soldiers who were involved in sexual offences, but he argued that this was the government's, not the police's, doing. He described police efforts to put an end to nightly incidents of British soldiers entering Jewish homes in Jerusalem in search of women, and of Indian soldiers wandering Jewish neighbourhoods trying to seduce children with candies. David Tidhar, *In My Homeland Service (1912–1960)* [in Hebrew](Tel Aviv: Yedidim, 1961), 61, 86–87.

[81] Jeremy Bentham and Oscar Wilde, for example, identified homosexuality with pederasty. Jeremy Bentham, *Of Sexual Irregularities, and Other Writings on Sexual Morality*, ed. Philip Schofield, Catherine Pease-Watkin and Michael Quinn, *Penology and Criminal Law, Religion and the Church* (Oxford: Clarendon Press, 2014), 97–98. For Wilde's testimony at his gross indecency trial, see http://law2.umkc.edu/faculty/projects/ftrials/wilde/Crimwilde.html.

[82] Michel Foucault, *The History of Sexuality: An Introduction*, Vol. 1 (New York: Vintage Books, 1990), 43.

embryonic in Mandate Palestine. Medicalization of practitioners of male sex was limited and related mostly to those who were penetrated (thus implicitly bolstering myths of inferior and 'blameable' sex roles). Penetrators were not classified as 'paedophiles'. Medical opinions employed vernacular terms, such as 'used' or 'habitual sodomist', to label the penetrated partner. The use of 'habitual sodomist' as a medical term signalled the emergence of homosexuality as pathology and a type of personality and at the same time it portrayed male sex as a 'habit' rather than a medical disorder. The medical discourse had a rather equivocal role in the formation of a homosexual identity. The British emphasis on the importance of medical evidence made a rhetorical claim for superiority based on science and progress. But attribution of personal pathology through the medical gaze conflicted with the imperial gaze, which deplored the sexuality of 'natives' in general.

Local dispositions also resisted the concept of male sex as pathology. Regulation of both forceful and consensual male sex leaned on existing sociocultural concepts and hierarchies and on sexual roles that were arranged along the local social power grid (an older and more affluent man penetrating a younger one). The meaning of male rape and the criminalization of homosexuality were neither dictated top-down by the drafters of criminal provisions nor exclusively shaped through the interpretations of British judges. This is not to say that the British did not effectuate an actual change. In a departure from the status quo in Ottoman days, under British jurisdiction, men who engaged in consensual sex with other men could end up in prison. However, the plausible narratives that unfolded during courtroom proceedings demonstrate that continuity was no less present than change.

# 3

# Plausibility of Children's Testimonies: Narrator's Identity

Most sex offence cases prosecuted in the courts of Mandate Palestine for which records exist concerned minor victims. Of 147 cases, 101 (69 per cent) involved children younger than 18.[1] Of 96 minor victims 81 (37 girls and 44 boys) were under 16, and 15 (5 girls and 10 boys) were aged 16 to 18.[2] Although conviction rates were similar in cases involving minor victims (63 per cent) and adult victims (64 per cent), child witnesses confronted special challenges that did not affect adult witnesses.[3]

The experience of being a child, and therefore the cultural meaning of 'childhood', varies over time and across space.[4] Current historical studies regard childhood not as a mere chronological span but as a concept that attains its meaning within a specific historical and cultural context.[5] Age does not simply represent 'natural' phenomena but is socially constructed similarly to categories of gender, race or class.

Children were considered competent witnesses, yet courts often distrusted them. Suspicion toward their testimony was built into evidentiary and procedural mechanisms. The credibility of young witnesses was often challenged on the basis of individual inadequacies as well as socially constructed misgivings regarding the testimony of children more generally. This chapter examines the special challenges faced by child witnesses in sexual offence cases, and this examination serves as a basis for exploring the interconnectivity of plausibility and credibility.

While credibility and plausibility are associated with different goals (the former truth and the latter persuasion), they occasionally overlap, as the

[1] Not included in this count is one victim whose age is recorded as sixteen to twenty-one. ISA Division 30 (Supreme Court Files), File B/374/143, original docket # Cr.A 143/44.

[2] Victims figuring in multiple cases (e.g. of separately indicted accused attackers or of perjury charges related to the original filing) are counted once in this tally.

[3] The results in cases involving minor victims break down as follows: unknown result – 7, stay of proceedings – 5, general amnesty – 1, acquitted – 23, convicted of lesser offence – 13, convicted as charged – 47. Results in cases with adult victims are: acquitted or convicted of assault instead of a sexual offence – 6, convicted of lesser offence – 4, convicted as charged – 24, unknown result – 3, stay of proceedings – 2, information quashed – 1.

[4] Heidi Morrison, *Childhood and Colonial Modernity in Egypt* (Houndmills: Palgrave Macmillan, 2015), 8.

[5] For a review of the historiographic debates about the significance of childhood as a category of historical analysis, see ibid., 7–10.

persuasive witness may be deemed more convincing. The assessment of credibility involves consideration of both individual criteria (the witness's observation and communication skills, possible interest or bias, etc.) and socially constructed characteristics. The latter, which might seem like individual traits at first glance (e.g. race, gender, profession, socio-economic status), are in fact attributed to the witness on the basis of his or her social or cultural affiliation. Some of what appear initially to be individual, objectively observable qualities are in effect standards seen as applicable to a whole social or cultural category. Can the members of this social group be trusted? Are they expected to speak, behave, feel in certain ways? Do the witness's actions and demeanour, as they unfold through testimony, make sense considering his or her gender, social status, ethnicity and other attributes?

The qualities ascribed to the witness as a member of a social group or sector are grounded in scripts of plausible narratives, roles and traits. Descriptions that are deemed implausible, bearing in mind the witness's categorical socio-cultural affiliation, can damage credibility. For example, if it is deemed implausible that a woman would remain calm after being raped, her testimony that she maintained her composure could compromise her credibility. Plausible behaviour or emotions (the latter are discussed in detail in Chapter 5) must conform with gendered, ethnic, aged-based and other social expectations, lest they undermine the witness's credibility.

The analytical distinction between individual and socially constructed criteria of credibility is often blurred. The child witness is a case in point, as chronological age is both an individual quality that may be correlated with level of maturity and cognitive development and a marker of membership in a cultural and social category, a socially constructed communal trait.

This chapter focuses on three legal mechanisms that reveal an institutionalized scepticism toward narratives told by child witnesses in sex offence cases: the preconditions of oath-taking, perjury charges against children and inquiry into the sexual history of child complainants. Doubtful plausibility of narratives of "children" as a cultural category resulted in diminished credibility of individual child witnesses. In other words, the assumption that children in general tended toward imagination, embellishment and outright fabrication – that is, narrative implausibility – diminished the credibility of individual child witnesses.

## The Victims

The charges and complaints in the cases I examined provide a complex picture of children's life realities in Mandate Palestine and reflect the prevalence of sexual assaults against children in diverse social circles. Children who complained of having been sexually assaulted included urban dwellers, villagers and nomads, Arabs and Jews, boys and girls, school students and working children. Their attackers were strangers, relatives, neighbours and acquaintances.

The attacks occurred while victims were playing outside or at their home or tent, while working in the fields, helping with the chores or just passing the time.

Jack (age three) was playing in a garden near his house in Haifa when a twenty-two-year-old unemployed man walking the streets in search of a job invited him to 'play'; the man then sodomized him under a pine tree up the road from his home.[6] Jamila (seven) was playing outside with a friend and her younger brother when a man approached her, took her to an isolated area and assaulted her.[7] Hava (ten) was picking flowers.[8] Omad (three) had gone to buy himself a balloon.[9] Shoshana (five) was raped while carrying a tin of water from a drainage pipe to her family's home in an orange grove near Hadera.[10] Mohammad (seven), sent by his mother to buy bread, was sodomized by a man who threatened him at knifepoint.[11] Amneh (ten) was gathering straw with her cousins on village lands.[12] Mustafa (ten) was grazing the family's two goats on village lands.[13] Saleh (seven)[14] and Mohammad (eight)[15] were herding cows. Nokha (fourteen) was grazing camels.[16]

Quite a few complaints were made against people familiar to the victims. Esther (ten) accused her neighbour,[17] Muna (ten) a cousin[18] and Samiha (thirteen) her father.[19] Nazmi (nine) named his elementary school teacher.[20] Nizar (eight) identified a young employee in his father's pharmacy as the one who sodomized him in a storage room.[21] Naifa (fourteen), a servant, reported a worker at the bakery where she used to buy bread.[22] A chewing gum seller was accused of assaulting Abdul (fourteen),[23] an itinerant Primus stove repairman of attacking Khana (twelve)[24] and a man whose job was to make sure lights were extinguished (an air raid precaution) of violating Suad (nine).[25]

6 ISA/RG 30/Law 2054 (original docket # Cr.C 155/46).
7 ISA Division 30 (Supreme Court Files), File B/269/79, original docket # Cr.A 79/38.
8 ISA/RG 30/Law 2053 (original docket # Cr.C 139/46).
9 ISA/RG 30/Law 2062 (original docket # Cr.C 179/47).
10 ISA/RG 30/Law 2039 (original docket # Cr.C 325/44).
11 ISA/RG 30/Law 2047 (original docket # Cr.C 264/45).
12 ISA/RG 30/Law 2045 (original docket # Cr.C 167/45).
13 ISA/RG 30/Law 2037 (original docket # Cr.C 257/44).
14 ISA/RG 30/Law 2015 (original docket # Cr.C 80/42).
15 ISA/RG 30/Law 2036 (original docket # Cr.C 234/44).
16 ISA/RG 30/Law 2048 (original docket # Cr.C 307/45).
17 ISA/RG 30/Law 2006 (original docket #Cr.C 127/39).
18 ISA/RG 30/Law 2034 (original docket # Cr.C 159/44).
19 ISA Division 30 (Supreme Court Files), File B/353/122, original docket # Cr.A 118/42.
20 ISA/RG 30/Law 2036 (original docket # Cr.C 200/44).
21 ISA Division 30 (Supreme Court Files), File B/269/71, original docket # Cr.A 71/38.
22 ISA/RG 30/Law 2010 (original docket # Cr.C 187/40).
23 ISA/RG 30/Law 2054 (original docket # Cr.C 175/46).
24 ISA/RG 30/Law 2033 (original docket # Cr.C 88/44).
25 ISA/RG 30/Law 2009 (original docket # Cr.C 170/40).

Some attacks occurred in the context of ongoing familial or social conflicts. Fatmeh (eight), for example, was raped in her tent near Gaza by three men whose family was feuding with her own.[26]

## Policy

The protection and care of children was a declared policy of British legislation and administration in Mandate Palestine (although execution and resources often lagged behind). The British regulated matters such as child labour, child marriage[27] and juvenile delinquency.[28] They established systems of probation, health and welfare.[29] Given the paternalistic nature of colonial rule, regulation of children's lives 'exposed better than did contract, tax, or any other kind of legislation the inherent tensions between tradition and change with which colonial rulers contended'.[30] By stressing their pro-child policy, the British explicitly distinguished themselves from their Ottoman predecessors, sought legitimacy not only among their subjects but also in the international arena and British public opinion and reiterated their self-laudatory narrative of instilling progress among the backward.[31] The explicit policy of protecting local children, however, was frequently not backed up by zealous practice. There were significant areas of legislative inaction, notably, the failure to enact compulsory education.[32] Seemingly progressive British legislation sometimes reflected acquiescence to local pressures.[33] Child protective legislation either was compromised by statutory mechanisms that significantly reduced its impact or was not effectively enforced.[34]

Mandate legislation in the area of criminal law reflects a dualistic image of the child. On the one hand, children were perceived as menaces to society, actual or potential delinquents who should be punished or 'reformed'. On the other hand, their youth and vulnerability rendered children prospective victims, justifying their special care and protection. The literature on children in Mandate Palestine dwells mostly on the first of these perceptions, describing

[26] SA Division 30 (Supreme Court Files), File B/186/40, original docket # Cr.A 40/34.

[27] Assaf Likhovski, *Law and Identity in Mandate Palestine*, ed. Thomas A. Green and Hendrik Hartog, Studies in Legal History (Chapel Hill: University of North Carolina Press, 2006), 13, chapter 14.

[28] Nava Elad and Anita Weiner, *The History of Youth Probation and Services for Disadvantaged Delinquent Children in Israel* [in Hebrew] (Tel Aviv, Ramot: Tel Aviv University, 1995), 29–35; Gad J. Bensinger, 'Criminal Justice in Israel', in *Crime and Criminal Justice in Israel: Assessing Knowledge Base toward the Twenty-First Century*, ed. Robert R. Friedmann (Albany: State University of New York Press, 1998), 44–45.

[29] Significantly complemented by Zionist and missionary institutions. Marcella Simoni, 'A Dangerous Legacy: Welfare in British Palestine, 1930-1939', *Jewish History* 13, no. 2 (1999): 83–84.

[30] Likhovski, 85. [31] Ibid., 86, 104.

[32] Tammy Razi, *Forsaken Children: The Backyard of Mandate Tel-Aviv* [in Hebrew] (Tel Aviv: Am Oved, 2009), 100.

[33] Likhovski, 89–90. [34] Ibid., ch. 4.

neglected children as social threats, potentially turning to crime and prostitution,[35] and emphasizing the dangers posed by young offenders.[36] Records of sex offence cases vividly demonstrate the ambivalent perception of children in Palestine.

## Sex Offences and Children

Whereas the Ottomans categorized sex offenders as 'persons who violate honour',[37] the British saw them as having committed 'offences against women and children and against decency'[38] (later, 'offences against morality'[39]). An explicit rationale behind Mandate's definitions of sexual offences was the protection of children. The offences of rape[40] and sodomy[41] required a sexual act against an individual's will. These offences were also constituted when the sexual act was committed with a child younger than sixteen, notwithstanding consent. The rationale is evident. Children were considered too immature to consent to sexual acts, and therefore they needed to be protected from deceit, trickery, short-sighted discretion and poor judgement.

The commitment to protect children from sexual assaults was not free from impediments. The criminal law in the area of sex offences incorporated incongruent images of the child, and the law in action was not always consistent with the explicit rationale of the law on the books. The declared goal of protecting children was somewhat frustrated by evidentiary mechanisms such as corroboration and oath preconditions that impeded proof of sexual offences against minors. Furthermore, the protection of child victims was undermined by culturally prototypical images of children that underlay the process of proof. The complainant might indeed have been a vulnerable violated child, but it was also plausible that he or she was fabricating, unreliable and seductive. The ambivalent cultural position of children's sexuality, simultaneously imperilled and perilous, endangered and dangerous, pure and corrupted, had a role in justifying existing age-based hierarchies and in regulating those perceived as a threat to the sanctity of childhood.[42]

I demonstrate the tensions associated with proving sex offences against children by highlighting three areas of suspicion regarding their testimony: the preconditions of oath-taking, perjury charges against children and inquiry into the sexual past of child complainants. These mechanisms clearly demonstrate British caution when it came to trusting the narratives of children.

[35] Razi. [36] Simoni, 96–104. [37] The title of Part III of the OPC.
[38] The title of the relevant section of the CLAO, 1927.
[39] The title of the sex offences chapter in the CCO, 1936. [40] Section 152(2)(a) of the CCO.
[41] Section 152(2)(b) of the CCO.
[42] R. Danielle Egan and Gail L. Hawkes, 'Imperiled and Perilous: Exploring the History of Childhood Sexuality', *Journal of Historical Sociology* 21, no. 4 (2008): 357, 360.

## Preconditions of Oath

On the face of it, statutory provisions made proof easier when the victim of a sex offence was a child. In cases of rape or sodomy, it was unnecessary to prove the use of force when the victim was younger than sixteen.[43] The punishment for an indecent act committed upon a child younger than sixteen was similar to punishment for a forced indecent act.[44] However, in practice, the proof of sex offences with a child victim was strewn with obstacles. The requirement of corroboration in all cases of sexual assaults, as I demonstrate in Chapter 6, disproportionately affected children.

Another evidentiary device that obstructed the prosecution of offences against children was oath-taking. Witnesses testifying in the courts of Mandate Palestine had to be examined under oath (except when the court was convinced oath-taking was at odds with their religious beliefs, in which case they could be examined on their own affirmation).[45] Child witnesses enjoyed the prima facie privilege of exemption from oath. Section 34(2) of the Criminal Procedure (Trial upon Information) Ordinance (hereinafter, TUI) proclaimed, 'A child too young to understand the nature of an oath may, if the court is satisfied that his evidence should be heard, be examined without oath.' Children, this section provided, were to be heard, even if they were too young to understand what an oath signified. While the age of consent was statutorily set at sixteen, the TUI provision did not establish a fixed age at which a child was 'too young' for such understanding. Nor were there judicial criteria for differentiating between babyhood, childhood and youth. The parsing of the young into age cohorts (e.g. toddlers, adolescents, etc.) can be related to the rise of child-centred scientific disciplines.[46] Apparently, in Mandate Palestine, it was judges rather than child experts who determined a minor's level of maturity. According to Ephraim Salant, a Mandate-era prosecutor and the author of a book on evidence law, the judge was supposed to establish the degree of mental development. He writes, for example, 'If the judge asks the minor what happens to a liar? and the minor answers that he goes to hell, it can be presumed that the minor acknowledges the duty to testify truthfully.'[47]

Section 34(2) enabled the testimony of very young witnesses. For example, the magistrate who held preliminary examination in the matter of the sodomy of five-year-old Shoshana from Hadera ordered she be heard 'without oath because she does not under[stand] what it is'. The record further stated that the

43 Section 152(1)(c) of the CCO.

44 Sections 159 (*Indecent act committed upon child*) and 157 (*Indecent act with force*) of the CCO.

45 Criminal Procedure (Trial upon Information) Ordinance, 1924 (the original section number, 32, was modified in later ordinances to 34. I use the latter).

46 Such categorization appeared in the twentieth-century United States. Leslie Paris, 'Through the Looking Glass: Age, Stages, and Historical Analysis', *The Journal of the History of Childhood and Youth* 1, no. 1 (2008): 108.

47 Ephraim Salent, *Evidence Law: In Criminal Trials* (Tel Aviv: Israel Print, 1952), 106.

child looked confused and did not answer questions. Her nine-year-old sister also testified without oath.[48] Although judges were expected to examine whether the child understood the duty to tell the truth, some relied on physical traits rather than cognitive level in making this determination. For example, seven-year-old Merriam from Acre was allowed to testify unsworn, the record stating that she was 'tall and well developed for her age'.[49]

Some judges explicitly reasoned that the demand for oath should not be 'constructed so strictly in the case of young children'.[50] They reckoned that since children under the age of criminal responsibility could not be charged with making false statements, formal oath-taking was not mandatory.[51]

Despite the oath-exemption mechanism, the voices of children, regrettably, were not always heard. Three-year-old Jack participated in an identification parade but was unable to single out his attacker. Jack was not called to testify in the preliminary examination or the trial, and his mother told his story. The accused was nevertheless convicted, on his own admission.[52]

Yehodit, a Jewish domestic servant of a Muslim family residing in a Carmelite building in Haifa, testified that one morning in October 1945, while she was going about her housework, she entered a room and saw her four-year-old son, Arie, sitting in the lap of Mustafa, a resident at the house.[53] As she picked up Arie (who was dressed in shorts), she noticed that Mustafa's trousers were open and his sexual organ exposed. The doctor who testified in the case against Mustafa reported finding a recent tear in Arie's rectum. At the preliminary examination, the defence attorney objected to the boy's testimony 'because the boy whose age is 4 years does not know what he says'. The objection relied on TUI section 34(2) and Phipson.[54] The magistrate, without even questioning Arie himself, ordered that his testimony not be heard: 'He is 4 years old. I don't believe that he understands what he says.' Later, when the prosecution called Arie to testify in District Court, the defence counsel again objected, this time on the ground that a witness who had not given evidence at the preliminary examination could not be called by the prosecution at trial. The objection was allowed. Arie was not heard, and the accused was eventually acquitted despite the medical evidence and the mother's testimony.

Often, parents stepped forward to describe the injuries done to their children. They were not eyewitnesses to the assaults, however, so their accounts amounted to hearsay. Furthermore, a conviction could not rest on the

[48] ISA/RG 30/Law 2039 (original docket # Cr.C 325/44).
[49] ISA/RG 30/Law 2004 (original docket # Cr.C 259/37).
[50] ISA Division 30 (Supreme Court Files), File B/269/71, original docket # Cr.A 71/38), ruling in page 7 of the transcripts.
[51] Ibid. [52] ISA/RG 30/Law 2054 (original docket # Cr.C 155/46).
[53] ISA/RG 30/Law 2050 (original docket # Cr.C 24/46).
[54] *Phipson on Evidence* is a leading textbook on evidence law. The first edition, by Sydney L. Phipson, was published in 1892. Updated editions followed, the last published by Sweet & Maxwell in 2013.

uncorroborated testimony of a single witness, and what children told their parents was not considered corroboration. Sometimes children other than victims served as witnesses, but if they too did not testify under oath, their accounts were not considered corroborative. In the rape case of seven-year-old Jamila, Abd, a neighbour boy of about the same age, testified that he saw the accused take Jamila by the hand at the time of the incident. The Supreme Court overturned the conviction in the case, reasoning that 'the evidence of that child, which was given unsworn, was corroborated only by the evidence of another unsworn child. On this becoming clear the Crown Counsel rightly stated that he could not support the conviction.' The court, it turned out, was mistaken about Abd's testimony – in fact, it was given under oath. The record duly states 'sworn: Will speak truth by God. Aged 7–8 years. Seems intelligent.' The Supreme Court's mistake possibly reflects the ubiquitous assumption that young children were unfit to take the oath.[55]

Even when children had the opportunity to tell their stories in court, their inability to swear under oath could jeopardize the chance of conviction. This consequence was sometimes explicitly denounced in judicial decisions, as it was in the acquittal of the accused in the sodomy case of seven-year-old Mohammad: 'the unsworn testimony of the second witness is not corroboration of the similarly unsworn testimony of the complainant, it appears most unfortunately and most unhappily impossible to bring to book the perpetrator of this revolting offence against a very young boy'.[56]

Frustrated judges lamented that the difficulty imposed by unsworn child testimony made it almost impossible to prove sex offences against children, despite their wide incidence in Palestine. Judge Weldon, the president of the Haifa District Court, was one who did so, summarizing one case in the following terms:

> the evidence of the boy Yousef is not sworn testimony; the evidence of the boy Elias is likewise not sworn testimony. What the boy told his mother is not corroboration in view of his unsworn testimony; what the boy showed the Police as regards the room and the bed is likewise not corroboration. I wish to say quite frankly that under application of English law to this country nearly all such offences as the present one cannot be proved; they are all too common in this country and unfortunately it is almost always impossible to bring to book the offender.[57]

This judgment maintains that in Palestine those accused in sexual attacks on children could rarely be convicted. Unsworn testimony of children could be formally admitted into evidence, but it was not considered corroborative. The reason given for this flawed practice was that the application of the

[55] Judgment of the Supreme Court. ISA Division 30 (Supreme Court Files), File B/269/79, original docket # Cr.A 79/38.

[56] ISA/RG 30/Law 2030 (original docket # Cr.C 252/43).

[57] ISA/RG 30/Law 2032 (original docket # Cr.C 50/44).

evidentiary standard of 'English law' did not fit 'this country'. The problem, Judge Weldon implies, lay not in transplanted English evidentiary standards but in the prevalence of sexual offences in Palestine. He insinuates that Palestine was not advanced enough for the application of British law. One can question the logic of his criticism, as he simultaneously points to legal English standards as the root of the injustice. One thing is clear: while children could be exempted from oath, their unsworn testimony was not sufficient to serve as a basis for conviction and thus made little difference in the outcome of a case.

The testimony of the child witness, even when sworn and corroborated, faced a further difficulty: it was weighed against the testimony of an adult. The testimony of an adult accused faced fewer evidentiary obstacles than that of a child victim, and the accused's age could sometimes work to his benefit. For instance, Dr Ohannes Torian, a government hospital doctor testifying as an expert witness in a 1944 rape case of a thirteen-year-old girl, opined that 'it is irrational that a man in such an age (60–70) can have an intercourse with a girl and to commit the act of sodomy on her within half an hour's time'.[58] It was plausible, to Dr Torian, at least, that an older man lacked the capacity to pose a sexual danger to others. For the child, age was a disadvantage in the courtroom, but for the accused of advanced years, it could become a line of defence.

## Perjury: An Accuser Becomes Accused

The distrust towards the testimony of the child who complained of sexual assault could ripen into charges of perjury against the child. Such was the case for twelve-year-old Mohammad, a poor Muslim boy from Acre.[59] Mohammad accused seventy-year-old Khaled of sexually attacking him. Khaled was a coachman who kept his horses in a store located between a carpenter's shop and a sea coffee-house. In his statement to the police, the boy recounted how he had been walking in the street near his home when Khaled, who was watering his horses, offered to pay him one piastre to fill a bucket of water. When he entered the stable/store, Mohammed said, Khaled locked the door, covered his mouth, threw him down and forcibly removed his underwear. Khaled took out his penis and lay on top of him while Mohammed shouted and struggled. Two men who heard the shouting from outside (one of them, a neighbour, recognized Mohammad's voice) broke through the door, interrupting the act. Mohammad also stated that on several previous occasions Khaled had offered to give him money for sex but that he had refused. Before the magistrate, Mohammad repeated the story, except for two details. He had told the police that the suspect had taken off his underpants by force and had

[58] ISA/RG 30/Law 2036 (original docket # Cr.C 197/44).
[59] ISA/RG 30/Law 2051 (original docket # Cr.C 64/46, 65/46, 66/46).

lain on top of him. To the magistrate, Mohammad said he had not been wearing underpants and that the suspect had not touched his body. In all other details (the accused locking the door, taking off the boy's trousers, etc.), the two accounts matched.

In altering his story, the boy might have been trying to protect what little remained of his reputation. One of the men who broke the door in and saved him, his neighbour Habush, also recanted his initial story. Originally he said he saw Khaled lying on the boy, but before the magistrate he claimed he had not seen anybody lying over the boy, that he had only heard the boy's voice through the door. Both Mohammad and Habush were charged with perjury for giving contradictory statements. The other witness who broke into the store/stable insisted that he found Khaled lying over the boy, and he was not charged with perjury. From the accuser, the boy Mohammad turned into the accused. Khaled was charged with attempted sodomy but was later acquitted in District Court, given the benefit of the doubt on the basis of the inconsistent witness testimony (although the judgment explicitly expressed doubts about his innocence).

Mohammad was convicted of perjury and sentenced to three years' detention in a reformatory institution for boys. The probation officer's report reveals the dire circumstances of his life. He was the second of six children, all dirty, neglected and given to loitering about. His entire family, parents and children alike, were illiterate. Mohammad had never been to school. The family lived in a filthy one-room apartment in Acre, where the parents quarrelled continuously. Mohammad's father, a fisherman and reputed drunkard, had deserted the family about a year before the incident. Afterwards, the family's sole provider was fourteen-year-old Omar, Mohammad's older brother, who worked as a restaurant boy. The probation officer's report describes the mother as 'a simple and ignorant woman' with 'a bad indecent character of bad fame and immoral reputation'. Mohammad's sexual reputation was similarly flawed. The officer writes that he had 'a bad name from a moral point of view (i.e. he lends himself to sodomites for sodomy and copulation acts). He represents the destitute and spoiled type of a boy.' The officer thus recommended that he be remanded to a reformatory school for boys, an institution that 'would render him a good benefit and serve his future'.

Mohammad successfully appealed to the Supreme Court, which rescinded the order for detention. That court held that since Mohammad did not testify under oath, he could not be convicted of perjury.[60] Although it quashed the boy's conviction on several legal grounds, the judges clearly were unsatisfied with the boy's prospects and ordered the authorities to further investigate whether he should be placed in supervised care.

Mohammad embodied the dual image of the child. On the one hand, he was a victim of desolate life circumstances. Growing up in poverty, illiteracy and

[60] Cr.A 47/46 *Muhammad Abdul Fattah el Moghrabi* v. *A.G.* (1 May 1946).

unhygienic conditions, with dysfunctional parents who were poor role models and with no access to education, he faced a bleak future. On the other hand, Mohammad could not be trusted. His age and background plausibly suggested he was manipulative and untruthful, a transgressor of social rules and sexual boundaries. Lacking 'respectability', he had little credibility. His word was insufficient foundation for legal sanctions against his attacker, and in fact he himself became a target of sanctions.

Mohammad's case involves a discounting of credibility that is based on both individual and socio-cultural characteristics. It is different from cases in which implausibility was imputed to the witness solely on the basis of membership in a social group or category (as the rule of corroboration did, for example, in undermining the trustworthiness of complainants concerning whom no individual flaw was attributed). Mohammad was disbelieved because of his incoherence and possibly because of what was perceived to be his murky social and familial background. From a sexual assault complainant, he was transformed into an accused perjurer. As the following section suggests, Mohammad's ability to persuade faced an additional, especially formidable, obstacle.

## The 'Used' Child

Cases of perjury are explicit attempts to establish lack of credibility and untrustworthiness. Contradictory statements were at the fore of the attempt in Mohammad's case, but circumstances such as the boy's sexual past, rumours about his prostitution and his mother's ill-reputed sexuality orbited the case. These circumstances, though not part of the official evidence against him, created an impression that nevertheless influenced determination of Mohammed's credibility and reliability. Notwithstanding its irrelevance to most cases, information about a child witness's sexual past was an influential rhetorical device. When children accused adults of sexual molestation, both their stories and their bodies were scrutinized.

Under the British definition of rape or sodomy, underage children were legally incompetent to give consent. Any sexual act with children under sixteen, even if they cooperated and no force was used, created an offence. In popular view, however, the consenting child could be regarded as blameable and as ripe for taking. These competing views are on display in a 1947 case in which fourteen-year-old Jamila testified that forty-year-old Said Sharqiya, her neighbour in Hawwase, abducted her and violently penetrated her body. Jamila testified she was a virgin. During his examination by police, Said did not deny engaging in a series of sexual acts with young Jamila. He did so, he claimed, after Jamila practically threw herself at him. First, he said, Jamila (who used to deliver his laundry and clean his hut) told him several times that she wanted him to marry her. Next, according to Said, Jamila showed up uninvited at his hut at night, but he sent her away. Later, Jamila absconded from her father's house, and after failed attempts on his part to find the girl and return her to her father (her family was simultaneously trying to retrieve her), Said alleged, she appeared at his village home in Imqa. When he urged her to return to her own home, she told him that if he forced her to do so she would spill kerosene over herself and implicate him. Said then replied, 'So long [as] you want me, I want you', and they had sex. Said described in detail how he had deflowered her and she had bled, and he said he had repeated the act about ten times that night and once again about four or five days later. In Said's view, his story was exonerating. 'She offered herself to me', he claimed. Whether or not Said's story was an outright lie, it was one that made sense to him and one that he thought would be persuasive and plausible in the eyes of investigators. Clearly, he believed Jamila's consent rendered his actions legitimate. Even had his story been believed, however, his actions constituted rape under the CCO. Indeed, at his trial he pleaded guilty and was sentenced to eighteen months' imprisonment.[61]

Although loss of virginity was not part of the definition of any form of sexual assault in Mandate Palestine, the judiciary regarded the deflowering of girls with abhorrence. In one case involving a twelve-year-old girl, the Supreme Court conveyed that it was 'fully conscious of its duty to protect young girls from lustful men'.[62] Whereas, in the above example, Said asserted that Jamila was a virgin when he had sex with her, the accused in other cases argued in their defence that their alleged victims were not virgins and thus that sex with them was permitted. The sexual past of a young girl was directly at issue only when the prosecution claimed that she had no previous sexual experience. In such cases, the defence pointed to evidence that the girl was no longer a virgin.[63] For example, when thirteen-year-old Samiha from Jaffa claimed she lost her virginity when her father raped her, the defence tried to use medical evidence to demonstrate that the rupture of her hymen occurred ten to fifteen days before the alleged rape.[64]

A child who claimed to be a virgin prior to a sexual assault opened the door to contradictory claims. Virginity was doctrinally inconsequential in most cases, but credibility was always an issue. In a 1947 case, fourteen-year-old Margalit claimed she had been a virgin until twenty-year-old Munir Tawfiq sexually assaulted her. The girl was examined by Dr Ohannes Torian, who testified that he found a tear in her hymen that was not recent as well as a deep contusion and haemorrhage in her vagina that implied recent penetration 'with use of violence and force'.[65] Although the question of virginity was doctrinally immaterial to the elements of the offence, the issue was often raised. Social pressures may have driven children to deny any former sexual experience, even when this was untrue, to avoid the

61 ISA/RG 30/Law 2067 (original docket # Cr.C 259/47).
62 ISA/RG 30/Law 2035 (original docket # Cr.C 184/44).
63 ISA/RG 30/Law 2048 (original docket # Cr.C 307/45).
64 ISA Division 30 (Supreme Court Files), File B/353/122, original docket # Cr.A 118/42.
65 ISA/RG 30/Law 2065 (original docket # Cr.C 321/47), page 8 of the preliminary inquiry.

social stigma and blame associated with such experience, especially when consensual.

Evidence of the promiscuity of the complainant was theoretically superfluous in criminal proceedings. The element of consent was immaterial to proof of sexual offences involving children younger than sixteen. However, reference to the sexual past of the complaining child was part of the cultural subtext scaffolding the process of proof.

The indirect bearing of a child's sexual past on criminal proceedings is hard to measure. Alya (fifteen), a servant girl, asserted that she had not consented to have sex with Khalil, a repairman from Damascus whom she had known for seven years while in service in Haifa. It is hard to tell whether the court's disbelief of her story was influenced by medical testimony that she may have had 'frequent intercourse' prior to the encounter with Khalil.[66] Likewise, it is hard to tell whether that evidence had any bearing on the court's conclusion that the accused reasonably believed, given the girl's 'developed' appearance, that she was eighteen years old. Here, the sexually active child was juxtaposed against the 'pure' naive victim. Childish bodies that did not emit signs of adult activity were deceptive and confusing. The construction of the child witness as a sexual person undermined his or her credibility – though indirectly, through its effect on plausibility. The less 'pure' the child's past, the less plausible the scenario of the child as victim became.

Clearly, some defendants regarded the child's sexual past as a mitigating factor. Mahammad, who was charged with (and eventually acquitted of) the rape of ten-year-old Deebeh, denied the accusation, claiming, '3 boys played with the complainant before me, and the desire of the parents of the complainant is to make me marry her.'[67] In this case, the doctor who examined the girl testified he had found two old tears in her hymen and some indication of recent intercourse. In another case, the accused in the rape of Nokkha (fourteen), a Bedouin girl whom he suspected of stealing watermelons from the vines he was watching, claimed she had consented.[68] He stated before the police investigator that 'I found her women [*sic*]. I told her who raped you she said her fiancé Suleiman Kharoubi. The reason which made me be certain that she is not virgin because no blood came out. I want a Govt. doctor to examine her and if he decides that she is raped recently I am ready then to accept any punishment.' According to the logic of his statement, a medical finding that the girl was not a virgin necessarily meant he was not a rapist. This statement conveys the perception that only a virgin could be raped and implies that a non-virgin was sexually available to anyone.

Evidence of past sexual activity was also introduced when alleged victims were boys. Subhi (thirteen), from a Galilee village near Nazareth, was living in

[66] ISA/RG 30/Law 2008 (original docket # Cr.C 134/40).
[67] ISA/RG 30/Law 2023 (original docket # Cr.C 515/42).
[68] ISA/RG 30/Law 2048 (original docket # Cr.C 307/45).

Haifa and earned his living by selling fruits on the beach. On 21 June 1940, at around 2 a.m., he was outside the cinema after the movie had ended, when he met Rashid. No buses operated at that hour, and the two began walking together. Subhi asserted that when they reached the football grounds, Rashid stunned him with a blow and sodomized him. Subhi's medical examination revealed injuries consistent with his story, and traces of what appeared to be semen were found in his underwear. Dr Ahmad Kamel emphasized that 'the boy had been used more than once for this purpose, as he had a funnel shaped rectum'.[69] Subhi's sexual past was irrelevant to the offence of sodomy. Because he was younger than sixteen, his involvement in anal sex was sufficient to establish an offence, even if he had consented. The judges of the Haifa District Court agreed with the defence attorney's claim that there was no case to answer, as Subhi's complaint could not be corroborated. The lack of corroboration, not Subhi's sexual past, figured in the formal reasoning behind the acquittal. But scaffolding the official distrust in his testimony, Subhi's sexual history was well integrated into the trial record.

The relevance of a child's sexual past was starkest in the case of the child prostitute.[70] Twenty-eight-year-old Zafer was charged with the sodomy of thirteen-year-old Aref.[71] On 8 February 1944, an anonymous phone call led police to the El Asry Hotel in Haifa. When they opened the door of Room 4, they found Zafer and Aref on the bed, both naked from the waist down. They had become acquainted a month earlier in Jaffa, where, Aref related, they had gone to an orange grove and Zafer had committed sodomy with him and paid him thirty piastres. After they met again in Haifa, they spent the day together, had a simple supper at a café and Aref agreed to accompany Zafer to the hotel. A medical examination of Aref revealed that 'the anus of the boy shows that he was used several times'. Aref did not have to testify at the trial, since Zafer pleaded guilty. Had he been summoned to testify, Aref's sexual past could have been used, though not directly, to damage his credibility.

Evidence of a child's past sexual activity, it must be stressed, was not necessarily detrimental; a conviction could still be obtained on the basis of his or her testimony, irrespective of such activity. A case in point is the assault of twelve-year-old Moshe, labelled a 'habitual sodomist' by the testifying doctor. The court believed Moshe's story of the attack against him and convicted Suleiman and Raja, the accused in that case (Raja's confession provided the necessary corroboration).[72]

[69] ISA/RG 30/Law 2010 (original docket # Cr.C 195/40).

[70] Child prostitution in Palestine took various forms, ranging from payment for individual, occasional sex to organized sex labour managed by procurers or taking place in brothels. Some children were trafficked to brothels outside Palestine. David Tidhar, *In My Homeland Service (1912–1960)* [in Hebrew] (Tel Aviv: Yedidim, 1961), 126–127.

[71] ISA/RG 30/Law 2032 (original docket # Cr.C 76/44).

[72] ISA/RG 30/Law 2009 (original docket # Cr.C 168/40).

## Conclusion

In Mandate Palestine, a story's power to convince depended in part on the identity of the narrator. British legislation explicitly purported to protect children. To enable them to tell their stories and bring those who victimized them to justice, children were regarded as competent witnesses and could be exempted from testifying under oath. Nevertheless, their stories often failed to convince, and their credibility was repeatedly questioned. A witness's inability to tell reality from imagination, or the existence of contradictory statements could harm his or her credibility, notwithstanding age. But credibility, or lack thereof, was also established through socially constructed categories. The British viewed children – as a cultural category – with suspicion. It was plausible to them that children would invent stories.

The judicial need to formally determine whether each child witness should testify under oath cast a priori doubt on all children. Unsworn children constituted an inferior category of witnesses, and the stories of all children, even those who eventually testified under oath, were treated with special caution.

The extreme manifestation of disbelief was the pursuit of perjury charges against minors who originally complained about sexual assaults. Contradictory statements served as objective criteria for assessing credibility, yet the nature of the contradictions was a matter of interpretation. Twelve-year-old Mohammad gave contradictory accounts about his attacker taking off his underwear and touching his body, but he was consistent in describing other elements of the sexual attack (that the attacker locked him in a room and took off his trousers). Nevertheless, the boy was charged with perjury. The most damaging inferences regarding his credibility may have been linked to his derelict existence and his sexual past.

It was plausible to British judges that children would invent stories, and it was especially plausible that a sexually active child would do so. Suspicion towards the credibility of a child deepened when he or she was assumed to be sexually active, as made evident by the concept of the 'used child'. Children's sexual histories were scrutinized and held against them. Their engagement in sexual behaviour clashed with social expectations of 'purity'. The image of a vulnerable, innocent and violated child coexisted with the image of a fabricating, unreliable and seductive being, and the resulting ambivalence rendered the narratives of child witnesses less plausible.

The identity of every witness affected the plausibility of his or her story, and children faced particular challenges in this regard. They were constructed as immature, as unable to distinguish reality from imagination and as likely fabricators. The sceptical view towards children might have had a spillover effect when adults were likened to children. The British Mandate was created in an era of significant shifts in imperial policy. The aggrandizing colonialism that had characterized the occupation of eighteenth-century India was no longer acceptable at the beginning of the twentieth century, and the Palestinian Mandate was shaped by the goal of developing a local population not yet ripe for independence and civilized self-government.[73] The mandated subjects were 'structurally disfranchised', and by definition 'dependent on colonial powers to cure their backwardness'.[74] Norman Bentwich, the first attorney-general of Mandate Palestine, clearly regarded mandates as internationally controlled structures of national responsibility for government, in which the guardianship of peoples resembled the guardianship of minors.[75] If all Mandate subjects resembled children, perhaps all of them should be doubted.

Furthermore, one can speculate whether the latent British view of 'natives' as minors led to increased doubts when witnesses were both oriental 'natives' and children. The identity of the narrator reflected on the plausibility of the tale, and intersecting elements of suspect identity might have had particularly deleterious effects on a story's plausibility.

[73] John Strawson, *Partitioning Palestine: Legal Fundamentalism in the Palestinian-Israeli Conflict* (London: Pluto Press, 2010), 66; Laura Robson, *Colonialism and Christianity in Mandate Palestine* (Austin: University of Texas Press, 2011), 50.

[74] Natasha Wheatley, 'Mandatory Interpretation: Legal Hermeneutics and the New International Order in Arab and Jewish Petitions to the League of Nations', *Past & Present* 227, no. 1 (2015): 214. About these inner tensions within the Iraqi context see Susan Pedersen, 'Getting Out of Iraq – in 1932: The League of Nations and the Road to Normative Statehood', *The American Historical Review* 115, no. 4 (2010).

[75] Strawson, 68.

# 4

# Plausibility and Ethnicity: Audience–Narrator Nexus

## Introduction

Plausibility is about persuasion, and persuasion is relational, the product of interaction between a speaker and an audience. To understand plausibility, one needs to note who is telling a story, to whom and why. As persuasion, by definition, emerges through interaction, the identity of all participants in an interaction plays a significant role in its creation. This chapter focuses on national and ethnic identity as the backdrop of speaker–audience interaction.

Nationality and ethnic origin are not elements of substantive criminal norms. On the contrary, considering them would be an affront to the principle of equality before the law.[1] Nevertheless, in practice, legal proceedings involving sex offences intersect with ethnic patterns and provide a public stage on which national sentiments may be stirred, expressed, shaped, opposed and sometimes silenced or repressed.

British, Arabs and Jews in Mandate Palestine acknowledged and mobilized the national or ethnic identity of the various participants in sex crime litigation in differing manners and for differing ends. To present themselves, both locally and internationally, as impartial administrators of the Mandate, the British downplayed the significance of ethnic origin in criminal proceedings. Nevertheless, occasional derogatory remarks slipped past British judges' facade of neutrality and betrayed their prejudice against their local subjects. In contrast, Arab defendants and defence witnesses liberally used ethnic labels. Arab defence lawyers sometimes tried to sway British judges by portraying their clients' ethnicity as a mitigating factor (thus, trying to manipulate the judges' possible prejudices).

The plausibility of stories about sex offences as perceived within the Jewish community is most productively examined outside the courtroom, in the Hebrew press, which paid much attention to incidents involving Arab sex offenders. The reporting at times seems to reflect conscious attempts to avoid sensationalizing coverage of interethnic sexual assaults so as not to stir political

[1] Unless such origin is specifically defined as an element of the offence (as in the case of hate crimes) or as an element constituting jurisdiction (e.g. sections 13–14 of the Israel Penal Code, 1977, establish exterritorial jurisdiction in cases of offences against Jews or Israeli citizens).

tension, and at other times it portrays Arabs as sexually aggressive, especially dangerous to innocent young boys and female Jewish immigrants.

Because a story's plausibility can rest, inter alia, on the identity of the speakers and audience, accounts of sex offences not only convey the details of criminal occurrences but also tell tales of identity. The social arenas in which such stories are told, whether inside or outside the courtroom, allow individuals and collectives not only to express their own identities and comment on the identities of 'others' but also to negotiate, reconstruct and modify those identities.

## Sex Offences and Ethnicity

Much has been written about the ways national, ethnic or racial patterns are interwoven into the complaints, investigation and prosecution of sexual crimes.[2] Statistical data demonstrate that sexual assaults tend to be committed against victims of the assailants' own racial, ethnic or national group.[3] Despite their relative infrequency, cases of interracial or interethnic rape draw much public and scholarly attention, their political significance being evident.

The association between rape and nationality is most vivid when rape is used as a weapon of war. Rape can be deployed by troops or militias as part of a war between nations, a civil war or an ethnic cleansing, or it can be a negative 'side effect' of contact between fighting forces and civilian populations.[4]

National and ethnic aspects of sexual assaults may be most glaring in war zones, but they also surface in criminal cases far from areas of military activity. They are most evident when the accused and the alleged victim belong to different nationalities or ethnic groups, but they can also be manifested when judges do not share the same nationality or ethnicity as the accused and witnesses (e.g. within a colonial context) or when general public debate is stirred by cases of sexual assaults.

The connection between racism and rape has been the subject of much research.[5] As an expression of power relations between collectives, rape can have a racial dimension, as seen historically in the United States in the

[2] On intersectionality and the effects of multiple subordination, see Kimberle Crenshaw, 'Mapping the Margins: Intersectionality, Identity Politics, and Violence against Women of Color', *Stanford Law Review* 43 (1991).

[3] Gary D. LaFree, 'Male Power and Female Victimization: Toward a Theory of Interracial Rape', *American Journal of Sociology* 88, no. 2 (1982): 323. Only 3–4 per cent of the rape cases in Philadelphia in 1958 and 1960 were interracial, according to Menachem Amir, *Patterns in Forcible Rape* (Chicago: University of Chicago Press, 1971), 44.

[4] Tal Nitzan, '"Controlled Occupation": The Rarity of Military Rape in the Israeli Palestinian Conflict' (MA thesis, The Hebrew University, 2006), 184.

[5] Lisa Lindquist Dorr, '"Another Negro-Did-It Crime": Black-on-White Rape and Protest in Virginia 1945–1960', in *Sex without Consent: Rape and Sexual Coercion in America*, ed. Merril D. Smith (New York: New York University Press, 2001); Crenshaw; Nicola Gavey, *Just Sex?: The Cultural Scaffolding of Rape* (New York: Routledge, 2004), 27.

widespread rape of black female slaves by their white owners.[6] Even today in the United States, cases brought against black men for raping white women are more likely than those brought against white men to result in conviction, consistent with cultural myths about 'real rape'.[7] The racial stereotype of the hypersexed black man endangering white women, especially prevalent in the southern United States, has been the focus of much scholarly attention.[8] Some of the scholarship emphasizes the role of such stereotypes in supporting and shaping rape myths, and some is more sceptical about the significance of rape myths.[9] Intersectional feminism has called for analysing rape through a broad research frame that takes into consideration various aspects of identity, such as race, gender and class.[10]

Such nuance characterizes microhistorical analysis of rape cases, which emphasizes their role in establishing national and ethnic identity and constituting a community's boundaries and collective memory.[11] This approach demonstrates how gender imbalance intersects with other social features such as class, age, race, disability and ethnicity.[12] One may add religion to this list. Other works concentrate on interracial rape cases (resolved by both legal means and extralegal means such as lynching) in which sexual offences by non-whites have historically been deployed to bolster racial hierarchy, protecting the privileged status of the white community.[13]

The reinforcement of social boundaries has also been examined from a theoretical perspective that focuses on interracial rape as a metaphor. This scholarly work examines linguistic and cultural aspects of legal discourse

[6] Gregory D. Smithers, *Slave Breeding: Sex, Violence, and Memory in African American History* (Gainesville: University Press of Florida, 2012); Danielle L. McGuire, '"It Was Like All of Us Had Been Raped": Sexual Violence, Community Mobilization, and the African American Freedom Struggle', *The Journal of American History* 91, no. 3 (2004): 908.

[7] Susan Ehrlich, *Representing Rape: Language and Sexual Consent* (London: Routledge, 2001), 19–20; Crenshaw, 1266; Gavey, 18, 26. Historically, some US states had lesser evidentiary demands when a black man was charged with the rape of a white woman. Stephen J. Schulhofer, *Unwanted Sex: The Culture of Intimidation and the Failure of Law* (Cambridge, MA: Harvard University Press, 1998), 24–25.

[8] Daniel A. Cohen, 'Social Injustice, Sexual Violence, Spiritual Transcendence: Constructions of Interracial Rape in Early American Crime Literature, 1767–1817', *The William and Mary Quarterly* 56, no. 3 (1999): 482–483. On the cultural narrative of 'black beasts', see Andrew E. Taslitz, *Rape and the Culture of the Courtroom* (New York: New York University Press, 1999), 28–31.

[9] Cohen, 485–486. [10] Gavey, 26; Crenshaw.

[11] Leora Bilsky, '"Rothstein's Affair": Nachum Guttman, Local Mythology and the First Attempted Rape in Tel Aviv' [in Hebrew], *Iyunei Mishpat* 26, no. 2 (2002); 'The City, the Woman and the Drifter: A New Reading of the Yaakobowitz Trial' [in Hebrew], *HaMishpat* 16 (2011).

[12] Constance Backhouse, *Carnal Crimes: Sexual Assault Law in Canada, 1900–1975* (Toronto: Osgoode Society, 2008).

[13] Bonni Cermak, 'Race, Honor, Citizenship: The Massie Rape/Murder Case', in *Sex without Consent: Rape and Sexual Coercion in America*, ed. Merril D. Smith (New York: New York University Press, 2001), 231.

rather than legal doctrine per se.[14] Literary representations of rape in the colonial context include the metaphor of the English colonizer raping the land, narratives of the dark-skinned native raping the Englishwoman and references to women's bodies as 'undiscovered' lands.[15] The European fear of interracial rape, it has been suggested, was related to the periodic instability of the colonial regime, and narratives like those mentioned above were used to neutralize colonizers' dominance by stressing the violence of native men and to perpetuate traditional gender roles within English society.[16] Yet intraracial rape cases too preserved the colonial power grid, by adopting evidentiary standards that constructed native complainants as untrustworthy.[17]

Since rape is closely associated with the social power grid, criminal cases that involve national or ethnic tensions can shed light on implicit and unacknowledged means of establishing plausibility. They reveal the significance of the national or ethnic identity of the narrator and the audience in making a story of sexual assault either 'right' or unconvincing.

## British Attitude towards Sex Offences

Focusing on plausibility sheds light on parallel or counterstories that exist alongside the story formally spelled out in an indictment. Examining British treatment of interethnic rape cases uncovers the story Mandate authorities told themselves and others about the justice system they created. The story was of a fair and just system, indifferent to nationality and ethnicity. The ideal of neutrality, however, was not always successfully achieved.

The British legal routine of specifying a defendant's age, religion, father's name and, sometimes, tribal membership on the titles of the hearings or information sheets provides basic data on the social and ethnic background of courtroom participants. Yet, other than applying this practical standard for ensuring the identity of the accused, the British tried to ignore ethnic characterization as much as possible. This is most evident in trials with the potential to be socially explosive, for instance, those involving brutal interethnic gang rape. The 1946 trial of those charged with the rape of Rachel from Kibbutz Eilon is a case in point. Rachel, a nineteen-year-old

14 Kristin Bumiller, 'Rape as a Legal Symbol: An Essay on Sexual Violence and Racism', *University of Miami Law Review* 42 (1988): 87.

15 Nancy L. Paxton, 'Mobilizing Chivalry: Rape in British Novels About the Indian Uprising of 1857', *Victorian Studies* 36, no. 1 (1992): 5–7; Elizabeth Philipose, 'Feminism, International Law, and the Spectacular Violence of the "Other": Decolonizing the Laws of War', in *Theorizing Sexual Violence*, ed. Renee J. Heberle and Victoria Grace (New York: Routledge, 2011), 184. For an example of the colonizer-as-rapist metaphor, see William B. Ziff, *The Rape of Palestine* (New York: Argus Books, Inc., 1946).

16 Jenny Sharpe, *Allegories of Empire: The Figure of Woman in the Colonial Text* (Minneapolis: University of Minnesota Press, 1993); Paxton, 7.

17 Elizabeth Kolsky, 'The Rule of Colonial Indifference: Rape on Trial in Early Colonial India, 1805–57', *The Journal of Asian Studies* 69, no. 4 (2010).

Jewish woman, had gone for a walk with her companions Yaacov and Raphael to nearby Wadi Karkava.[18] They were stopped by four armed men, who led them off the road down into the wadi. The men were ordered to take off their wristwatches and strip off their shirts and were then made to lie face down on the ground with their hands tied behind them. The armed men then threatened Rachel and forced her into some bushes with them, where they tore her shorts and took turns raping her for 30–40 minutes. Rachel was not the first Jewish woman from Eilon to have been sexually assaulted in the nearby wadi. The previous year, Sholamit, who was hiking there with her husband, had been attacked by Fawzi Rashed El Taher, who caught her and tried to throw her to the ground. Sholamit took advantage of a stone-throwing exchange between Fawzi and her husband to flee.[19] Fawzi may also have participated in Rachel's gang rape.[20]

The investigation into Rachel's rape led to the indictment of two Bedouins, Fahed Musa and Musa Ahmad, on charges of robbery and rape. Although much of the case revolved around the issue of identification, the formal legal presentation by the prosecution appears to have been indifferent to the ethnic identities of the protagonists. In contrast, the testimony of defence witnesses demonstrated that the ethnicity of the protagonists did matter and that the charge of rape of a Jewish woman by a Bedouin had political significance. Rachel and her companions, who testified for the prosecution, did not specify that they were attacked by Arabs but rather provided details from which this identity could be inferred. They stated that some of their attackers wore 'Arab dress' or 'fellahin dress' and that they spoke Arabic. The complainants described specific items of clothing worn by their assailants, such as *kafiyyeh, hattats* and *agals* (head coverings), *gumbaz* (robes) and *libas* (drawers). Although much of the testimony related to the identification of the accused, insofar as their ethnicity was concerned, the prosecution witnesses used quite neutral language. Thus, British police inspector Daniel Day testified that the identification parades he oversaw included persons of 'similar appearance, dress and race'. He stated that, in the first parade, all participants wore fellahin dress and that,

[18] Unless otherwise mentioned, the details of the incident are taken from the Supreme Court file containing the transcripts of all the proceedings connected to the case (including Cr.C 229/46, District Court of Haifa, *A.G.* v. *Fahed Kathem & Musa Ahmed* (1947)). ISA Division 30 (Supreme Court Files), File B/441, original docket # Cr.A 31/47 (*Fahed Kathem & Musa Ahmed* v. *A.G.*).

[19] Fawzi subsequently admitted to attempting an indecent act and was sentenced to four months' imprisonment. ISA/RG 30/Law 2046 (original docket # Cr.C 206/45).

[20] Of the four men who attacked Rachel and her male companions, only two were indicted in Cr.C 229/46. The others may have been charged in a separate case. Kibbutz Eilon's *mukhtar* (the Ottoman term for a village head) remembered Fawzi as one of her attackers. Kobi Peled, *Noura's Dream: A Historical Portrait of a Bedouin Tribe* (Tel Aviv: University of Haifa Press, 2015), 115.

in the second parade, some wore fellahin dress and others Bedouin dress. He did not explain how 'race' was determined.[21]

When the accused in this case were convicted, Judge Weldon of the District Court stated, 'Now the evidence in this case is purely one [a matter] of identity.' He was referring here to 'identification' and not 'ethnic identity', consistent with the dictum that the sufficiency of evidence, under a legal doctrine enshrining 'the rule of law', should not depend on political, social or cultural considerations. At the close of the trial, Fahed was found guilty of robbery and attempted rape and was sentenced to fifteen years' imprisonment for the former offence and five years for the latter (the terms to run concurrently). Musa was found guilty of robbery and rape and was sentenced to fifteen years' imprisonment for the robbery and ten years for the rape (again, the terms to run concurrently). The Supreme Court upheld Fahed's conviction but reduced the sentence imposed for the robbery to ten years, to run consecutively to a five-year term for attempted rape (the overall term thus remaining the same). Musa's conviction was overturned by the Supreme Court. I turn to the judgment of that court to see whether the judiciary really was indifferent to issues of social identity.

The Supreme Court agreed that the 'case rests entirely upon the evidence of identification', but the majority opinion, written by Justice Shaw with Arab Justice Abdulhadi concurring, found reason to doubt the identification of Musa as one of the perpetrators. Some of the doubt, it seems, arose from Musa's ethnic identity. Justice Shaw referred directly to the ethnicity of the offenders, whom he dubbed 'Arabs' or 'these Arabs'. He did not, however, refer to the complainants as 'Jews' but, rather, called them by their names or described them as 'the two men' and 'the girl'. Unlike the defendants, the complainants were identified by their personal traits and not essentially by their ethnicity. In laying out the specific reasons for Musa's acquittal, Justice Shaw found it significant that 'the two appellants do not belong to the same tribe. The first appellant being a member of the Kheilitat Arabs, while the second appellant is a member of the Arab Muwassi.' The judge apparently found it implausible that gang rape would be jointly committed by members of different tribes.[22] The Supreme Court did not go so far as to cast doubt on Rachel's credibility but remarked that the trial court had failed to consider whether Rachel might have been 'honestly mistaken' about Musa's identity.

[21] Both Jews and Arabs are of Semitic origin, and did not see themselves as belonging to different 'races' but to different peoples (a concept that involves ethnicity and nationality and that intersects with religion). The reference to the category of 'race' by Inspector Day is interesting. One can surmise whether he was trying to be more 'scientific' and 'objective', or perhaps such reference was just symptomatic of European colonizers' automatic registering of phenotype regardless of context.

[22] In fact, the different Bedouin tribes frequently interacted and even intermarried. The originally nomadic Bedouins also maintained complicated ties of friendship with and commitment to their farming neighbours, the fellahin. Peled, 58, 64, 68–73, 97.

Having raised these concerns, the majority opinion found reasonable doubt and overturned Musa's rape conviction.

Acting Justice Curry's dissent more obviously engaged ethnic stereotypes. Curry relied on Palestinian precedents, which urged careful scrutiny of evidence in rape cases (*Abu Zeid* v. *A.G.* (1942)) and required corroborative testimony (Cr. A 138/40, not published). His reasoning relied on a stereotypical view of the 'natives': 'It is quite a common thing in this country for complainants to add a charge of rape to one of assault or robbery and it is not easy for an accused to defend himself successfully against such a fabricated charge.'[23] Curry argued here that the need for corroboration was not grounded in the nature of the crime but rather in the dubious integrity of Palestine's inhabitants, both Jews and Arabs. Given his view of the credibility of native rape complainants, it is no wonder that, unlike his fellow judges, Curry found suspicious elements in Rachel's story and supported the acquittal of the defendants.

On the surface, British prosecutors projected indifference to the ethnic and national identities of the participants in criminal trials. Judicial impartiality and neutrality were cornerstones of the British effort to gain legitimacy as just rulers. Yet occasional judicial statements demonstrate that assessing the plausibility of rape stories did in fact rest, inter alia, on the ethnic identity of the protagonists, betraying British prejudice against local inhabitants. The following case exemplifies such an instance.

Edith, a Jewish woman, accused two men, a taxi driver and his friend, of raping her.[24] Both of the accused, Emil Naddi and Munjid Faris, were Arab Christians, twenty and twenty-two years old, respectively. In her testimony for the prosecution, Edith did not mention the men's nationality or ethnicity. She did not call them 'Arabs', instead referring to them as 'the driver' and 'another man' (in contrast, she referred to the previous passenger in the taxi as 'an Englishman'). The bench, however, did not display the same indifference to the ethnicity of either the complainant or the accused. Judge Dickinson opened his judgment on the case by stating that '[t]he complainant was an admitted prostitute. She was obviously a nervous psychopathic case.' Her lack of credibility, according to Judge Dickinson, stemmed partly from her undignified occupation and disturbed personality, but it was also tied to the ethnic attributes of both the complainant and the two accused. The judgment declared that '[f]or a Jewish girl to get alone into an Arab taxi with 2 Arabs at 4 a.m. was inviting immoral advances'.

Judicial prejudice sometimes targeted particular ethnic groups and sometimes locals in general. Furthermore, despite their cultivation of an air of ethnic disinterest, the British were well aware of the disruptive potential of

[23] Judge Curry's minority opinion in the Supreme Court's judgment of 4 June 1947.
[24] ISA/RG 30/Law 2048 (original docket # Cr.C 320/45).

interethnic sexual assaults[25] as well as of possible allegations against them of discriminating against local victims.[26]

Other parties to legal proceedings, it seems, expected British judges to hold ethnic stereotypes and, on occasion, tried to sway judicial decisions by appealing to possible ethnic prejudice. For example, in a 1944 case in which a fifteen-year-old Arab boy was accused of committing sodomy on a five-year-old Jewish girl, the probation officer recommended lenient treatment of the accused:

> At the time when the offence was committed Jamil was staying with his married sister in Hadera, and was working in an orange grove, where he was left much by himself. Since then he was returned to his family at Tulkarm, and in the opinion of our officer, it does not seem likely that the boy will again misbehave, especially in a place where he is well known, and where the local traditions and customs are much stricter than at Hadera.[27]

To persuade the judges to forego sanctions, the probation officer employs an ethnic stereotype as a mitigating factor. The return of the boy to reside with his parents in the Arab town of Tulkarm implies his return to the conservative tradition and strict surveillance that are implicitly compatible with his ethnicity, enabling the officer to recommend probation instead of prison. Arab Tulkarm is portrayed as a stabilizing anchor of tradition, unlike Jewish Hadera, where the boy went morally astray in the absence of sufficient family and community support. The ethnic characterization in this final probation report diverges somewhat from that in an earlier report, in which the boy and his family are described as outsiders to Tulkarm society: 'Originally the accused father is a gypsy (Nouri) came to Tulkarm settled and worked as a blacksmith. The boy has never been to any school and naturally he is illeterate [*sic*].'[28] Here, the boy and his family are presented as atypical in the community – their ethnic roots are unusual (gypsy), they are newcomers and the boy has never attended school with other children of the community. This report presents a family that is only partially integrated into the community. The final report addressing the judges, however, presents the family as a link in a chain of traditions and customs, implicitly employing ethnic stereotypes about Arabs to support mitigating circumstances. As the next section demonstrates, such persuasion sometimes took more explicit forms.

25 For example, a 21 August 1947 telegram instructed all criminal investigation departments to immediately report to headquarters any cases relating to a list of offences, including sexual offences, in which Jews complained about Arabs. HA 47–891.

26 On occasion, the British were accused of treating local victims of sexual offences differently than they did foreign victims. See, for example, a newspaper article protesting selective enforcement and claiming that when the victim was an American woman, the perpetrators were instantly caught, tried and convicted but that when the victim was a Jewish girl, the authorities dragged their feet. *Davar*, 23 May 1928, p. 3.

27 ISA/RG 30/Law 2039 (original docket # Cr.C 325/44), Senior Welfare Officer's report, dated 13 February 1945.

28 Ibid., Probation Investigation Report, 10 October 1944.

## Arab Attitude towards Sex Offences

Because the British authorities orchestrated the prosecution, prosecution witnesses, not surprisingly, tended to use neutral terminology to allude to ethnicity. In contrast, Arab defence attorneys and Arab witnesses for the defence in interethnic rape cases used explicit ethnic labels. The accused in the rape of Edith dubbed her 'the Jewess' or 'the Jewish woman' throughout their testimonies. The Bedouin accused of Rachel's rape started their testimony by introducing their tribal identity. Fahed's first statement was 'I am of Kleitat Arabs'. Musa's first words asserted he was 'of Arab Mowassi in Bassa lands'. They also referenced ethnic or national identity when speaking of others, as did Arab witnesses during the trial. Fahed referred to the 'British Inspector', and he testified that 'a Jew now identified me'. Musa's uncle described the harvest day when the police requested that his reapers (his nephew included) come for identification in 'a case of the rape of a Jewish girl'. He told the court he had seen the police collecting the 'Bedouin Arabs' and had heard from his nephew about 'the rape of the Jewish girl'. The latter statement contradicted his earlier statement that the police had informed him of the rape, but he was consistent in referring to the incident as 'the rape of the Jewish girl'. At the end of the trial, Musa stated, 'I have lived near to Jews for the past seven years and never done anything of this sort.' These words acknowledge a context in which rape was part of regional politics, that interethnic rape was not merely an offence committed by an individual man against an individual woman but an injury committed by the Arab collective against the Jewish collective. Fawzi Rashed El Taher, who eventually pleaded guilty to an attempted indecent act against Sholamit from Kibbutz Eilon, initially stated in the preliminary inquiry that the accusation was a Jewish plot, prompted by his dispute with the *mukhtar* of Kibbutz Eilon and that 'the Jews help each other. I do not know what they have in their hearts.'[29] It made sense to Fawzi, then, that the story of the purported crime be interpreted against the backdrop of the Jewish-Arab conflict.

It is evident that, at least for defendants, cases of interethnic rape had political and social significance within the broader context of Arab-Jewish relations. Within this context, sexual relations between Jews and Arabs were perceived by both communities as threatening.[30] Forcible rape of a Jewish woman by a group of Arab men was an explosive event. It could be interpreted not only as a threat to Jewish women but also to Jewish masculinity. Rachel's friends, Yacov and Raphael, on top of being robbed, were also victims of the sex offence, tied up and lying face down on the ground, aware of what was

[29] The preliminary inquiry is documented in ISA/RG 30/Law 2046 (original docket # Cr.C 206/45).

[30] Tammy Razi, 'Jewish-Arab Women? Ethnicity, Nationality and Gender in Mandate Tel Aviv', *Theory and Criticism*, no. 38–39 (2011): 147, 150.

happening to Rachel behind the bushes but completely helpless to protect her. The perception that Jewish masculinity was also ravaged by such crimes might have intensified the ethnic tension.

Arab lawyers went beyond ethnic labelling and actively invoked ethnic stereotypes in defence of their clients. Jamal Eff. Hamad, the Arab attorney who defended the accused in Rachel's rape case, argued for mitigating circumstances based on the men's origin. Contradicting the denials of his Bedouin clients, he described them as 'young men. Shaken by seeing a girl in shorts with two young men. Provocation for men such as accused, who are ignorant and fanatical and led away by inflammatory propaganda.' These short, meaning-laden statements were tailored to a stereotypical narrative that might have swayed the British judge to find mitigating circumstances.[31] The mitigating arguments in Rachel's rape case might not have reflected Hamad's own views but, rather, his assessment of the judges' prejudice about what made a narrative plausible. The implication here was that the guilt of the accused – illiterate Bedouin from the Galilee – was lessened by their backward upbringing, which made them vulnerable both to provocative sights such as women wearing shorts in the company of men and to 'inflammatory propaganda'. The susceptibility of the accused to propaganda hinted at a context of tense Jewish-Arab relations. Rape, the defence lawyer insinuated, was a political and even nationalistic act.

The lawyers' courtroom arguments may not have represented their personal views.[32] It may very well be the case that an advocate would tailor his argument according to his assessment of where British prejudice might lie. Persuasion is relational, and the speaker who wishes to persuade takes into account what the listener is apt to find plausible. This calculation may help explain the outcome in a case in which three family members were accused of raping an eight-year-old girl.[33] The men pleaded guilty, and their lawyer argued that the assault was an act of revenge based on an 'old custom', as the girl's father had raped the sister of two of the accused two years earlier. The rape was committed 'not to satisfy carnal desire but to wash away dishonour'. The district court judges (two Arab judges and a presiding British judge) remained sceptical: 'should such a custom in fact exist, the Courts cannot for a moment accept it or give it recognition; it is a custom which should . . . be uprooted forthwith'. The appeal to the Supreme Court that was drafted by prominent Arab lawyer Naseeb Abcarius Bey (a Coptic Christian who worked in Sudan and Egypt as well as Mandate Palestine)[34] repeated the argument about old custom. The appeal was

[31] An example of such mitigating rationale is found in the following statement by Judge Curry in a manslaughter case: 'I feel that in this case there are good grounds for mitigation of punishment. . . . he should not of course have hit the deceased on the head, but accused is a young Bedouin and one cannot expect a high degree of judgment from such a person.' ISA/RG 30/Law 2024 (original docket # Cr.C 13/43).

[32] Mitra Sharafi, 'A New History of Colonial Lawyering: Likhovski and Legal Identities in the British Empire', *Law & Social Inquiry* 32, no. 4 (2007): 1080.

[33] ISA Division 30 (Supreme Court Files), File B/186/40, original docket # Cr.A 40/34.

[34] Nathan Brun, *Judges and Lawyers in Eretz Israel* (Jerusalem: The Magnes Press, 2008), 341 n. 9.

heard by Micheal McDonnell, the British chief justice of the Supreme Court, the Arab justice Khaldi and the Jewish justice Frumkin. In his judgment, chief justice McDonnell denied the existence of such custom:

> The members of the Court are familiar with the custom among fellahin of killing in revenge for deflowering of a woman who is related to the murderers but not one of the members has ever heard of the alleged custom of avenging one's sister's rape by the rape of a female relation of the ravisher let alone a brutal ravishment as in this case by two men of a little girl of eight.

The perceived gravity of a crime could vary depending on the victim's ethnic or national identity. For instance, the rape of an Englishwoman was sometimes regarded as far worse than the rape of a Jewish woman. Thus, Hassan Zein, who robbed and attempted to rape an English countess, explained that he thought she was a 'Jewess'.[35] For the story of his mistake to be plausible, it had to make sense to listeners. Arguably, Jews who heard the explanation would have been less likely to share the sentiment that raping a Jewish woman was a lesser evil, but they could have been aware that such beliefs existed outside the community, as the following example demonstrates. A Hebrew newspaper article reporting the sexual harassment by a group of local children of the British governor's wife and her Arab friend on a visit to Hebron during Ramadan supposed the ruffians took them for Jewish women (an assumption that implies they thought it permissible to sexually harass Jewish women but not British women).[36]

The Arab press in Mandate Palestine was active and covered diverse issues, but it generally did not discuss the subject of rape. This reticence may reflect a general tendency in Arab societies to avoid discussion of deviations from normative behavioural standards.[37] Reports of sexual assault were extremely rare in Arab newspapers, even though the vast majority of those accused of sex offences as well as victims were Arab. One rare report of sexual assault was published in *Palestine*,[38] a newspaper whose front page was generally devoted to opinion, the latest developments in pan-Arabic issues and amusing stories. The report in question is about an arrogant young man who was riding his horse down a street in Gaza when he noticed a woman staring at his horse from her window. Thinking she was staring at him, he tied up the horse, went up to her flat and tried to hug her. Hearing the woman's screams, her neighbours came to her rescue and rebuked the young man. After her husband returned home, the woman told him what had happened, and he decided to confront the young man's father. He met the father in the market and laid down his accusations, whereupon the father hit him. The article goes on to speculate whether the young man belonged to the class of those who called themselves

35 ISA/RG 30/Law 2036 (original docket # Cr.C 213/44). 36 *Haaretz*, 28 May 1923, p. 2.

37 Stephen O. Murray, 'The Will Not to Know', in *Islamic Homosexualities: Culture, History, and Literature*, ed. Stephen O. Murray and Will Roscoe (New York: New York University Press, 1997), 15.

38 *Palestine*, 11 September 1931, p. 1. I thank Janan Basoul for bringing this story to my attention.

'princes of the land'. The focus of the story, then, is not sexual harassment but rather class degeneracy. The gravity of the incident is downplayed – the assault is described as a 'hug', though the screams of the wife imply that a more serious attack had occurred.

While Arab victims of sex offences, in many cases, did not hesitate to complain to the Mandate authorities, it appears that within the Arab community sexual assault was not considered a 'proper' subject for public discussion. The situation in the Jewish community seems to have been reversed, as sex offences were reported and discussed in the press, but Jewish complainants were few.[39]

## Jewish Attitude towards Sex Offences

Because plausibility is context bound and dependent on speaker–audience interaction, what is viewed as plausible varies from one forum to another. What made sense within the boundaries of one of Palestine's communities, for example, might have been different from what made sense to a British judge. In this section, I leave the courtroom setting to examine sex offence stories as they were told within an ethnically defined forum, the Jewish community. To do so, I analyse the rhetoric of the Hebrew press. Newspapers are publicly disseminated yet accessible only to readers who understand the language of publication. The digitized Historical Jewish Press collection in the National Library of Israel, one of my principal archival sources, allows searches using Hebrew key words. Unlike their Arab counterparts, Hebrew newspapers did not shy away from articles and news items about sex offences. Their reports had distinctive patterns in terms of format and content and shed light on what was considered plausible within the bounds of the Jewish community.

Even the shortest items in the criminal sections of Mandate-era Hebrew newspapers referred to the ethnicity of suspects and accused. Ethnicity was sometimes explicitly mentioned, as in the following examples: 'The court sentenced an Arab for seven years imprisonment for the offence of rape',[40] and 'in recent days a Jewish woman was raped in the afternoon in the vicinity of Bnai Brak, by two Arabs after they had robbed her purse that contained money'.[41] Sometimes a report included information (such as a name or residential details) that left little room for doubt as to the ethnicity of either the suspect or the victim. For example, a report about the preliminary inquiry into the rape of a young Jewish woman stated, 'Eventually the Magistrate decided to indict the accused, Samaan Arafat', the name revealing his Arab identity.[42] Some articles blended more obvious with less explicit ethnic characterizations. For example, an article titled 'Arab Rape Suspect Arrested'

[39] Data on the ethnicity of complainants are included in the next chapter.

[40] *Haboker*, 15 May 1944, p. 2 (identical text pertaining to this case as well as to other criminal cases appeared on the same date in the daily *Hatzofe*).

[41] *Davar*, 31 March 1946, p. 4. [42] *Haboker*, 21 October 1940, p. 3.

reported that 'a nineteen-year-old Arab from Salame Village was arrested in Ramat Gan on suspicion of attempted rape of a woman who walked with her girlfriend between Kfar Azar and Ramat Issac'.[43] The article clearly identifies the suspect as an Arab. It does not mention the victim's ethnicity, but readers could easily deduce that she was Jewish (and therefore, that the sexual assault was an interethnic one), from the names of the Jewish settlements between which she and her girlfriend were hiking.

The Mandate-era Hebrew press routinely reported sexual offences. Victims were variously reported to have been Jews and Arabs, females and males, adults and children, but the perpetrators were most often identified as Arab men.[44] I do not claim that the Hebrew press deliberately focused on cases of Arab sex offenders and ignored Jewish offenders. First, newspapers did publish accounts of Jews charged with sex offences, although such accounts were few in number.[45] Second, available statistics from the British Mandate period attest that the majority of suspects and defendants were Arab.[46] Third, my own

43 *Haboker*, 27 March 1945, p. 4.

44 A representative sample of news items includes the following: three Arab policemen suspected of raping a Jewish boy were released, as the boy later recanted (*Davar*, 12 June 1938, p. 4), two Arabs raped a male train employee at gunpoint (*Davar*, 9 July 1928, p. 4), a young woman who was strolling with an Arab man was raped by three Arabs (*Doar Hayom*, 11 April 1932, p. 4), an Arab raped an orphaned Jewish child (*Doar Hayom*, 11 June 1928, p. 4), Arab defendants were charged in four cases of rape and sodomy (*Doar Hayom*, 20 May 1932, p. 8), an Arab was convicted for attempted rape (*Davar*, 22 June 1934, p. 3), a recent immigrant woman was raped by an Arab policeman (*Davar*, 19 October 1936, p. 3), an Arab raped his twelve-year-old daughter (*Davar*, 18 March 1937), an Arab was investigated for tempting and raping four Jewish girls (*Davar*, 7 December 1939, p. 6), an Arab raped an Arab virgin (*Al Hamismar*, 14 November 1943), an Arab was imprisoned for raping a woman (*Davar*, 15 May 1944, p. 2), a Jewish woman was raped by Arabs (*Davar*, 31 July 1946, p. 3), Arabs attempted to rape a six-year-old girl and stabbed the policeman who tried to protect her (*Davar*, 7 October 1947, p. 3).

45 See the following examples: Jew arrested on suspicion of rape (*Doar Hayom*, 5 September 1928, p. 4), Jewish defendant acquitted (*Davar*, 31 July 1929, p. 4), Binkvitz and Urich convicted (*Davar*, 1 August 1935, p. 7), Yemenite girl raped by a Yemenite man (*Davar*, 11 November 1935, p. 6), Zecharia Cohen acquitted (*Davar*, 30 January 1936, p. 5), Max Trichter acquitted (*Davar*, 9 October 1936, p. 10), David Cohan convicted (*Davar*, 1 November 1939, p. 6), Meir Neustein imprisoned for two years for rape (*Davar*, 24 December 1939, p. 5), Hans Neustein acquitted by the Supreme Court (*Hamashkif*, 16 January 1940, p. 4), Chief Magistrate issued a warrant for the arrest of a Jewish suspect in the rape of a girl (*Hamashkif*, 23 October 1941, p. 3), preliminary inquiry of Feibish Kupilev for raping a girl (*Hamashkif*, 21 April 1942, p. 3). See also the following legal reports: Cr. A 75/39 *Hans Neustein* v. *A.G.* (7 P.L.R. 15) (acquitted by the Supreme Court; apparently the same case reported in *Davar* on 24 December 1939), see Shalom Kassan, *Convicted and Acquitted* [in Hebrew] (Tel Aviv: Dvir, 1960), 227.

46 In 1942, of 6,376 persons convicted of and sentenced for offences against the person, 5,314 were Muslims, 293 were Christians and 765 (11 per cent) were Jews (4 were categorized as 'others'). ISA Statistical Abstract of Palestine 1943, p. 165. The offences of rape and sodomy are not specified in the available statistics, but for some years the number of cases of 'unnatural offences' is recorded. For example, in all cases of 'unnatural offences' decided in the district courts in the first half of 1943, the defendants were Muslim. ISA/M 5302/9, table 5. The existence of 'unnatural offences' as a separate statistical category within the broader category of 'offences against the person' implies that consensual anal sex was regarded as essentially different from other sexual offences.

corpus of criminal cases suggests the vast majority of suspects were Arab. Of the 147 sexual assault cases in my corpus, the accused in 136 (93 per cent) were Arab. In the remaining 11 cases, 2 accused were Jewish, 2 British, 2 Druze, 1 Armenian, 1 Greek and 3 of unknown origin.

Generalizations about the ethnicity of sex offenders in Mandate Palestine on the basis of these data should be qualified. First, criminal cases probably reflect patterns of enforcement and prosecution rather than actual incidence. It is highly improbable that only or mostly Arabs committed sexual assaults. Second, my corpus includes criminal files of cases that were heard primarily by the Haifa District Court between 1939 and 1948, and situations might have been different in other districts. Had the Mandate-era files of the Tel Aviv District Court survived, we would have a better indication of the extent of prosecution of Jewish defendants in sexual assault cases, since, given the district make-up, this court primarily served Jewish litigants.[47] However, the preponderance of cases heard in district courts in manifestly Arab areas probably involved Arab defendants.[48] The Haifa District Court presided over an ethnically mixed population, and the explanation of the prevalence of Arab defendants there does not lie in the district's demographic composition.[49] Therefore, while one would expect more Jews than reflected in the data to be accused of sex offences (the next chapter examines their near absence in court records), the prevalence of Arab suspects and defendants in Hebrew press accounts seems to reflect a high rate of actual prosecution, and it can be safely assumed that the majority of suspects and defendants who were investigated and brought to trial were Arab.

Nevertheless, even if the recurrent reports in the Hebrew press about Arab suspects and perpetrators were not the result of bias, they still have value for the study of plausibility. The mere fact that ethnicity was always enunciated implies that it was a relevant fact (the reports did not mention, e.g., race or economic status). Simply for that reason, then, even succinct reports about sexual offences can help us in the study of plausibility. Other facts routinely mentioned in news reports were the gender(s) of perpetrator and of victim[50] and the geographic locale of a crime. The brevity of the reports highlights what details were considered essential. The habitual mention of ethnicity stands in

[47] Nathan Brun, *Law, Passions and Politics: Judges and Lawyers between the British Mandate and the State of Israel* (Tel Aviv: Steimatzky, 2014), 141, 144–145.

[48] For criticism in the Hebrew press of the official Mandate statistics as partial and distorted and as reflecting discriminatory enforcement against the Jews, see 'In the Courtrooms across the Country', *Hamashkif*, 27 July 1939, p. 3.

[49] In 1922 Jews made up about 25 per cent of Haifa residents and Arabs around 75 per cent. By 1944 Arabs composed only 46 per cent of the city's residents. May Seikaly, *Haifa: Transformation of a Palestinian Arab Society 1918–1939* (London: I.B. Tauris, 1995). Haifa was the largest city in a broader legal district. Taking into account Acre and the Arab villages in the Galilee, the ratio of Arabs to Jews in the district as a whole was probably different.

[50] Hebrew grammar dictates the use of either male or female declension of verbs, nouns and adjectives.

clear contrast to the legalistic view that the ethnicity of the parties involved was irrelevant to the definition of the offence.

The identity of the protagonists (both perpetrators and victims) is part of what makes a story plausible or implausible, and the insistent mention of ethnicity instructs us that this aspect of identity was significant. Its significance increased when certain behaviours were consistently affiliated with certain ethnic identities. The Jewish press attributed to Arabs a tendency to commit base, violent and crude criminal offences in general and sex offences in particular. For example, an article that characterizes the criminality of the 'Canaanites' – namely, Arabs – states,

> When the Jewish state will be established, there will be no 'market' of selling kids to slaves . . . It is not poverty that causes the patriarch to sell one of his sons or daughters. This is just one trait of an atmosphere in which exist murder, and crude meanness and all the obscene vices of debauchery. . . . where sodomy and rape abounds and fear to go out alone, the selling of children to slavery is not so 'terrible'.[51]

Another article, about the 'new face' of the courtroom in Rehovot after the court became a venue for Jewish rather than Arab litigants, contends, inter alia, that

> the honourable judge is no longer overburdened with work. The absence of Arabs is noticeable. They no longer crowd in the main road outside the entrance, and their shouts are no longer heard . . . No more criminal trials, murder trials, stabbing, beating and thievery . . . no more. No more trials for smuggling Hashish, tobacco, rape and sodomy trials . . .[52]

After associating Arabs with sexual offences in particular and criminal trials and criminal behaviour in general, the article claims that, having become a venue for Jewish litigants, the Rehovot court hears mostly commercial and fiscal matters – landlord–tenant cases and the like.

An association between ethnicity and crime is also found in Hebrew legal scholarship of the period. In his treatise on the criminal law in Mandate Palestine, Paltiel Dikshtein distinguishes between typical Arab and typical Jewish criminal activity. Arabs, many of whom, he says, are of a 'low cultural level', engage in serious crimes as 'the fruit of crude passions, bestial tendencies and simple, primal and primitive urges'.[53] In contrast, though still dangerous, the criminality of Jews is 'the fruit of mental complexes of immigrants from superior cultures [i.e. Western countries], their subtle sentiments, developed desires and stressed nerves, that reached delicate mental development, sometimes pathological'. Their offences are thus highly complex and complicated

[51] 'One Trait of the Canaanites', *Doar Hayom*, 5 February 1931, p. 1. For another article that deplores the prevalence of rape and sodomy among Palestine's Muslim youth, see David Tidhar, 'On Sin', *Doar Hayom*, 17 February 1930, p. 2.

[52] 'New Face to Rehovot Court', *Hamashkif*, 19 October 1938, p. 4.

[53] Paltiel Dikshtein, *Criminal Law*, vol. 1 (Tel Aviv: School of Law and Economics, 1938), 22.

and, because of devious planning, have a prima facie appearance of legality. These insights, Dikshtein explains, are based on what he dubs the 'colonial criminology'.[54]

A similar association between ethnicity and type of criminality is repeated in other Jewish sources. In his memoirs, Eliyahu Zeev Halevi Lewin-Epstein, one of the founders of the Jewish colony of Rehovot in the late nineteenth century, claims that the ignorance and illiteracy of the destitute Arab fellahin 'brought them to such a low moral degree, so that they possess almost all vices the bible calls "the ways of the Emorites"'.[55]

One of the recurring themes in the Hebrew press is Arab sexual assault of young Jewish women. This theme is present in journalistic reports in the criminal section and further articulated in opinion articles. In an article titled 'Caution!', one daily laments the prevalence of rape by Arabs and the reluctance of the Jewish public to complain.[56] The article claims that, in many cases, victims inform neither the British authorities nor community institutions, out of fear, embarrassment or a wish to preserve family honour. The stereotypical scenario is described as follows:

> Most calamities fall on new immigrants ... the girl recklessly travels to a location, distant from a Hebrew settlement, with an Arab driver, without knowing the environment and road. The Arab driver does not take her to the Hebrew location, but on side roads – if she has the strength to struggle she saves her soul, and if she is weak, she keeps the secret lest anyone would discover the shame of her disaster.

The article that offers this generic scenario further condemns the frivolity of newcomers who travel unknown roads and the reluctance of victims to complain. 'Saving one's honour' is not justified, the author proclaims, if doing so endangers the whole community. The article draws very sharp lines between the Jewish and Arab communities. Failure by naive, young female immigrants to keep their distance from Arabs might lead to their personal destruction. Their unwillingness to complain (a trend discussed in further detail in the next chapter) risks the whole community. More than the fear of rape is expressed in this article; so too is the fear that Jews, as newcomers in the land, will be exploited by the native Arabs. The article assumes as axiomatic that, within the Jewish community, a rape is a well-kept secret and that publicizing it will shame the victim.

A 1945 article titled 'They Did Not Learn a Lesson' offers a similar view. It blames two university students attacked in Jerusalem at around 1 a.m. for bringing the assault on themselves. The article rhetorically asks, 'Why would a young man and woman go so late to a non-Jewish isolated area? Why aren't they more careful after so many incidents of rape and violence? Why didn't they learn the lesson?'[57] This article takes for granted that rape is typically

[54] Ibid. [55] Eliyahu Zeev Halevi Lewin-Epstein, *Memoirs* (Tel Aviv: Lewin-Epstein, 1932), 240.
[56] *Davar*, 18 July 1935, p. 3. [57] *Doar Hayom*, 5 June 1928, p. 1.

committed by Arabs (and thus, perhaps, it insinuates that Arabs are naturally disposed to commit rape).

The failure of Jewish men to protect Jewish women is another recurring theme. One newspaper report from 1923 provides an extreme example:

> One Jewish man from Haifa, Nathan Tzvi, accompanied two girls on their way from the Technikum to the city. On their way two Arabs attacked the girls. Tzvi meant to protect them but one of the Arabs held him and began to smother him. Hearing the girls screaming a crowd gathered – Jews and Arabs. A fight broke. Meanwhile Police arrived and arrested the Arab attacker and another Jewish young man who participated in the fight. But hear out the end of the event. On March 14 the matter came before the magistrate. Arabs testified (including the friend of the attacker) that neither Tzvi nor the other Jewish man hit the attacker, yet the Magistrate ruled as followed: Tzvi, who protected the Hebrew girls was sentenced to 3LP. Fine or a twelve day imprisonment, the other Jewish man, who handed the Arab to the hands of the police got an identical punishment, and the Arab attacker was acquitted.[58]

In this story, the Arab aggressor overpowered Nathan Tzvi, the Jewish man accompanying the girls. The girls managed to summon help by screaming, but Tzvi and another Jewish man who tried to fight off the attackers ended up victims of the British justice system (which apparently found it plausible to view the two as guilty of misconduct rather than as the girls' saviours).

Most press reports were not sensational (even when they referred to the most brutal cases of rape, including interethnic rape) but rather took the form of concise items in the criminal sections.[59] The portrayal of Arabs as dangerously hypersexed was sometimes deliberately toned down to avoid exacerbating interethnic tensions, as reactions to a spate of minor assaults demonstrate. In June 1928 in Jerusalem, a series of acts of sexual harassment of Jewish women by Arab men was the subject of public debate. One newspaper article, titled 'Protect the Daughters of Jerusalem', not only protests that it was unsafe for young Jewish women to walk alone at night but also complains that acts like patting, pinching and pushing were openly committed and that rude language was used in the most central locations of the city.[60] Such acts, the author claims, were no less offensive to the women of Jerusalem and their companions than actual rape would be. Most such acts went unreported to the public or the

[58] *Haaretz*, 27 March 1923, p. 3.

[59] One example of such matter-of-fact reporting was the appearance of an item about a Jewish defendant who was convicted and sentenced to two years' imprisonment for the rape of a twenty-five-year-old woman alongside an item about a ten-year-old boy who was injured when he fell off his bike. *Davar*, 24 December 1939, p. 5. The rape conviction was later overturned on appeal by the Supreme Court. Another Hebrew paper, which published a detailed account of that case, opened with the statement that the accused, 'Hans Neustein, "the German youngster"', was acquitted on appeal. The characterization of the perpetrator as 'German' rather than 'Jewish' serves as an alienating rhetorical device. *Haboker*, 16 January 1940, p. 6.

[60] *Doar Hayom*, 5 June 1928, p. 1, *Doar Hayom*, 8 June 1928, p. 5.

police, and they were not prohibited by law. The article's author gives the example of a young Jewish woman who was pinched on her bottom by an Arab in full view of a police officer, who wanted to arrest the man. The young woman, however, refused to complain, to save herself from embarrassment. The tension ignited by such articles' vehement and dramatic rhetoric can be better appreciated in the context of other articles that reproached the authorities for their incompetence and discriminatory attitude in dealing with sexual harassment of Jewish women in Jerusalem.[61] It is conceivable that the authors of such critical attacks aimed to influence public opinion even in the international arena.[62] The numerous instances of sexual harassment, on the one hand, and the confrontational attitude towards the authorities, on the other hand, worried the leadership of Jewish institutions, who took action to improve security and tone down the sensational tone.

The Hebrew press was aware of the political sensitivity of interethnic rape. Two letters written in 1928 by Henrietta Szold, head of the Zionist Organization Department of Health, Education and Welfare, had explicitly addressed the problem of 'molestation' of Jewish women by Arab men in Jerusalem.[63]

The police maintained that public perception of widespread sexual harassment of Jewish women by Arab men was 'due to the particularity and insistence with which every such incident is reported, and to the vehemence of the editorial comment upon the misdemeanours'.[64] The Zionist National Committee (Vaad Ha-Leumi) sent a delegation to complain to the British high commissioner, who subsequently met with Muslim and Arab authorities to discuss the matter. As Szold noted, the high commissioner's efforts to calm emotions were coupled with a request that the Jewish press be more restrained in its coverage. The Zionist National Committee met with representatives of the Jewish press and offered to provide them with a 'trustworthy' person to investigate reports of sexual assault. The offer was rejected as an infringement on freedom of the press, but journalists agreed to exercise 'very great restraint' in future reporting of such incidents.[65] It may be that not reporting interethnic rapes such as the brutal gang rape of Rachel from Kibbutz Eilon was an

61 The accusations against the British included the claim that when the victim was Jewish the authorities were slow to act, whereas foreign subjects got speedy justice. Other charges were that the British let many Arab suspects get away and that they sometimes even brought charges against Jews who attempted to protect Jewish women rather than against the women's Arab assailants. *Davar*, 23 May 1928, p. 3, *Doar Hayom*, 8 June 1928, p. 5.

62 One author who describes a series of sexual attacks on the Jewish women of Jerusalem sarcastically writes, 'I imagine the kind of impression all the good news of salvation and comforts from Zion and Jerusalem could make on the Jews from abroad who will see our newspapers.' *Doar Hayom*, 8 June 1928, p. 5.

63 CZA S28/46 A letter to the Executive, Zionist Organization (21 June 1928) 992/sz/389, and a letter to the Secretary, Zionist Organization (22 June 1928) 992/sz/396.

64 CZA S28/46 A letter to the Executive, Zionist Organization (21 June 1928), pp. 2–3.

65 CZA 992/sz/396, Szold's letter to the Secretary, Zionist Organization (22 June 1928).

example of this 'great restraint', aimed at reducing tensions between Arabs, Jews and their British rulers.[66]

In general, then, the Hebrew press exhibited ambivalence toward Arabs suspected or accused of sexual assaults. On the one hand, it reported many incidents of sexual offences committed by Arabs but relatively few incidents committed by Jews.[67] Within the bounds of the Jewish community, it made sense that a sex offender would be a hypersexed aggressive Arab male. The ethnic identity of the victim had a rhetorical significance, and stories of interethnic rape reflected anxieties about the self-definition of the Jewish collective, its relationship with its Arab counterpart and the fragility of Jewish masculinity. On the other hand, many reports (though not all) were not sensationalized, and there is evidence to suggest that the coverage of interethnic sexual assaults was deliberately restrained. The restraint, prompted by a wish to avoid inflaming interethnic tensions, attests to the persuasive power of the reports.

## Conclusion

National identity is most clearly constituted through law in the course of celebrated political trials and in the establishment of national systems of jurisdiction. Definition of self and 'other' also occurs, however, in mundane criminal cases that allegedly have nothing to do with ethnicity or nationality. An analysis of sex offence cases heard by the Mandate-era Palestine courts demonstrates that the British, the Arab and the Jewish sectors displayed distinctive attitudes towards and mobilized the proceedings in different ways. To gain legitimacy in the eyes of Arabs and Jews, the British judiciary had to display impartiality. The British tried to tell stories of sexual offences in a way that would neutralize the significance of ethnic or national identities. Nevertheless, sporadic condescending and outright derogatory remarks directed at locals reveal their prejudice toward them. In courtroom proceedings, Arab witnesses and advocates made copious use of ethnic labels in reference to the various participants and displayed awareness of the political significance of interethnic rape. In a climate in which rape was not a legitimate tactic in military conflict, use of ethnic and national labels possibly served as a rhetorical device emphasizing the implausibility of interethnic rape, thus distancing the accused from the charges against them. Arab lawyers did not hesitate to point to ethnic attributes when arguing mitigating circumstances. Trying to sway British judges, Arab advocates were likely to tailor their arguments to conform to what the British might find plausible, however unflattering their portrayal of their clients. Outside the courtroom, in the

[66] Rachel's rape received only brief mention in a notice of Musa and Fahed's escape from prison a month after their conviction (*Palestine Post*, 11 May 1947, p. 3). They appear to have been caught, since the record of their appeal makes no mention of their absence.

[67] Of ten references to cases against Jews, three relate to acquittals. Supra fn. 42.

Hebrew press, national and ethnic identities were relevant elements of reports of sex offences. Plausibility of ethnicity-based stories is demonstrated, on the one hand, by repeated depictions of Arab suspects and accused as sexually aggressive, dangerous to young children and Jewish women, and, on the other hand, by deliberate restraint in coverage, to avoid national tensions.

Law may be employed in subtle ways to construct social boundaries and create social hierarchies. Identity is relational, and constructing the 'other' is also an act of self-definition, and vice versa. Differences between British and 'natives', Jews and Arabs in Mandate Palestine were constructed through cases of both inter-ethnic and intra-ethnic sexual offences. From a doctrinal point of view, ethnic or national identity is not an element of sexual offences. Nevertheless, the capacity of a story to convince is inseparable from the identities of the story's protagonists, the person telling it and the audience hearing it. Implicit and indistinct yet significant elements of persuasion, these culturally constructed differences are naturalized and essentialized.

# 5

# Plausible Emotions

## The Significance of Emotional Expression in Investigatory and Judicial Proceedings

The emotions that accompany a crime story – those of its narrator, its audience and its protagonists – are part of what constitutes its plausibility. Emotions are inseparable from social conventions that address matters such as

> what kinds of emotions should people show on trial, and how [is] this dependent on gender, age, and social status? What emotions [are] seen as mitigating factors in committing a crime, and what emotions [are] deemed to be legally punishable or worthy of legal protection? How [do] these understandings of emotions interact with societal and cultural notions of moral responsibility, free will, and conscience?[1]

A witness whose testimony is unaccompanied by 'appropriate' emotions, adequately corresponding to the content of the testimony, might be regarded as untruthful. A protagonist's display of a 'wrong' emotion can make the testimony of a witness who describes it implausible – a 'wrong' story to tell.

Acting Justice Curry of the Supreme Court of Palestine, for example, doubted that Rachel from Kibbutz Eilon had indeed been raped, as her emotional reaction to the alleged offence did not match what he expected of a rape victim. A group of four armed men attacked nineteen-year-old Rachel and her two male companions while they were hiking. The attackers took turns raping Rachel behind some bushes, while her friends lay tied up on the ground. Rachel testified that she resisted but did not scream. She explained that screaming would not have made any difference, as her friends, although able to hear what was happening to her, were unable to help. Afterward, a dishevelled Rachel and her two companions walked home in silence. Rachel's rational explanation about the futility of shouting made no sense to Acting Justice Curry, who wrote,

> I am extremely surprised that a girl of 19 ½ was not in much more distressed state after having been raped by three ruffians than this girl apparently was. One

[1] Laura Kounine, 'Emotions, Mind, and Body on Trial: A Cross-Cultural Perspective', *Journal of Social History* 51, no. 2(2017): 224.

> would have expected the reaction to have made her hysterical and to have reduced her to tears – but apart from statements by the men that she was excited and in a disarranged state there is no other sign of rape.[2]

Clearly, in this judge's opinion, a victim's hysteria was a 'sign of rape', whereas the demonstration of rationality and emotional restraint was not. Without the appropriate emotional supplement, in the form of crying or shouting, Rachel's story failed to persuade Acting Justice Curry.

Perpetrators as well as victims are expected to feel and display emotion 'befitting' their role. Sixteen-year-old Acre resident Mustafa Naif, suspected of having sex with another young man, recanted his original claim that 'I used to love him and he used to love me, and that this man had a sexual intercourse with me twice with my consent and free will, because he loves me and I love him'.[3] As a self-incriminating admission, this version was, of course, a 'wrong' story to tell the authorities. But it was also 'wrong' because it ascribed to the protagonist an emotion (love) that made little sense in the context of prevailing notions regarding relationships between men. Romantic love was not a plausible option.

Mohamad Sunji, an eyewitness to the sexual act, tells a completely different story. His story should be taken with a grain of salt, not only because he himself was indicted for perjury for making contradictory statements about the case but also because he may have been motivated by jealousy. Mohamad's account of how that eventful night began reveals that he himself probably fancied Mustafa Naif and that their cosy interaction was disrupted by the appearance of Mustafa Zahran.[4] My concern here is not the facts of the case but the way Mohamad tailored his story to the authorities' expectations. His account of what transpired between Mustafa Naif and Mustafa Zahran is not a love story but rather a story of male sex obtained through exploitation and threats. Mohamad said that on the night in question he was hanging out with Mustafa Naif in a series of hashish bars. The two were subsequently joined by Mustafa Zahran and, later, by another man. En route to another café, Mustafa Zahran told Mohamad and the fourth man to wait at a distance while he entered a cemetery with Mustafa Naif. Once inside, Mohamad said, the two took off their trousers and Mustafa Zahran spread his jacket under Mustafa Naif (a detail that indicates possible tenderness). He then provided a meticulous description of Mustafa Zahran penetrating Mustafa Naif. Mohamad later added that, after the act, Mustafa Zahran paid Mustafa Naif

[2] ISA Division 30 (Supreme Court Files), File B/441, original docket # Cr.A 31/47 (*Fahed Kathem & Musa Ahmed* v. *A.G.*), page 13 of Acting Justice Curry's opinion. Justice Curry mentioned 'three ruffians'. Rachel reported an attack by four men, two of whom were charged in this file, and another man apparently in a different case. The fourth was not charged, probably because he had never been caught.

[3] ISA/RG 30/Law 2029 (original docket # Cr.C 222/43).

[4] See his evidence before the police investigator on 11 June 1943. ISA/RG 30/Law 2029 (original docket # Cr.C 221/43).

thirteen piastres, claiming that that was all the money he had. According to Mohamad, the group then moved on. At one point, Mustafa Zahran went into his house and re-emerged with a pistol. Threatening to shoot Mustafa Naif, he forced him to agree to another sexual act:

> He returned and had a pistol with him . . . and said to the child Mustafa Naif: I want to ride over you once more, the child said, no, you have just rode on me; Mustafa Zahran said I was not pleased in the first time, you must walk, and he drew the pistol on him, and said I shall drill holes in you now, and we walked in the direction of the eucalyptus trees that are near the [police station], and there Mustafa Zahran acted with the child Mustafa for a second time in my presence, and when he finished he said to us go peace be with you, and did not pay money to the child, and we went.

This is no romantic tale about the natural outcome of mutual tender feelings but rather a story of brutal forced sex instigated solely for the enjoyment of the stronger party. Mustafa Naif is described as 'the child' and not as an equal, consenting partner. His satisfaction or wishes are of no consequence. He had less agency than a prostitute – Mustafa Zahran decided whether to pay him and how much. The sexual act is a 'ride', not lovemaking. Mustafa Zahran was so brazen as to declare to a police inspector the group encountered later that night, 'I shall have the child sleep by me tonight'. In his initial statement, Mustafa Naif described the sexual encounter with Mustafa Zahran as an expression of love, but his companion Mohamad did not see any love or tenderness. The possibility of love between men was not acknowledged either by the authorities (as Mustafa Naif's later repudiation may indicate) or by his peer, another Arab youth from Acre.

Interestingly, in some cases, love was a plausible motive for rape. George Georgiades, who was accused of raping nineteen-year-old Magdalene in 1933, explained that he was motivated by love for the girl, whom he forcibly married after sexually assaulting her.[5] Twenty-three-year-old Ali Saleh Mohammad, accused in the rape-cum-manslaughter of his sixteen-year-old cousin, explained to the police investigator that he had loved the girl for three years. Her parents, he said, would not allow him to marry her, 'so I thought of abducting her by force'. He described how he forcefully dragged her, struck her with a stick and repeatedly told her, 'You must marry me.'[6] In his view, apparently, love for the girl did not preclude the use of violence against her. After he forcibly raped his cousin in the swampy forest of Houleh, Ali kept her there until she died about five hours later.

If love was a plausible motivation for rape, marriage between the rapist and the victim made sense to some as a way to nullify the violation. David Cohen from Nachliel, a Yemenite Jewish neighbourhood in Hadera, was charged with

5 ISA/RG 66/M/188/33 (original docket # Cr.C 44/33).

6 ISA/RG 30/Law 2053 (original docket # Cr.C 120/46), on his police investigation on 28 November 1945.

rape. Judge Kassan proposed that the twenty-four-year-old Cohen, married and a father of one, divorce his wife and marry the victim to mitigate his punishment. The accused rejected the offer and was sentenced to one year's imprisonment and a fine of L.P. 30.[7] In another case, the rapist's agreement to marry his victim was regarded as grounds for his lenient punishment. In that case two young men, Qasem and Muhammad (aged twenty-two and twenty-three, respectively), were indicted for the abduction and rape of a girl under sixteen.[8] They took the girl by force from her father's home – she could see that Qasem had a pistol and her abductors also threatened her with knives. Later, Qasem raped her violently as she screamed and kicked. Qasem and Muhammad pleaded guilty to the charges of abduction and rape. However, Judge Shehade found mitigating circumstances: 'In the express understanding that the first accused will in addition to such damage as has been paid get married to his victim, I am inclined to take [a] somewhat lenient view, whereby the victim herself will not suffer and the family honour will be safe-guarded.'[9] Both the Jewish Judge Kassan and the Arab Judge Shehade regarded the marriage of the rapist to the victim as a mitigating factor in sentencing. It made sense to these local judges that the social disruption created by the offence for the victim and her kin could be resolved by uniting the victim with her attacker through the intimate bond of marriage.

The legal ideology that portrays law as 'rational' and as unaffected by emotions overlooks the role emotions actually play in criminal proceedings.[10] Their implicit nature is what makes emotions effective. Communication through emotion takes place on a less conscious level than explicit verbal interaction. When George described his love for Magdalene, whom he brutally raped and sodomized, he implicitly attempted to excuse his behaviour. Had he plainly stated that rape driven by love is justified, he likely would have been harshly rebuked. However, merely by describing his emotions, he conveyed this message. The tacit nature of such communication gives emotions the appearance of 'natural' instincts and conceals their socially constructed features.

By treating emotions and desires as uncontrollable instincts, lawyers could translate 'natural' reaction into a line of defence or an argument for mitigating circumstances. When Jamal Eff. Hamad, the attorney for the accused in the rape of Rachel from Kibbutz Eilon argued for mitigating circumstances, he described his clients as '[s]haken by seeing a girl in shorts with two young men. Provocation for men such as accused, who are ignorant and fanatical and led away by inflammatory propaganda.'[11] The implication here is that their vulnerable

[7] 'A Trial for Rape', *Davar*, 1 November 1939, p. 6. Judge Kassan was a magistrate, and the offence of rape fell under the jurisdiction of the district court. It is likely that the newspaper article is inaccurate and that the actual charges were for a lesser sexual offence. L.P. (Palestinian Lira) was officially termed 'Palestine Pound'.

[8] ISA/RG 30/Law 2063 (original docket # Cr.C 208/47).

[9] Page 1 of Judge Shehade's judgment from 20 October 1947.

[10] Kounine, 2.

[11] ISA/RG 30/Law 2046 (original docket # Cr.C 206/45).

emotional construction rendered the accused susceptible to even slightly arousing stimulation.

The emotional expression that takes place in court is the product of interaction between the procedural and evidentiary conventions that control the criminal proceedings and the extrajudicial beliefs, norms and dispositions of the participants in those proceedings. To historicize emotions one needs 'to historicize the psychological, physical, and material context in which a person experiences her emotions'.[12] It is therefore important to review what the participants bring with them from the cultural worlds that surround the court, not just the emotions they express in court.

## Modes and Arenas of Emotional Expression within Mandate Palestine's Jewish Community

I now turn to the extrajudicial context. I focus my gaze on the Jewish community in Mandate Palestine, scrutinizing two arenas in which emotion played a significant role: first, the making of a criminal complaint, in which shame was a salient concern, and second, acts of revenge for inter-ethnic rape, in which anger loomed large. I make three arguments with respect to shame and anger. First, both emotions were integral to 'plausible' stories about sexual assaults. Second, emotions underpinning 'plausible' narratives could be powerfully transmitted without words, through actions and demeanour. Shame was non-verbally communicated, for instance, through reluctance to file complaints, and anger was expressed through violent behaviour. Third, shame and anger were shared within ethnic and national communities, a phenomenon that highlights their social construction.

In this chapter, I draw extensively on extralegal sources, such as newspaper articles and intelligence reports, and I read the absence of complaints as indexing silence and lack of emotional display. Such materials may provide 'vivid insight into the emotional worlds of those participating in the legal systems'.[13] I begin my investigation by considering silence. Preceding the question of what is a wrong or a right story to tell is the question of whether a story should be told at all and, if so, to whom. Yet muted expression is still expression, and silence too conveys emotions that underpin 'plausible' stories about sexual assaults.

Jewish victims were less forthcoming than Arab victims with complaints about sexual assault, most noticeably within their own community. Out of 139 known complainants in my corpus, 107 (77 per cent) were Arab, and 25 (18 per cent) were Jewish (of the remaining victims, 3 were British, 1 was Polish, 1 Italian, 1 Greek and 1 Druze).[14] Only 2 of the Jewish complainants

[12] Kounine, 3.

[13] Merridee L. Bailey and Kimberley-Joy Knight, 'Writing Histories of Law and Emotion', *The Journal of Legal History* 38, no. 2 (2017): 125.

[14] These figures reflect the exclusion of bestiality and perjury charges in my 147-case corpus.

(1.4 per cent of the total number of complainants, 8 per cent of Jewish complainants) pointed the finger at fellow Jews. Why was rape a 'wrong' story for Jews to tell before the authorities?

As I note in Chapter 4, the rarity of Jewish complainants is not explainable by demographics, and I therefore assume that it reflects a social pattern. Much has been written about the deterrent effect of the ignominy that awaits sexual offence complainants, including a humiliating investigation by the police and painful exposure on the witness stand (sometimes described as a 'second rape').[15] Is it possible that Arabs and Jews were differently affected by these prospects?[16] In a traditional society that cherishes virginity, its loss, even through no fault of the victim, may injure the victim's social standing and chances of marriage. Both Jewish and Arab communities in Mandate Palestine included traditional sectors in which virginity was highly valued; factors other than, or in addition to, traditionalism, then, appear to be relevant to understanding the higher rate of sexual assault reporting in the Arab community.

Information is scarce about cases in which the victims were too timid or ashamed to complain. Documented complaints of Jews from the pre-Mandate era are particularly hard to come by, as the Orthodox Jewish community that resided in the Holy Land in the second half of the nineteenth century (dubbed the 'old Yishuv') was reluctant to openly discuss sexuality and violence.[17] Four complaints from the Ottoman period, however, provide us with some insight into the mentality of that community on the subject of sexual offences. One incident dating to the beginning of the twentieth century is described in the memoir of Eliyahu Zeev Halevi Lewin-Epstein, one of the founders of the Jewish colony of Rehovot.[18] Lewin-Epstein recounts that one of the colonists, married and the father of sons, had a carriage with which he transported passengers from Rehovot to Jaffa on a daily basis. One day, upon returning to Rehovot, he found himself alone with the wife of one of the colony's labourers, and he raped her. Two days later the incident became known, and the victim's husband threatened to stab the rapist. He was pacified only after being promised that the offender would be brought to trial. A hearing was held

15 Nazife Bashar, 'Rape in England between 1550 and 1700', in *The Sexual Dynamics of History*, ed. The London Feminist History Group (London: Pluto Press, 1983), 35; Sarah E. Ullman and Henrietta H. Filipas, 'Correlates of Formal and Informal Support Seeking in Sexual Assault Victims', *Journal of Interpersonal Violence* 16, no. 10 (2001); Susan Estrich, *Real Rape* (Cambridge, MA: Harvard University Press, 1987), 23; Julia R. Schwendinger and Herman Schwendinger, *Rape and Inequality* (Beverly Hills: Sage, 1983), 23–24. For more on reluctance to complain, see Jennifer Temkin, *Rape and the Legal Process*, 2nd ed. (Oxford: Oxford University Press, 2002), 3–4, 17–19.

16 On ethnicity and willingness to file a sexual assault complaint, see Nicola Gavey, *Just Sex?: The Cultural Scaffolding of Rape* (New York: Routledge, 2004), 26–27, 51–52.

17 Margalit Shilo, *Princess or Captive? Jewish Women in Jerusalem, 1840–1914* [in Hebrew] (Haifa: Haifa University Press, 2001), 20.

18 He does not specify the year, but the text implies the incident occurred about a decade after Rehovot's founding in 1891. Eliyahu Zeev Halevi Lewin-Epstein, *Memoirs* [in Hebrew] (Tel Aviv: Lewin-Epstein, 1932), 186.

before the colony's board. The accused refuted the charges, but the board believed he was guilty. Lewin-Epstein writes,

> This was the first and last criminal case during the ten years I headed the board. We had no example on how to behave in such an impure matter. The board did not want to assume responsibility, therefore it summoned all members of the general assembly of the colony. Each stated his opinion, and all the 'opinions' were noted in the transcript and affirmed by signatures. All but two opined that the accused must leave the colony for eternity within two weeks.[19]

As there was no mechanism of enforcement, however, the board had no way to make the accused comply with this decision. Eventually, informal sanctions forced the man and his family out of Rehovot. The board maintained a firm position despite the accused's threat to kill Lewin-Epstein and his complaints to the Russian consul, to a Jaffa rabbi, to Ottoman officials and to members of another early colony, Rishon Le-Zion. Despite his obstinacy and threats, the board did not consider bringing the matter before the Ottoman authorities.[20]

In a second incident, reported in the press in 1903, the mother of a seven-year-old girl spread her daughter's (presumably incriminating) dress before the rabbis and demanded that they investigate the rape of her daughter by a yeshiva student.[21] The press report did not use the word 'rape', instead describing the incident through allusion to the biblical story of Dinah.[22] The account stirred outrage, not because of the injury done to the child but rather because of the embarrassment and shame to which it exposed the Orthodox community.[23]

A third rape incident within the Orthodox community of Jerusalem was reported in 1912.[24] A privately printed pamphlet accused a hotel owner from the city's ultra-Orthodox sector of raping a fourteen-year-old girl who was a guest in his hotel, and the ensuing debate led the hotel owner to charge his accuser with libel.[25] The case was heard neither by an official Ottoman court nor by a religious Jewish court but by a voluntary tribunal of the Jewish community. The tribunal was headed by Rav Kook, a distinguished religious authority, who appointed six more members, three from the modern Jewish intelligentsia and three affluent businessmen. The case stirred fierce debate within the Jewish community, but Ottoman authorities were not involved.

[19] Ibid., 187.

[20] The accused, by contrast, did turn to the Ottoman authorities, possibly to protest the banishment and the loss of property it entailed.

[21] Shilo, 231. *Hashkafa*, 27 November 1903, p. 2. [22] Genesis 34.

[23] Shilo, 233. *Hashkafa*, 4 December 1903, p. 3.

[24] The information about the case is taken from Nathan Brun, 'Jaffa 1912: Rape of a Girl in Mea-Shearim Jerusalem', *Katedra*, no. 142 (2012).

[25] For reference to the seventy-page pamphlet in the Yiddish language, see ibid., fn. 16. Brun also reconstructed the trial transcripts (the originals were lost) on the basis of secondary materials. www.ybz.org.il/?CategoryID=235&ArticleID=3680#.Wg_08kojTIU.

The fourth incident involves a case of attempted rape reported in Tel Aviv in 1913. A Jewish labourer entered a home by breaking a bath window and attempted to rape a sixteen-year-old girl, who screamed and was saved by her neighbours. The Tel Aviv council, a voluntary body of the then newly established Jewish neighbourhood, faced a stressful dilemma.[26] On the one hand, criminal enforcement required police, detention facilities, courts and jurisdiction, all of which the small Hebrew community lacked; on the other hand, handing the suspect over to the Ottoman authorities would have compromised the community's autonomy.[27] The council resolved not to inform the Ottoman authorities but to deport the accused abroad.

These examples reflect the Jewish community's tendency to handle sexual offence cases internally. Even on those rare occasions when community members demanded inquiry, they did not bring the matter before the state authorities but rather before the community's voluntary tribunals.

Five waves of Jewish immigration to Palestine beginning around the turn of the twentieth century changed the composition of the local community.[28] The first wave (1881–1903) doubled the Jewish population through the influx of roughly twenty-five thousand people, mostly lower-middle-class families from Russia, Romania and Yemen who left behind deteriorating political and economic conditions in their countries of origin. The second wave (1904–1914) brought around thirty-five thousand Jews, mostly from eastern Europe. Among the immigrants in this wave were pioneers, young people committed to Jewish nationalism and socialism (many had belonged to revolutionary parties in Russia) who clearly embodied the Zionist ethos.[29] The 1917 Balfour Declaration expressed British commitment to establishing a national home for Jews in Palestine. After the First World War and the constitution of the British Mandate in Palestine, around thirty-five thousand Jews arrived in a third wave of immigration (1919–1923); young pioneers accounted for substantial numbers of these newcomers until 1921. About sixty-two thousand immigrants, mostly from Poland, arrived in the fourth wave (1924–1931). Many of them settled in cities. The fifth wave (1931–1939) included close to three hundred thousand mostly middle-class immigrants who were driven from Europe by the rise of the Nazi regime. Most of these immigrants, whether socialist pioneers or urban bourgeoisie, were more 'modern' than the ultra-Orthodox Jews of the Ottoman period. One would expect them to have been

[26] The description is based on Leora Bilsky, '"Rothstein's Affair": Nachum Guttman, Local Mythology and the First Attempted Rape in Tel Aviv' [in Hebrew], *Iyunei Mishpat* 26, no. 2 (2002).

[27] Ibid., 428.

[28] On the scholarly debate on the issue of the periodization of Jewish immigration see Nahum Gross, 'A Note on the Periodization to the History of the Yishuv during the Mandatory Period' [in Hebrew], *Cathedra* 18 (1981): 174; Hizky Shoham, 'From "Great History" to "Small History": The Genesis of the Zionist Periodization', *Israel Studies* 18, no. 1 (2013): 32 ; Gur Alroey, *An Unpromising Land: Jewish Migration to Palestine in the Early Twentieth Century* (Stanford, CA: Stanford University Press, 2014), 5, 11.

[29] Alroey, 20–21.

more open about matters of sexuality, less worried about their reputations or those of their families or community should it be known that they had been victims of sexual offences.

This expectation, however, is not corroborated by documentary evidence. Pioneer women, for example, shied away from making sexual abuse complaints, and those who exposed such incidents faced significant social sanctions.[30] In 1927, under British rule, an official of the Jaffa Worker's Council was accused of misdoings, including sexual harassment of female comrades: attempting to kiss them, making indecent proposals and paying them night-time visits.[31] The council appointed a board of inquiry, which prepared a secret report concluding that the charges, except of general indecency, were mostly unfounded. One board member dissented, claiming that the conclusions were politically biased and that a number of female comrades were too embarrassed to testify. The dissenter published his opinion in an opposition magazine and was subsequently brought before a Comrades Law Tribunal,[32] which found him guilty of 'unlawfully publicizing secrets from a judicial chamber'.[33] Just like the old-Yishuv ultra-Orthodox community, Zionist socialists displayed dismay at allegations of sexual abuse and were concerned about their effect on the community's reputation.

Agricultural settlers belonging to the second wave of immigration were also expected not to report criminal behaviour by fellow members of their community, even if rape was suspected. In 1923, Tzvi Shmushkin, from the Galilee settlement of Segera, complained to the police that three local young men, returning drunk from a Purim party, attempted to rape his sister Haya.[34] The police arrested the suspects and drove them shackled to the Tiberias police station on the Sabbath, shocking the Orthodox settlers of Segera. Tzvi was forced by the community to retract his complaint, which violated an unwritten social code forbidding exposure of honour-related conflicts to strangers. His complaint and countercomplaints by the three youngsters were eventually heard by the legal committee of the settlers union, the community's tribunal.

In her autobiography *The Life of a Worker in Her Homeland* (originally published in 1935), pioneer Henya Pekelman writes of her rape by fellow

[30] A literary example reflecting this atmosphere is found in an unpublished manuscript by pioneer author Rivka Alper that tells the story of Dinah (purposely named after the biblical rape victim), who blamed herself for being raped and who never considered complaining to the authorities. Alper's first book had met with hostility – one reviewer sarcastically asked if it was proper for a woman pioneer, one who laboured as hard as men did, to also be a pioneer of sexual description. Alper's story and biographic information by Ruth Beckie Colodny were published in *Haaretz*, 11 April 2014 (www.haaretz.co.il/literature/prose/.premium-1.2291395).

[31] The description of the incident draws on Ronen Shamir, *The Colonies of Law: Colonialism, Zionism, and Law in Early Mandate Palestine* (Cambridge: Cambridge University Press, 2000), 140.

[32] For background on the Comrades Law system, see ibid., 135. [33] Ibid., 140.

[34] The description of the case draws on Yair Seltenreich, 'Masculinity, Respect and Body in the Pjca Settlements of the Galilee During the Settlement Period', *Israeli Sociology* 11, no. 1 (2009): 144–145.

pioneer Yeruham Mirkin.[35] Henya described Mirkin as corrupt, lazy and self-indulgent. She worked with him on a tobacco farm he established and testified against him when he was sued for irregularities involving investors' money. Yet, when he later raped her, she did not pursue legal proceedings.[36] It is obvious from Henya's writing that presenting oneself as a rape victim was perceived by pioneer society as a violation of the codes of sexual modesty.[37] When Henya found out she was pregnant, she was distraught to the point of suicide.[38] She moved out of the area and lived under an assumed name until the birth of her daughter. Had she not become pregnant, the rape might have remained unknown, a well-kept secret, but having a child exposed unmarried Henya, who courageously confronted her old friends with her story, to social pressures. After her daughter's birth, Henya even considered complaining to the authorities about the rape:

> I started to think what should I do now. I decided to go to the government and ask for advice, can I seek revenge. All I wanted was revenge. I came to the police and told everything to officer Cohen. First he asked me why didn't I go to the government immediately after the act. I answered that I was very naive and was too ashamed to tell anyone. The officer responded that the government can find out the truth, but can take no action without witnesses. I must go to the offices of the Rabbinate, and the government could intervene on the basis of their judgment. I left the police, but did not go to the Rabbinate: I knew what the verdict would be: he should either marry me or pay compensation. I did not want to marry such a villain nor did I want money from his hand. Can money heal my misery? No! Should he pay he'd feel as if he had atoned for his sin, and I did not want that.[39]

After finally bracing herself to complain, Henya was sorely disappointed by the response of the justice system. Her account suggests one possible reason for the scarcity of Jewish complainants and Jewish suspects in the corpus of cases I was able to examine: like Henya, other victims may have been dissuaded from complaining. Henya did not follow the government officer's suggestion to seek the help of the Rabbinate, a patriarchal institution that could only offer her

[35] Henya M. Pekelman, *The Life of a Worker in Her Homeland* (Or-Yehuda: Kinnert, Zmora-Bitan, Dvir, 2007).

[36] Henya's normally straightforward and candid writing becomes oblique when she describes the rape, which she represents by a few dashed lines:

> 'Why are you locking the door?' I asked. 'The landlady does not allow strangers to enter the room', he responded. I immediately felt his deceit and wanted to exit the room, but Yeruham forcefully held me. We began to struggle until I got a hard blow on my head and fell to the floor. ------------------------------------------ I remember nothing more. I only remember myself pacing on the beach like crazy.

Ibid., 163.

[37] Tamar B. Hess, 'I Am Not Alone in the World: The Memoirs of Henya Pekelman', in *The Life of a Worker in Her Homeland* (Or-Yehuda: Kinneret, Zmora-Bitan, Dvir, 2007), 227.

[38] Pekelman, 166–167. [39] Ibid., 188.

solutions that would preserve her inferiority. Instead, she sought justice her way. She published her story in a book and plainly stated on its first page, 'I do not intend to blame anyone or demonstrate my righteousness. But I could not surrender to society's requirements and taste.' Reporting the rape publicly was an act of defiance. Society, it seems, was not ready. Henya's testimony stood in brilliant solitude for many years and got no notice until the end of the twentieth century.[40]

Henya's insistence that her voice be heard was exceptional, but, forthright as she was, even she had no words to describe the rape. The event made her wish she were dead. In fact, she committed suicide fifteen years later. Others, with less strength, did not last that long. Chaya Probtzam, a recent immigrant from Germany, committed suicide four days before she was scheduled to testify against her rapist in court. Unfortunately for Chaya, following a visit to Ramat Hakovesh, the kibbutz where she planned to settle, she got a ride with Shafiq George Halaby, a serial rapist. A newspaper article described what happened:

> The life of Chaya Probtzam was destroyed. The terrible experience in her first days in the country . . . the loss of her chances to enter Ramat Hakovesh, meeting the rapist before the police and before the magistrate, and the rapist's confidence that nothing bad would happen to him, his cynical laughter, lack of help in the matter of her disaster, sadness from every direction in the Tel Aviv turmoil depressed her. . . . She said she had no energy to go to court, that she could not bear it all.[41]

The article lays bare the informal sanctions the rape victim faced both within and outside the Jewish community. Chaya's chances of becoming a kibbutz member were ruined, and the investigatory and criminal proceedings offered little hope of justice and were emotionally unbearable.

The data reflect little tendency for Jews to name and testify against fellow Jews in cases of sexual offences. It is hard to tell whether the community's volunteer tribunals imposed sanctions on Jewish transgressors. Inbar describes a 1940 case in which a Haganah (an underground resistance organization; the name means 'defence') member was tried before a court-martial for rape.[42] He left his guard post without permission and walked to an adjacent lot with his friend, where the two saw a couple having sex. The two men pointed a gun at the couple and agreed to release them only if the woman had sex with them. Then they took turns raping the woman while holding the man at gunpoint. The accused Haganah member was permanently expelled from the organization. I have no evidence of other informal proceedings within the Jewish community, but this does not mean that they did not exist.

There are several possible explanations for the reluctance of Jewish victims to complain about sexual aggressors, especially if they were fellow Jews.

[40] Hess, 219. [41] 'Rape which Caused Suicide', *Davar*, 4 July 1935, p. 8.
[42] Zvi Inbar, *Scales and Sword: The Foundations of Military Law in Israel* (Tel Aviv: Ministry of Defense Publishing, 2005), 57.

Litigation in the Palestine courts may have been perceived as an avenue available to local Arabs, a continuation of tradition dating back to the Ottoman period. For Jews, the local system had to be an acquired taste. Most Jewish immigrants came from countries where they had viewed the authorities with caution and suspicion and where internal debates were kept within the community. The reluctance to report the sexual crimes of fellow Jews also may have been instilled by the long Jewish tradition of *din moser* (the law of the informant). This Halachic rule forbids Jews from turning co-religionists over to secular authorities, especially non-Jewish authorities, for violations of the law, whether Jewish or secular. Another possible explanation for the disproportion between Jewish and Arab complainants is the greater number of Arabs serving on the police forces and as forensic physicians, prosecutors and judges (reflecting their larger proportion in the population).[43] Jewish sex offence victims, we may speculate, would have felt more comfortable about complaining had there been more Jews in the police and justice system.

Still another explanation might lie in the Jewish concern for the reputation of the community. As demonstrated in the previous chapter, Jews referenced a propensity for sexual assault when characterizing Arabs, thus creating a distinction and bolstering the boundaries between the two communities. The image of the sexually dangerous Arab male was counterposed to that of the sexually non-aggressive Jewish male, an opposition undermined by complaints about Jewish sexual offenders.

Whatever the explanation, the reluctance of Jews to tell the authorities about incidents of sexual assault conveys a strong sense of shame. A story of rape was a 'wrong' story to tell, especially to 'outsiders'. Rape was perceived as shameful and humiliating to the victim and to the victim's collective. Accompanying the shame was a sense of guilt. The victim was to blame for not being careful, and the collective, especially its men, were guilty of not being able to protect the victim.

Failure to file an official complaint was a manifestation of shame but also of unwillingness to acknowledge dependency. Complaining to government authorities meant not only exposing stories of sexual offences to 'outsiders' but also giving those outsiders authorization to handle these matters. The Jewish disinclination to trust the British occupiers with the mission of securing justice went hand in hand with an aspiration to act as autonomously as possible.[44] This combination of suspicion and determination to be self-reliant sometimes resulted in community members taking the law into their

[43] In 1946 the regular police forces in Palestine consisted of 6,285 policemen (3,259 British, 2,376 Arabs, 650 Jewish). In December 1945, out of 48 government attorneys, 22 were Arabs and 17 Jews, and out of 533 employees of the civil courts, 341 were Arabs and 166 were Jews. Jacob Reuveny, *The Administration of Palestine under the British Mandate 1920–1948: An Institutional Analysis* (Ramat Gan: Bar Ilan University Press, 1993), 154, 235.

[44] On the Jewish tradition of reluctance to submit to the jurisdiction of foreign sovereigns, see Shamir, 58.

own hands. The reluctance to turn to the authorities blocked a significant outlet for the anger felt towards sexual offenders who attacked members of the Jewish community. Thus, while silence expressed embarrassment and shame, violent acts of revenge expressed anger and frustration as well as political independence.

Documentary records refer to a few instances in which representatives of the Jewish community committed horrifying acts of revenge against Arabs suspected of raping Jewish women. These non-verbal expressions of extreme anger sent a powerful message about the meaning of inter-ethnic rape and were aimed at re-establishing the boundaries between the Jewish and Arab communities. Like silence, non-verbal acts are significant rhetorical tools for expressing emotions that speak to the plausibility of stories about sexual assaults.

On one occasion, members of Irgun (an underground resistance organization) opened fire on British Army soldiers (including an officer) in retaliation for the rape of a young Jewish woman in Jerusalem by British soldiers.[45] The indiscriminate nature of the shooting (those targeted were not the rapists) reveals that the rape was framed in national terms. The fact that those involved in the shooting were self-appointed does cancel out their perception of inter-ethnic rape as an injury that justified revenge in the name of the whole community. According to this perception, inter-ethnic rape was not merely an injury to an individual woman by an individual man but an assault against the Jewish people by the British collective. The anger, therefore, was felt by the community, and the revenge, though carried out by self-appointed representatives, expressed this shared emotion.

Acts of revenge against individual suspects also had a national aspect. Around 1942, a Jewish mother and her daughter lost their way in the upper Galilee and reached an army camp near Mahanayim. Two Arab guards from the camp raped both women, who were illegal immigrants and thus unable to file a complaint.[46] The Haganah conducted a trial of the rapists in their absence and sentenced them to death. The men managed to escape detection for several years. Eventually, one of them was found to be working as a policeman in Haifa and the other as a guard in his uncle's orchard in the north. Three members of the Palmach (the military force of the Haganah) disguised as policemen travelled to the orchard and asked the guard to accompany them on a pretext. They then killed and buried him in a grave they had dug the day before. The uncle went to the police the next day to find out why his nephew had not come home, only to realize that those who had taken him had not been police. Rumours began to spread, and tensions between Jews and Arabs began to rise. The Jews denied involvement in the man's disappearance, and as he had a criminal record and was known to be

[45] *Davar*, 22 December 1947, p. 1, *Palestine Post*, 22 December 1947, p. 1.
[46] HA 49-38, HA 169-2.

a weapons smuggler, uncertainty persisted about his fate. The second rapist again escaped reprisal.

In September 1946, *Hamashkif*, a right-wing Hebrew newspaper and the unofficial platform of the Irgun, published a series of stories of retaliation for rape. The first report concerned twelve Jewish men from Pardes Hanah, who, armed with rifles and pistols, sought revenge for the rape of a young girl by a Bedouin youth. When they did not find the boy in his family's tent, they ordered the family out of the tent and set it afire.[47] The mother of the family identified two of the attackers, whom she knew as guards. A few days later, the newspaper reported another case in which fifteen Jews dressed in khaki pants and white shirts and armed with pistols entered the orange grove of an Arab man in Sheick Munes. They attacked the man and his son, Hassan, who had been involved in the rape of a Jewish woman in the same orange grove several weeks earlier. After pistol-whipping Hassan and his father, they shot Hassan, injuring his arm.[48] The revenge had a clear nationalist implication: Jews, armed, organized and dressed in uniform, were responding as a group in military fashion to the rape of a Jewish woman. The anger was directed at a specific offender and his father. The avengers, however, as made clear by their paramilitary appearance and demeanour, represented not just the individual victim but the Jewish community as well. Their expression of anger was meant to display national force.

In at least three cases, members of the Haganah employed castration in avenging the rape of Jewish women by Arab men.[49] Around 1935, a Jewish female physician who had taken a taxi from Haifa to Nahariya to treat her patients, was raped by the Arab taxi driver.[50] Upon hearing her story, some Haganah members demanded revenge. Haifa's Haganah commander[51] approved the revenge, and high-ranking leaders also approved it.[52] In a sting

47 'Arson of an Arab Tent as Revenge of Rape', *Hamashkif*, 4 September 1946, p. 4. Footprints led from the family's encampment to Pardes Hana, where a ten-year-old child had been raped by a sixteen-year-old boy named Hassan, a charge for which he was tried earlier that year. The record of the case is found in ISA/RG 30/Law 2053 (original docket # Cr.C 139/46).

48 'Did 15 Jews Attack an Arab Rapist?', *Hamashkif*, 9 September 1946, p. 4.

49 I was able to find documentation of a case in which the Jewish poet Y. Z. Rimon was castrated by Arabs in October 1922. This early case, it appears, was part of a series of incidents in which Jews were victims of violent attacks by Arabs and had no sexual implications. *Doar Hayom*, 22 October 1922, p. 3; Shmuel Giller, 'The Poet of God, Yosef Zvi Rimon and the Murder of the Officer Tauffic Bey', http://samgiler.weebly.com/uploads/6/8/1/9/6819339/rimon.pdf (in Hebrew).

50 HA 178-28, interview with Gershon Ritov.

51 Yaacov Dori was the Haifa commander. In 1939, he became the Haganah's commander in chief, and with the establishment of Israel, he became the first commander in chief of the Israeli Army.

52 HA 80-134-2, Berl Raptor's testimony, pp. 3–4. Berl consulted with high-ranking Haganah officials, who advised him, 'We don't interfere in such matters.' He also consulted with two socialist political leaders, Berl Katznelson (editor of the leading newspaper, *Davar*) and Isaac Tabenkin, who advised him that a response to the rape was appropriate but that killing should be avoided.

operation, three Haganah members entered the driver's taxi as passengers, attacked him and tied him to an electricity pole. They castrated him and left him tied to the pole.

In 1945 a series of sexual assaults troubled the Jewish inhabitants of Beit She'an Valley. The attempted rapes of two kibbutz women and the rape of a third, who was attacked by two armed men as she was walking with her companion, motivated the regional commander of the Haganah to react.[53] The suspect was identified shortly after the first incident by the victim, an eighteen-year-old girl named Matti who had been attacked while walking from the bus stop to her kibbutz, Sdeh Nahum. She was crossing a creek where two young Arabs were fishing, when one of them embraced and kissed her forcefully and tried to take off her underwear. After a few minutes' struggle, she managed to escape. Pursuant to her complaint, Aref Ben Ahmad Esh Sharida, a nineteen-year-old Arab from Biesan, was arrested, identified by Matti in an identification parade, and charged with attempted rape and an indecent act. While he was released on bail pending his trial, members of the Palmach made their own inquiries about the identity and whereabouts of the suspect and resolved to castrate him (after two more sexual assaults had occurred).[54] The operation was approved by the Palmach's chief commander, Isaac Sadeh, who decided the avengers should teach a lesson but not kill.[55] A Palmach unit prepared for the operation. Undercover agents gathered information about the suspect and consulted with a doctor, who instructed them how to use ether and which veins to cut. Disguised as Arabs, they went to the suspect's house and persuaded him to accompany them to a wadi.[56] Despite the anaesthesia administered to him, their victim remained confused and active and was eventually rendered unconscious by a blow to the head. The primitive operation was performed with a shaving knife; the veins were tied with a shoelace. Several Jews were subsequently investigated by the police, but no arrests were made.[57] When Aref was brought to trial, he pleaded guilty to an indecent act and not guilty to attempted rape. He was convicted of an indecent act, yet the Arab prosecutor offered no evidence supporting the more serious and contested charge of attempted rape, and Aref was consequently acquitted on that count. The British judge expressed horror and repulsion at what Aref had gone through:

> The accused has had a sufficient punishment by the abhorrent and bestial offence committed on his person by those who have taken the law into their

[53] HA 214-1, HA 115-7, HA 140-4, HA 101-6, HA 25-30; Amos Nevo, 'The Punishment', *Yediot Ahronot*, 30 April 1993.

[54] This is another manifestation of the lack of trust in British justice and the desire to act autonomously. See also Gamliel Cohen, *Under Cover* (Tel Aviv: Ministry of Defence, 2002), 44. For particulars on the case against the suspect, see ISA/RG 30/Law 2043 (original docket # Cr.C 104/45).

[55] HA 214-1, interview with Jacob Cohen, p. 24.

[56] HA 178-28, interview with Gershon Ritov.

[57] Kurt Weil, who guided the Palmach team, participated in an identification parade. He whispered to the castrated victim, who recognized him, 'Didn't you have enough?' preventing the man from identifying him. HA 115-7.

> own hands in such an unjustifiable and uncivilized manner without awaiting the trial and punishment of the accused by the Courts of Justice who are the sole and proper persons to try such offences.[58]

The judge clearly perceived the Palmach unit's actions as a bold challenge to the authority of the British justice system. Notwithstanding the conviction, Aref was discharged on bond for one year. The brutal castration was commemorated in a popular Hebrew song, 'We Castrated You, Mohammed!'[59] The substitution of a common Arabic name for Aref's name and the use of the first-person plural pronoun implies the castration was perceived in the context of the broader national conflict and was not merely punishment meted out to an individual wrongdoer.

A similar occurrence took place in late 1946, when a mentally ill Jewish woman was raped near Ramat Gan. An Arab greengrocer from Sheik Munes was arrested but was released on bail despite his admission of guilt.[60] The Haganah abducted the man, Mahmoud Mohammad Shoulabi, upon his release, and he was subsequently castrated in a forest near a governmental hospital (Bellinson Hospital, in Petach Tiqva) by Dr Reuven (Rudolph) Meir, a psychiatrist.[61] After the operation, an anonymous caller notified the police about a wounded Arab in the forest, and Mahmoud was found and hospitalized. He was eventually convicted of rape but was given a short sentence in consideration of what he had gone through. Reportedly, Mahmoud became a Haganah informant and was subsequently murdered by Arabs who suspected him of disloyalty.[62] A critical Jewish

58 ISA/RG 30/Law 2043 (original docket # Cr.C 104/45).

59 Richard Silverstein, 'Amos Horev: Castrated Palestinian in Blood Vengeance', www.richardsilverstein.com/2010/06/17/amos-horev-castrated-palestinian-in-blood-vengeance/. There is some uncertainty regarding the identity of the castrated victim. The prosecutor and judge take it for a fact that Aref was the victim. See also the testimony of Jacob Cohen, one of the participants in the Palmach operation, who stated,

> The British arrested one person, I think it was Aref Ahmad Shakawi, whom they arrested and released, without indictment, nothing. As far as the British were concerned, they were done. Then we made up our mind to work on this guy. Apparently this guy, the one we castrated, was accomplice in all three [rape] cases. The guards of Kibbutz Mesiloth brought us information about this guy. We knew his name. We knew more or less where he lives. . . . He was not hiding.

HA 214-1, p. 25. However, Amos Nevo, a journalist who interviewed Palmachniks who participated in the operation, identifies the rapist as Mohammad Tawash. This discrepancy might be attributed to the fact that the rapist had an accomplice. Amos Nevo, 'The Punishment', *Yediot Ahronot*, 30 April 1993.

60 HA 173-23, HA 177-27.

61 Dr Meir may have instructed others in performing the actual castration. See the confession of Meir Lavertovski and Isaac Weinstein, members of a special unit of the Palmach, about their participation in the operation, in the documentary 'Villains – the Real Story', https://vimeo.com/46188145 from minute 20:30.

62 This testimony, of Hilel Levin, seems inaccurate, as it implies that the rape had occurred around 1940 and that the accused became an informer only years later, while in fact the rape took place around the end of 1946. HA 177-27, pp. 8–10.

newspaper article titled 'Rascals Take the Law into Their Own Hands' denounced the Haganah's actions in this case.[63]

Acts of revenge express anger without using words. They do not involve a spontaneous eruption of emotion but are carefully styled rituals aimed at delivering a message and modifying reality. The act of castration transforms both the castrated and the castrator.[64] The castrated, from the attacker's viewpoint, receives a punishment that befits the crime – having used his genitalia to attack women, he has his genitalia mutilated and his virility permanently destroyed. The castrator commits a brutal act and is transformed into a ruthless oppressor. In the context of a national battle, preventing a member of the 'other' group from procreating is a powerful symbolic act. While acts of castration attempted to re-establish the boundaries between the Jewish and Arab communities, they were not disruptive of gender hierarchies. Emasculation through castration 'both reinforces and threatens masculinity'.[65] The rape of a Jewish woman was perceived as an injury to Jewish men, and it was men who retaliated for rape by mutilating other men.

## Conclusion

The expression of emotions varies across social arenas, and in each arena specific conventions govern the emotions befitting a situation, whether their expression is allowable and, if so, in what manner and to what intensity. Emotional display that may be legitimate outside the court may not be permissible during judicial proceedings. What can be expressed within the bounds of community may be withheld in the presence of outsiders and vice versa. This variation demonstrates that emotions and their display are subject to considerable social construction and are not merely spontaneous or natural eruptions.

The courtroom is an arena of emotional restraint, but it is not buffered from emotions. On the contrary, emotional expression underpins the plausibility of evidence. Emotions are part of a story and its believability. Even when they do not articulate them verbally, those narrating stories exhibit emotions, and they invoke feelings in their audiences. When emotions deviate from conventional patterns (for example, if a female rape victim behaves calmly), they render a rape story less plausible. Likewise, when they adhere to conventional patterns, emotions contribute to its plausibility.

Emotional display in court is an outcome of the interaction of influences from two sources: the first is legal convention that restrains emotional expression, and the second is the cultural conditioning participants in the proceedings (judges, lawyers, witnesses, defendants) bring with them from the outside

63 *Hatzofe*, 14 January 1947, p. 1.

64 Larissa Tracy, 'Introduction: A History of Calamities: The Culture of Castration', in *Castration and Culture in the Middle Ages*, ed. Larissa Tracy (Cambridge: D.S. Brewer, 2013), 9.

65 Ibid., 7.

world. Therefore, a fuller understanding of the emotions associated with sex offences and their role in legal proceedings requires their investigation in extrajudicial spheres.

In my examination of the emotions displayed outside the courthouse within the Jewish community in Mandate Palestine, I found shame and anger to be salient. The intensity of these emotions can be powerfully communicated, with or without words. Neither can be freely vented in court. Shame is no excuse for silence on the witness stand, where victims and witnesses are expected to relate their stories and submit to scrutiny, no matter how embarrassing the process may be for them. In the words of Acting Justice Curry in the case against Rachel's rapists: 'One must not suffer from a false sense of modesty in such case, for it is only by getting exact details of the act from the complainant one is able to test the truthfulness of her story.'[66] Anger too must be restrained. Criminal proceedings are predicated on the assumption that deciding guilt and meting out just punishment are matters for the authorities. Unruly anger and private punishments are illegitimate. An angry witness may appear less credible, as anger may be interpreted as an indication of bias or cloudy judgement.

Outside the courtroom, however, shame and anger can be freely expressed, either verbally or non-verbally. The silence of Jewish victims conveyed a deep sense of shame. Jews, it appears, were less likely than Arabs to complain of sexual assaults and were even less inclined to point the finger at assailants in their own community. Yet refusal to complain to the police did not necessarily equate with passivity or acquiescence, as incidents of 'private justice' illustrate. Rape, by definition, is imposed on an individual victim. In Mandate Palestine, shame was ascribed to that victim, who became the bearer of social stigma and blameable for her or his own misfortune. This was stated point-blank in newspaper articles in the Hebrew press that accused victims of carelessness. Yet shame was also a collective sentiment. The members of the Jewish community were reluctant to share stories of assault with outsiders. Rape was perceived as injurious not just to the individual victim but also to the victim's community, and some notion of blameability, weakness and humiliation was shared by the community as a whole. An official complaint was often a wrong story to tell to the Mandate authorities, as it could expose to outsiders what was perceived as a communal embarrassment. Furthermore, it signalled the community's lack of national autonomy.

Shame was greater when members of the community itself were sexually aggressive perpetrators. It is interesting to note that the small number of official complaints filed by Jewish victims related almost exclusively to inter-ethnic rape. Intra-ethnic rape involved not only the humiliation of the victim but also the degradation of the perpetrator. A complaint would have made public that Jews too could be sexually aggressive and morally flawed. Silence expressed shame and was an attempt to ignore unpleasant possibilities.

[66] Judge Curry's minority opinion in the Supreme Court's judgment of 4 June 1947.

Both inter-ethnic and intra-ethnic sexual assaults were building blocks in the construction of national and ethnic identity in Mandate Palestine. The silence concerning rape within the Jewish community demonstrates overriding collective considerations and reluctance to have 'outsiders' meddle in what was perceived to be a community affair.

Anger and shame delineated the boundaries of the collective, as these emotions were shared by its members, a fact that highlights their socially constructed nature. The collective nature of the anger triggered by the rape of Jewish women is evidenced in acts of revenge carried out by representatives of the collective, members of paramilitary organizations fighting for national liberation. The expression of anger through acts of revenge was meant to send a message from one collective to another, to construct social boundaries and create social hierarchies.

The story that the Jewish community wished to tell through its handling of sex offences was a story of national strength. Rape symbolized weakness, and incidents of rape were mostly silenced and occasionally responded to with extreme violence. These deliberate attempts to send a message of strength demonstrate a belief that the rape of an individual community member could plausibly be viewed as an indication of national weakness.

Common emotions are predicated on socially constructed knowledge. The display of shared emotions, therefore, helps define the boundaries of the community in which the knowledge is created and shared. The anger and shame shared by the Jewish community in Mandate Palestine were based on common social knowledge about sex offences. The instances of their expression reveal that it was plausible to regard rape within a broad national and ethnic context. These emotions outline a distinct ethnic community that regarded itself as separate and different from the Arab community.

Focusing on the anger and shame sex offences triggered within the Jewish community in Mandate Palestine reveals that these emotions underpinned various stories the community regarded as plausible: that rape victims and their community were both blameable; that Arabs were sexually dangerous; that inter-ethnic rape encapsulated an antagonistic distinction between the Jewish and the Arab communities; that females were vulnerable and needed male protection; and that a Jewish sense of weakness could be overcome through the use of extreme violence.

Narratives of sex offences are deemed more plausible when they correspond to socially validated knowledge about the world, and this knowledge includes the emotions that fit the narratives being told and whether, how and under what circumstances they should be expressed or restrained.

# 6

# Corroboration: Plausibility Embedded in Evidentiary Standards

In the introduction to this book, we met young Nafiseh, whose story of her night-time sexual assault by her village neighbour Nimr Judge Curry found implausible.[1] The implausibility of her story, as elaborated by the judge, was anchored not only in the elements of the 'plot', which he depicted as 'strange', but also in the evidentiary rule of corroboration. Nafiseh's testimony, he held, was not corroborated, even though it was supported by the accounts of two additional witnesses: her father, who testified that Nafiseh immediately complained to him, and Khalil, her brother-in-law, who testified that he was awakened by Nasifeh's screams. Subsequently, Khalil said, he saw a man running from Nasifeh's roof to Nimr's house. He also testified that he heard Nimr's mother asking 'Who is that?' and Nimr, in reply, telling her to be quiet. Judge Curry explained that this additional testimony did not establish the required corroboration, as it did not support Nafiseh's claim that Nimr acted without her consent.[2]

This chapter examines the rule of corroboration in demonstrating that plausibility can be embedded in evidentiary mechanisms. The narratives that witnesses relate in court are plausible when they are grounded in common knowledge or implausible when they deviate from culturally accepted patterns. The socially constructed knowledge on which plausibility is predicated, however, does not have to be expressed in the form of narrative testimony. It can also be moulded into a rather formal evidentiary standard. This chapter demonstrates how, in Mandate Palestine, the requirement of corroboration in cases of sexual assault enveloped socially constructed perceptions about (the implausibility of) such offences.

## The Rule of Corroboration and its Origins

The common-law rule of corroboration prevents the adjudicator from convicting the accused on the basis of a single witness's testimony, credible as that witness may be, unless an additional, independent piece of incriminating evidence is available.[3] Inherent in the rule of corroboration (often implicitly)

[1] ISA/RG 30/Law 2036 (original docket # Cr.C 208/44).

[2] See the judgment given 16 December 1944.

[3] Mirjan R. Damaska, *Evidence Law Adrift* (New Haven, CT: Yale University Press, 1997), 18.

is categorization of certain categories of witnesses as untrustworthy. Even when fact finders regard specific witnesses as truthful, honest and credible, their testimony alone is insufficient for conviction if they are members of 'suspicious' groups. Implicit in the evidentiary arrangement requiring that the testimony of each and every complainant in a case of sexual offence be corroborated is the assumption that the stories of all complainants should be treated with suspicion. In other words, the plausibility of complaints of sexual assaults is constructed as questionable.

The original goal of corroboration was to sift out false testimony. However, treating the members of a certain social category as potentially flawed witnesses constructs all group members as inherently flawed, their testimony insufficient for conviction. Controversy over corroboration goes to the question of which categories of witnesses should be believed and under what conditions.

Some jurisdictions (e.g. Scotland and the Netherlands) require corroboration of all testimony in all criminal cases. Yet the corroboration rule in common-law jurisdictions is typically limited to cases involving the testimony of an accomplice and to cases of sexual offences. In the first instance, the accomplice's interest in shifting blame onto a partner to the crime is the rationale behind the requirement to corroborate his or her testimony.[4] When it comes to sexual offences, the standard explanation for the requirement is that such crimes are often committed in private and, therefore, that special care against false accusations is warranted.

A long British common-law tradition pointed to the evidentiary difficulties inherent in proving sexual crimes and demanded evidentiary precautions that would prevent false convictions on the basis of fabricated charges. Any conviction that rested on a single person's testimony with no supporting evidence could create doubts.[5] Sex offences, however, were often described as particularly problematic to prove. The renowned judge Sir Matthew Hale referred to both rape and witchcraft as 'crimes that give the greatest difficulty . . . wherein many times persons are really guilty, yet such an evidence, as is satisfactory to prove it, can hardly be found; and on the other side persons really innocent may be entangled under such presumptions, that many times carry great probabilities of guilt'.[6]

[4] For the rationale and history of accomplice corroboration, John H. Langbein, *The Origins of Adversary Criminal Trial,* Oxford Studies in Modern Legal History (Oxford: Oxford University Press, 2003), 203.

[5] Sir Geoffrey Gilbert, *The Law of Evidence*, 3rd ed. (London: W. Owen, 1769), 150.

[6] v. 2, Sir Matthew Hale, *Historia Placitorum Coronae. The History of the Pleas of the Crown, by Sir Matthew Hale . . . Now First Published from His Lordship's Original Manuscript, and the Several References to the Records Examined by the Originals, with Large Notes. By Sollom Emlyn . . . To Which Is Added a Table of the Principal Matters. In Two Volumes. . . .* (London: F. Gyles, T. Woodward, and C. Davis, 1736), 290. For more about Hale on rape, see also Gilbert Geis and Ivan Bunn, *A Trial of Witches: A Seventeenth-Century Witchcraft Prosecution* (London: Routledge, 1997), 121.

Hale also maintained that rape 'is an accusation easily to be made and hard to be proved, and harder to be defended by the party accused, tho never so innocent'.[7] His assertion later became the target of much criticism on the grounds of inaccuracy[8] and prejudice against female accusers.[9] The criticism for inaccuracy was double edged. First, critics called the fear of false convictions unwarranted, pointing to the low prosecution rate and to the high acquittal rate in rape cases during Hale's time.[10] Second, accusations of sexual assault were not that easy to make, as the accuser was likely to be embarrassed or criticized and scrutinized for sexual frivolity.[11] Another deterrent to bringing rape charges in early modern England was the expense, as the accusing party had to bear the costs of legal action.[12] Given all these obstacles, Laurie Edelstein doubts that rape was a crime that would have been chosen for malicious charges.[13]

Yet those who have criticized Hale as showing 'concern for the male defendant and a prejudicial attitude toward his female accuser'[14] or, more blatantly, as a 'misogynist'[15] may have unjustly caricatured his analysis. Judging a seventeenth-century jurist by feminist standards formed 300 years later is clearly biased and oversimplifies Hale's argument. It should be remembered that Hale also cautioned against false convictions in witchcraft cases, in which most defendants were women. Hale did not state that female accusers in rape cases should be assumed to have made false accusations (in fact, he listed several rules that enhanced the possibility of achieving convictions in cases of rape under the contemporary law).[16] He also made clear that female victims of rape were competent witnesses.[17] His view was that children 'of tender years', those who were too young to take an oath (the testimony of children under

[7] v. 1, Hale, 631.

[8] Constance Backhouse, *Carnal Crimes: Sexual Assault Law in Canada, 1900–1975* (Toronto: Osgoode Society 2008), 171; Gilbert Geis, 'Lord Hale, Witches, and Rape', *British Journal of Law and Society* 5, no. 1 (1978): 26.

[9] Elizabeth Kolsky, '"The Body Evidencing the Crime": Rape on Trial in Colonial India, 1860–1947', *Gender & History* 22, no. 1 (2010): 111.

[10] Ibid.; Geis, 27; Garthine Walker, *Crime, Gender and Social Order in Early Modern England* (Cambridge: Cambridge University Press, 2003), 55; Laurie Edelstein, 'An Accusation Easily to Be Made? Rape and Malicious Prosecution in Eighteenth-Century England', *American Journal of Legal History* 42, no. 4 (1998): 351, 362.

[11] Geis, 27; Edelstein, 364. [12] Edelstein, 373. [13] Ibid., 375. [14] Kolsky, 111.

[15] Geis, 27.

[16] For example, despite the Elizabethan prohibition against 'carnally know[ing]' a girl under ten years of age (18 Eliz. Ch. 7 [1576]), Hale maintained that the age of consent was twelve. Although the conviction of rape demanded proof of penetration, Hale asserted that anyone present who was aiding and abetting should be punished like the principal offender; he also maintained that consent obtained by threat of death was no consent, that despite the presumption of matrimonial consent, the Crown could indict a man for prostituting his wife, that a woman could bring charges of rape against a man who compelled her to marry him and had forceful sex with her once the marriage was dissolved and that the Crown and the victim's relatives could bring charges even when the woman gave her consent after the rape. v. 1 Hale, 628. See also Edelstein, 356.

[17] v. 1 Hale, 633.

fourteen was generally inadmissible), should still be heard by the court; however, he maintained, their testimony should be corroborated.[18] Whereas Hale's use of corroboration was aimed at giving children more leeway to testify, application of the rule in the courts of Mandate Palestine resulted in routine rejection of their testimony. Notably, Hale's recommendation of corroboration was limited to child witnesses. He creatively constructed corroboration as a device allowing their otherwise inadmissible testimony. In Hale's opinion, the secretive nature of sexual offences entailed a special challenge of proof and justified a departure from the standard evidentiary mode. Yet Hale differentiated between competence and credibility and asserted that the latter should be a matter for the jury. He also listed circumstances that might support the credibility of a female complainant or raise doubts about her reliability.[19] Although Hale himself advocated for corroboration only with regard to children's testimony, in the following centuries his articulation of the general probative problem and of the criteria of reliability underpinned the corroboration rule for adult victims as well.

The troublesome issue of proving rape continued to occupy English jurists throughout the modern era. Victorian treatment of sexual offences reflected some transformation of early modern ideas and included changes in the substantive law, criminal procedure and evidence that facilitated proof and conviction in cases of rape. Juries' reluctance to convict was softened in 1837, when prosecutors were legally allowed to bring lesser charges together with the primary charge of rape, thus giving jurors the option to convict on a charge of assault rather than having to choose solely between conviction or acquittal on rape. It was further eroded in 1841 by the removal of the death penalty.[20] The Victorian courts developed an interpretative framework narrowing the notion of women's consent, including limiting inquiry about the victim's sexual past and demanding less resistance on her part to the assault, thus broadening the scope of situations that were considered non-consensual and that warranted conviction for rape.[21] Proof was also facilitated by the abandonment of the requirement that emission of semen be shown.[22] Another significant change was the conceptual shift from the notion of 'against her will' to 'without her consent', the former being a concealed element and, therefore, hard to prove.[23] The result was that, despite expanding legal representation, the likelihood of conviction rose markedly in comparison with earlier times (although conviction rates remained relatively low for some years into the

[18] v. 1 ibid., 634.

[19] v. 1 ibid., 633. William Blackstone drew on Hale in his analysis of the evidence required to prove the crime of rape. See William Blackstone, *Commentaries on the Laws of England*, 4 vols. (Dublin: John Exshaw, Henry Saunders, Boulter Grierson, James Williams and John Milliken, 1769), Book IV.

[20] 4 & 5 Vic. Punishment of Death Repeal Act C. 56 (1841); 1 Vic. Offences against the Person Act c. 85 S. 11 (1837); Martin J. Wiener, *Men of Blood: Violence, Manliness and Criminal Justice in Victorian England* (Cambridge: Cambridge University Press, 2004), 91.

[21] Ibid., 92. [22] Ibid., 89. [23] Ibid.

nineteenth century).[24] Although Victorian judges facilitated proof of rape, complainants in sexual offence cases continued to be scrutinized more closely than victims of other offences, and their testimony still required corroboration.

A leading precedent that emerged in a 'gross indecency' case, *R. v. Baskerville* (1916),[25] held that corroboration must come from an independent source and that it should implicate the accused by confirming in some material particular not only that the crime had been committed but also that the accused had committed it.[26] The Baskerville case influenced the British Commonwealth for decades to come. The rationale behind the demand for corroboration, explicitly voiced in cases of homosexuality, was hidden and disguised in cases of sexual assault – with the victim being implicitly viewed as some sort of an accomplice, a willing party in the commission of the crime.[27] The demand for corroboration, which implies categorical distrust of complainants of sexual assaults, is a manifestation of the suspicion underlying their treatment.

By the time the British occupied Palestine, the elements of reliability listed by Hale had become rooted in English law.[28] It became standard practice to warn the jury about the necessity of corroborating the testimony of the alleged victim.[29] Corroboration was not essential by law but was

24 Ibid., 77.

25 Harry G. Cocks, *Nameless Offences: Homosexual Desire in the Nineteenth Century* (London: I. B. Tauris, 2003), 33. Baskerville precursors include the cases of Tate and Meunier, which acknowledged the well-settled practice of corroboration, although opinion diverged about whether conviction subsequent to a failure to caution the jury amounted to miscarriage of justice justifying a reversal. *R.* v. *Tate*, [1908] 2 K.B. 680; *R.* v. *Meunier*, [1894] 2 Q.B. 415.

26 Constance Backhouse, 'The Doctrine of Corroboration in Sexual Assault Trials in Early Twentieth-Century Canada and Australia', *Queen's Law Journal* 26 (2001): 300; *R.* v. *Baskerville*, [1916] 2 K.B. 658.

27 For an analysis of the elements of rape as a reflection of defences available to women charged in cases of fornication and adultery, see Anne M. Coughlin, 'Sex and Guilt', *Virginia Law Review* 84, no. 1 (1998): 1.

28 The twenty-fifth edition of Archbold, published in 1922, states criteria similar to those listed by Hale two centuries earlier:

> If the witness is of good fame; if she presently discovered the offence, and made search for the offender; if the party accused fled for it; these and the like are concurring circumstances which give greater probability to her evidence. But, on the other hand, if she is of evil fame, and stands unsupported by the testimony of others; if she concealed the injury for any considerable time after she had opportunity to complain; if the place where the act was alleged to have been committed were such that it was possible she might have been heard, and she made no outcry; these and the like circumstances carry a strong but not conclusive presumption that her testimony is false or feigned.

John Frederick Archbold et al., *Archbold's Pleading, Evidence & Practice in Criminal Cases* (London: Sweet & Maxwell, 1922), http://ia700408.us.archive.org/2/items/cu31924021698281/cu31924021698281.pdf, 1022.

29 Glanville Williams, *The Proof of Guilt: A Study of the English Criminal Trial*, The Hamlyn Lectures (London: Stevens & Sons, 1955), 117. By the time of the Mandate, corroboration was required not just for rape but for all sexual offences, including indecent assault and homosexuality. Ibid. at 117.

required in practice,[30] and it spread with the British Empire to other jurisdictions that adhered to the common law, including Mandate Palestine.[31] Hale's mistrust of female complainants is just one example of bias that became encoded in procedural and evidentiary rules. In Palestine, this evidentiary tool was infused with a new dimension of bias that designated legal participants in some categories as less worthy than others.

## Corroboration in Mandate Palestine

The Evidence Ordinance that went into effect in 1924 declared that 'all persons are competent to give evidence in all cases'.[32] The ordinance also maintained that '[n]o judgment shall be given in any case on the evidence of a single witness'.[33] This requirement mandated that all testimony in both civil and criminal cases be corroborated (unless it was satisfactorily proven that the criminal accused made a 'free and voluntary' admission).[34]

The blanket demand for corroboration did not exist in English law, and the motivation for such a demand in Palestine was probably British fear of widespread perjury among witnesses from the local population.[35] In the words of the attorney-general, 'I do not consider that the standard of credibility of witnesses in Palestine is very high.'[36] The drop in conviction rates during the Arab revolt of 1936 was the backdrop for an amendment that obliterated the statutory corroboration requirement in criminal cases.[37] Crossing out the corroboration requirement in criminal cases could have resulted in enhanced

30 Archbold et al., 58.

31 Hale's phrasing continued to echo in Palestine's judgments. See CrimA 118/42 *Abu Zeid* v. *A.G.*, ASC. 472, [1942], at 1 ('Rape is one of those offences a charge of which it is very easy to make and which, although entirely innocent, an accused may find it very difficult to refute'); CrimA 54/38 *Shafiq George Halaby* v. *A.G.* [1938] ('[C]harges could be made which it might be very difficult for an innocent person to refute'); ISA/RG 30/Law 268/54, CrimA 54/38 *Shafiq Halaby* v. *A.G.* [1938], at 3.

32 The Law of Evidence Amendment Ordinance, No. 13, 1924, Art. 3. The ordinance contained two exceptions: parents and children and spouses were not competent to testify against each other.

33 Ibid. at Art. 6.

34 L. Sebba, 'The Requirement of Corroboration in Sex Offences', *Israel Law Review* 3 (1968): 75.

35 Ibid. It is also possible that a British misreading of the Ottoman two-witness rule and a wish to adopt the *Mejelle*'s (the Ottoman Code of Obligations) sufficiency standards led to the adoption of the general corroboration requirement.

36 Ibid., a fine example of English understatement.

37 Vol. 2, Eliahu Harnon, *Law of Evidence* [in Hebrew] (Jerusalem: Hebrew University of Jerusalem, Faculty of Law, 1977), 5 § 2. Evidence Ordinance No. 68 of 1936 replaced section 6 with the following provision: 'Corroboration in civil cases. 6. No judgment shall be given in any civil case on the evidence of a single witness unless such evidence is uncontradicted or is corroborated by some other material evidence which, in the opinion of the Court, is sufficient to establish the truth.' The amended ordinance demanded corroboration in civil cases only and was put into effect on 11 October 1937. For a review of the Arab revolt, see Matthew Hughes, 'The Banality of Brutality: British Armed Forces and the Repression of the Arab Revolt in Palestine, 1936–39', *English Historical Review* 124, no. 507 (2009): 313.

judiciary discretion. However, judges continued to apply English precedents and to demand that single-witness testimony in sexual offence cases be corroborated.[38] The British judges did not perceive the amendment as an opportunity for freer evaluation of testimony but, rather, as a signal that English case law should be applied. By letter, Harry Herbert Trusted, the chief justice of the Supreme Court at the time of the publication of the amendment, instructed lower-court judges as follows:

> I would draw your attention to the notice published in Gazette No. 725 of the 4th of October, bringing into operation the Law of Evidence (Amendment) Ordinance, 1936.
>
> Prima facie, the effect of this would seem to be that English Common Law of Evidence will apply in criminal cases.
>
> I think it well that the attention of Palestinian Judges and Magistrates should be called to this notice and, in cases where you think it necessary, the general provisions of the English Law explained, particular regard being had as to necessity of corroboration of an accomplice, of a young child, and of the prosecutrix in sexual offences.[39]

Justice Trusted, however, in an instruction that sounds like a default to familiar rules, misstated the English law,[40] which, as noted, merely obligated a cautionary warning to the jury against accepting the testimony of a single witness unless it was supported by other incriminating evidence. In England, facts are found by laymen, jurors who give unreasoned verdict. Corroboration, like many other common-law evidentiary rules, was created to facilitate the processing of the evidence by laypersons. It is not obvious why a jury-related evidentiary concept should be grafted onto local law when the fact finders were professional judges. Corroboration, even in England, was not mandatory, and a jury properly directed could still have convicted solely on the basis of uncorroborated testimony.[41]

Although the written law, as it was amended in 1936, made no such explicit demand, the Mandate judges routinely required corroboration in cases of

[38] Hannah Avnoor, 'Corroboration in Sexual Offences – What For' [in Hebrew], *Hapraklit* 26 (1970–1971): 79.

[39] I found the original undated letter to the presidents of the District Court and the chief magistrates in Jerusalem, Jaffa, Haifa, Nablus and Tel Aviv, marked No. J/1/10, affixed to p. 84 of a library copy (University of Haifa KA792.P3 1943) of H. Kantrovitch, ed., *The Law of Criminal Procedure in Palestine* (Tel Aviv: Mizpah, 1943). The volume bears the stamps 'the Supreme Court Jerusalem Feb. 1943' and 'The District Court Haifa Palestine 1 Mar. 1943', indicating that it was used by the Mandate judges.

[40] This misapprehension was also expressed in Justice Trusted's judgments. For example: 'It is quite clear that according to English Law which for this purpose now applies, in order to convict for sexual offences, the evidence of the complainant must be, to some extent, corroborated.' ISA/RG 30/ Law 268/54, CrimA 54/38 *Shafiq Halaby* v. *A.G.* [1938], at 3.

[41] The statutory corroboration requirement in cases of procurement of women by threats, false pretences or administering drugs to obtain or facilitate intercourse, Criminal Law Amendment Act, 1885, 48 & 49 Vic., c. 69, §§ 2–4, was repealed in 1994. In some exceptional cases the Court of Criminal Appeal refrained from quashing a conviction despite the lack of warning. Sebba, 77.

sexual offences. They presumed that corroboration was mandatory, and the question became what could constitute the necessary corroboration and what could not.

According to Hale, the immediacy of a complaint lent it more probability while delay gave it less. The courts of Mandate Palestine considered a delayed complaint less credible than an immediate one but did not regard immediacy as corroborative.[42] In other words, the criterion of immediacy could be used only to devalue the complainant, not to constitute corroboration.[43] It was usually assumed that the corroboration had to be external to the testimony of the victim. The Mandate judges clarified that identification of the rapist by the victim in an identification parade[44] or the complainant's statements to others also constituted insufficient corroboration:

> Corroboration may of course be found in the appearance of the prosecutrix, the state of her clothes, the result of an examination by a medical man, or the conduct or statement of the prisoner. Evidence of a complaint made by the girl or woman shortly after the alleged offence is not the required corroboration of her story as it does not come from an independent quarter. Putting it in other words she cannot corroborate herself.[45]

Medical reports and forensic evidence figured prominently in the rhetoric related to corroboration. Physical evidence 'spoke for itself', and scientific evidence was seemingly objective, unconnected to witnesses of suspicious reliability and therefore particularly probative. Furthermore, such evidence fit well into the colonial narrative of the British as the avatars of progress. Some judges explicitly stated that

> [i]n rape cases the most usual and most important corroborative evidence is that of a doctor . . . [O]ne would expect if her story is true, medical evidence showing that intercourse had in fact taken place; evidence of stains of semen on her underclothes; evidence of bruises on her thighs and other parts of her body when she resisted and struggled. If a doctor did examine her and found no such signs, it would be very strong evidence indeed to discredit her complaint.[46]

[42] The expectation of immediate complaint presumes a 'normal' reaction by rape victims and ignores the various reasons that may deter a victim from immediately reporting the crime. Yuval Merin, 'A Feminist Perspective on Evidence Law: The Gendered Truth and the Silencing of the Different Voice' [in Hebrew], *HaMishpat* 16 (2011): 108 n. 139.

[43] One extreme example is from the rape case of Rachel from Kibbutz Eilon which I discussed at length in Chapter 4. The minority judge hearing the appeal found Rachel's testimony lacking in credibility because she did not state she had been raped to her friends who saw her immediately after the event, although the fact of rape was obvious to them, considering, among other things, that they saw Rachel's attackers forcibly take her behind nearby bushes and heard their voices during the assault. ISA/RG 30/Law 441/31, CrimA 31/47 *Khatem & Ahmed* v. *A.G.* [1947], at 12 (Acting Justice Curry's minority opinion).

[44] ISA/RG 30/ Law 268/54, CrimA 54/38 *Shafiq Halaby* v. *A.G.* [1938], at 4.

[45] ISA/RG 30/Law 441/31, CrimA 31/47 *Khatem & Ahmed* v. *A.G.* [1947].

[46] ISA/RG 30/Law 441/31, CrimA 31/47 *Khatem & Ahmed* v. *A.G.* [1947] (Acting Justice Curry's minority opinion).

Yet a close reading of rape cases demonstrates that even ample medical and forensic evidence was often insufficient to corroborate the victim's testimony.[47] Examination of the actual implementation of the doctrine of corroboration reveals recurring gaps between the narrative of instituting progressive criminal law, protecting women and children and relying on scientific evidence, on the one hand, and on the other, the low trust of local complainants and the corroborative insufficiency of medical and forensic evidence.

## Inflexible Demand for Corroboration and the Plausibility of Fabricated Charges

The Palestine Supreme Court overturned Mohammad Youssef's conviction for sodomy because of lack of corroboration.[48] Mohammad, originally from the Jenin area, was charged with sodomizing eight-year-old Nizar, the son of his employer, a well-to-do Haifa pharmacist. The events described by Nizar occurred in his family's busy pharmacy, where five people worked (Nizar's father, the father's brother and three other employees, including the accused). Nizar's mother described Mohammad's position as that of 'servant'. He had started working for the family when he was a boy himself (one of the disputed issues at the trial was whether he was seventeen, as he claimed, or over eighteen, as the prosecution argued; the court held the latter). At first, he had worked both in the business and at the family's house, later working only at the pharmacy as an errand boy. He was 'promoted' to work in the storage room after a new servant, a fifteen-year-old from Africa, replaced him as errand boy. This boy was also named Mohammed and was, therefore, dubbed by the family 'the other Mohammad'.

Nizar and his brother grew up in a protective environment. They did not go out much, and servants escorted them to and from school. Only their mother and a servant helped them get dressed. In the words of Nizar's mother, 'I permit no one to look after my children except myself.' Nizar, a first-year school pupil, asserted that the accused sometimes took him and his younger brother to a back room in the pharmacy, where medicines, bottles and other sales goods were stored, and there took off Nizar's pants and committed sodomy on him. Mohammad Youssef had been employed by Nizar's father for eight years and had known Nizar since he was a baby. Among the witnesses for the prosecution were Nizar, his parents, 'the other Mohammad', who also testified that he sometimes saw Nizar and his brother sitting in the accused's lap while he was teaching them the Arabic alphabet, and a doctor who examined both Nizar (finding indications of sodomy) and the accused (to

[47] For a similar observation regarding Australia, see Backhouse, 'The Doctrine of Corroboration in Sexual Assault Trials in Early Twentieth-Century Canada and Australia', 311.

[48] ISA/RG 30/Law 269/71, CrimA 71/38 *Mohammad Abdel Ghani* v. *A.G.* [1938].

verify his age and ability to commit the offence). The conviction obtained in the Haifa District Court was quashed on appeal for insufficient corroboration. Medical proof of the commission of a sex offence was not enough. The Supreme Court stated that '[t]he fact that the mother saw bruises on the child is corroboration of an offence having been committed, but not necessarily that the accused had committed the offence'.[49] It did not even mention the medical evidence. The identification of the accused, according to the court, remained uncorroborated.[50] It did not matter that Nizar could not have mistakenly identified someone he had known since he was a baby. The court's decision suggests that the concern behind the insistence on corroboration was probably not the fear of an honest mistake but rather of a deliberate lie.

Despite the medical evidence, the Supreme Court did 'not think that there [was] corroboration of the child's tale', the very use of the term 'tale' implying a concocted story. Embedded in the formal requirement for corroboration was a perception that a true complaint of sexual assault was much less plausible than a fabricated complaint. The judgment further states that '[i]t may be that sodomy is one of the cases which are difficult to prove, but difficulty in proof does not dispense with the proof'. The complainant's testimony alone was not 'proof', as its fabrication was more plausible than its veracity. Built into the demand for corroboration was socially constructed knowledge according to which fabrication of a complaint of sexual assault was highly plausible. When corroboration is necessary for establishing facts, these perceptions of socially valid knowledge are perpetuated.

Similar reasoning was voiced in a case in which Muhammad Agha was charged with raping Samiha, his thirteen-year-old daughter.[51] The family lived in the old city of Jaffa. Samiha's mother had died, and her father had been divorced for a few years from his second wife, Zahara. Muhammad's marriage to Zahara had been part of an arrangement that included the marriage of his son to Zahara's daughter. Following the divorce of their parents, the son and the daughter-in-law had to move from the house of the accused, and Zahara remarried her first husband. Familial tensions, then, formed the backdrop of the case. Samiha's household was poor and did not have enough mattresses for everyone to sleep on, so Samiha had to share a mattress with her father. Two younger brothers slept in the same room with them.

Samiha said that, one night, after arriving home late from the café, her father took off her underwear and had intercourse with her. In the morning, weeping, Samiha went to the house of her married brother and told his wife about the incident. Her brother took her to a doctor and then to the police station. The next day, a policeman took the girl to another doctor for examination.

49 CrimA 71/38 in ISA/RG 30/Law 269/71, at 2.
50 See Cr.C 27/38 (Haifa District Court) and CrimA 71/38 in ISA/RG 30/Law 269/71.
51 Cr.C 173/43 (Jaffa District Court) *A.G.* v. *Agha* [1943] in ISA/RG 30/Law 353/122.

The doctor who examined the girl at the request of the police testified that her hymen had recently been ruptured. The first doctor testified for the defence. His opinion was that her hymen had been ruptured about fifteen days prior to his examination and that scratches in the vagina could have been caused up to ten hours before the examination. The District Court regarded the testimony of both doctors corroborative (since the question was not when the girl's hymen was ruptured but whether she was subjected to sexual intercourse). The picture changed at the Supreme Court, however, which held that the medical evidence alone was insufficient to corroborate the girl's complaint against her father. The Supreme Court agreed the girl was probably sexually assaulted but found insufficient corroboration of the identity of the attacker.[52] The father's admission that he slept on the same mattress with his daughter was not regarded as sufficient corroboration.[53] Again, corroboration was required not just of the sexual assault but also of the identity of the perpetrator.

The requirement that the identification made by the victim be corroborated when the accused was familiar (here, the girl's own father) demonstrates that the court's concern was not the possibility of mistaken identification but fabricated charges. Rape was very hard to prosecute against the backdrop of such mistrust. The court stated that it was 'a most unfortunate and deplorable matter in which the young daughter of the appellant, a girl of some 13 years of age, had apparently been assaulted by some person'.[54] Despite its acceptance of Samiha's claim that she had been raped, the court was reluctant to abandon the rule of corroboration and believe her statement that her father was the perpetrator. In this case, the court was offered an opportunity to moderate the rule, the attorney-general advocate urging that, as a matter of law, corroboration was not required in cases of sexual offences in Palestine. The Supreme Court rejected the argument, saying '[t]hat may or may not be so, but we are of opinion that, at the very least as a matter of practice followed, and rightly followed, by Courts in these matters in this class of cases corroboration implicating the accused is necessary'. In this case as well it seems that the Supreme Court did not regard corroboration as limiting its capacity to convict the guilty but, rather, as a tool whose use was both justified and necessary.

Another prosecutorial attempt to curb the application of the corroboration rule was made in a 1944 Haifa case, in which a twenty-five-year-old teacher was charged with sodomizing Nazmi, a nine-year-old former pupil.[55] Before the magistrate at the preliminary inquiry, the defendant's attorney moved to dismiss the charges due to insufficient corroboration. In response, the Prosecution Officer opined that the corroboration rule was applicable to 'cases which occurs [*sic*] between a male and female and not between a male and male'. The Prosecution Officer also claimed that the amended Evidence Ordinance called for an unqualified abandonment of the corroboration

52 CrimA 122/43 *Agha* v. *A.G.* [1943], ISA/RG 30/Law 353/122. 53 Ibid. 54 Ibid., at 1.
55 ISA/RG 30/Law 2036 (original docket # Cr.C 200/44).

demand. In addition, he pointed to various pieces of evidence that supported the boy's testimony. In this case, two other boys stated that when they were with Nazmi on the playground the teacher approached them and called Nazmi to come with him and that a little while later Nazmi returned crying. The boy's father described the events Nazmi reported upon returning home and how the teacher had asked for his forgiveness. The forensic evidence included semen stains on the boy's trousers, and Dr Torian testified to finding a recent tear on the opening of the boy's anus. The District Court, pointing to the medical evidence, was convinced that young Nazmi was 'interfered with'. Nevertheless, the judgment proclaimed, there was no corroboration that it was the accused who had committed the act of sodomy. Finding that there was 'no evidence' and that there was no case to answer, the District Court thus acquitted the accused. Similar to the other cases described above, here there was no ambiguity as to the identification of the accused by Nazmi and his friends. They knew the teacher well. The doubt that justified insistence on corroboration can only be explained by concern about perjury.[56]

Embedded in the corroboration requirement, one can argue, were socially constructed perceptions about the plausibility of fabricated charges. The examples above demonstrate that these concerns affected the proof of sexual assaults notwithstanding the existence of medical evidence. It should be noted that when the victim was under sixteen, the use of force was not an element of the offence, and when the sexual act was proved, an offence existed regardless of consent. One could hypothesize that the demand for corroboration, which rendered accusers fabricators by definition, increased the plausibility that they were blameable willing partners. The following example demonstrates, however, that the distrust built into the demand for corroboration existed even when the medical and forensic evidence pointed to a violent rape.

Jamila was the seven-year-old daughter of a Haifa shoemaker who had his own shop near the Istiklal mosque downtown.[57] On the afternoon of 14 June 1938, while Jamila was playing outside with her three-year-old brother, Yusef, and another boy, a man approached the children. He gave Jamila two piastres and told her to accompany him to buy sweets for her brother. He then took her outside the area to a spot near a Jewish neighbourhood, put her in a pit and raped her. Jamila's parents noticed her unusual appearance upon her return and took her to be medically examined. Jamila recognized her rapist as Mahmoud Khalil, a man who sometimes visited the family's neighbours. He was arrested and charged with rape. Mahmoud, a Jenin resident, was by his own account a chauffeur and electrician and was employed by the Haifa lawyer Fuad Atallah, who provided him with food in lieu of wages. He denied the rape charge and claimed an alibi, which was rejected by the District Court.[58]

[56] Indeed, the teacher claimed the accusations were revenge for Nazmi's expulsion from school.
[57] ISA/RG 30/269/79, CrimA 79/38 *Khalil* v. *A.G.* [1938].
[58] His employer testified in his defence at the hearing in the District Court and also argued before the Supreme Court in his appeal.

The evidence included the testimony of Jamila and her parents, the testimony of a boy (too young to be sworn) who saw the accused take Jamila by the hand on the day in question and who later picked him out of an identification parade and the testimony of a physician as to the physical injury caused by the rape.[59] Despite the significant medical evidence offered, the conviction of the accused was overturned by the Supreme Court for insufficient corroboration.[60] There was no doubt that little Jamila was raped. The severe injuries she sustained necessitated surgery. The issue that required corroboration was the identity of the accused. Jamila's identification of her attacker was not considered sufficient corroboration nor was the testimony of an unsworn boy. The medical evidence could affirm the occurrence of rape but not the identity of the rapist.

It is not only the demand for corroboration that encumbered the proof of sexual assaults but also the content of what was considered acceptable as corroboration. Given that medical evidence did not confirm the rapist's identity, it is no wonder that an accuser's distressed appearance, disarranged clothes or bruised body encountered a similar evidentiary barrier. The case of Batia, fifteen and a half, provides an example. Batia was waiting for a bus in Tel Aviv one night when a man subsequently identified as George Halaby from Jaffa, a grocer's chauffeur and a recidivist sex offender, offered her a ride in the Dodge he was driving.[61] Batia accepted and later testified that instead of driving her where she wanted to go, the man drove in the direction of Jerusalem, stopped the car near an orange grove and attacked her. He threw her to the ground, beat her and threatened her with a knife. Batia struggled fiercely, and the man did not manage to complete the act. After she returned with her attacker to Tel Aviv, a friend noticed her injuries, her disorganized appearance and her distress. Batia told her friend what had happened, and the following morning he accompanied her to the police station, where she gave a detailed description of the suspect and the car. After Halaby was arrested later that day, Batia identified him in an identification parade and picked his car out of a group of vehicles she was shown. Batia also underwent a medical examination. The Supreme Court overturned Halaby's conviction, explaining that the girl's statement to her friend that she could identify the suspect and the friend's testimony that she was distressed and had a wound in her eye,

59 See the transcripts of Cr.C 94/38 (Haifa District Court) in ISA/RG 30/269/79.

60 Judgment of the Supreme Court in CrimA 79/38.

61 Two of Halaby's four previous convictions were for sex offences, and local newspapers had reported on his violent treatment of women. On 28 August 1934, he reportedly offered a young woman a ride, took her to a secluded spot and attempted to assault her. On 4 July 1935, papers reported that a Jewish immigrant from Germany committed suicide after Halaby raped her. Again, he had picked her up and driven her to an out-of-the-way place, where he attacked her. According to the news accounts, the police officer who received the complaint knew immediately who Halaby was, since many similar complaints about him had been made in the past. 'Driver Charged with Violence', *Palestine Post*, 28 August 1934, at 5; 'An Act of Rape Prompted a Suicide', *Davar*, 4 July 1935, at 8; ISA/RG 30/ Law 268/54, CrimA 54/38 *Shafiq Halaby* v. *A.G.* [1938].

disarranged clothes, disordered hair and blood on her hand were 'not sufficient to corroborate her story'.[62] It is noteworthy that the Supreme Court completely ignored the testimony of the physician who examined Batia and found bruises and marks on her body. Batia's distress was not considered corroboration of her assault; lack of distress on her part, however, could have been seen as undermining her credibility.[63]

The complainants in the above examples were disbelieved not for any personal reasons but because they belonged to a category of witnesses that was, by definition, suspicious: complainants in cases of sexual assaults. In Chapter 3, I discuss the even more suspicious category of non-English child complainants and additional evidentiary and procedural tools embodying disbelief in their testimony. It should be stressed that the suspicion incorporated in the demand for corroboration was not personal but was, rather, levelled at the social category to which a witness belonged. Complainants who were personally suspected of being untruthful could fare worse than the categorically untrustworthy and could face charges of perjury, as I discuss in Chapter 3 in my analysis of the plausibility of the child-narrator's testimony.

## Conclusion

The requirement of corroboration in cases of sexual assault was intended to solve the evidentiary challenge posed by such hard-to-prove crimes. The probative difficulty related to sexual charges should not be underestimated, especially in cases in which the only available evidence was the word of the alleged victim against the word of the defendant. Nevertheless, he-said-she-said situations could occur in non-sexual crimes as well. Perpetrators of all sorts of offences tried to avoid eyewitnesses as much as possible. Even so, the application of the evidentiary solution of corroboration was not universal. Cases of sexual assaults were singled out as especially problematic. Scrutinizing this riddle from the perspective of plausibility, it may be concluded that facing the contradictory narratives of the complainant and the defendant, the courts approached the dilemma with an evidentiary rule that subsumed social misgiving about the former.

At the explicit, rhetorical level, the doctrine of corroboration as applied by the Palestinian judiciary was a tool for promoting justice and ascertaining guilt in hard-to-prove sex offence cases. However, corroboration in such cases was not a neutral evidentiary tool but, rather, a tool for signifying 'others', those belonging to a category of social players who should not be believed. The blanket demand for corroboration with respect to all complainants in

[62] ISA/RG 30/ Law 268/54, CrimA 54/38 *Shafiq Halaby* v. A.G. [1938], at 3.

[63] As was the case in CrimA 31/47 *Khatem & Ahmed* v. *A.G.* (Acting Justice Curry's minority opinion, at 12).

cases of sexual assaults implied that the plausibility of such assaults, in general, was questioned. It was often more plausible, as demonstrated above, that a story of sexual assault was a fabrication than a truthful account.

While complaints of sexual assaults in general were treated with suspicion, the characterization of the complainants diverged across time and place. In England, those labelled 'others' by the corroboration rule were females and homosexuals, and in the colonial context, they were non-English, especially non-English children. In contexts where most complainants in cases of sexual assaults were female, mistrust of the complainant's testimony, as expressed through the doctrine of corroboration, had an apparent gendered aspect. In Mandate Palestine, however, complainants were not predominantly female (in the cases I was able to trace, seventy-two complainants were male and seventy-four female). The Mandate British judges did not explicitly voice bias against women for their supposed lack of veracity, unlike the American evidence law scholar, John Henry Wigmore, whose writings warned against the credibility of female complainants in sexual cases on the basis of perverse psychological pathology.[64]

Originally based on a prejudice specifically against female complainants in cases of sexual offences, the rule of corroboration as applied in the colonial setting of Mandate Palestine expressed prejudice concerning the truthfulness of locals, especially the young, irrespective of gender. British perceptions of the locals could not help but affect what went on inside the courtroom, and, in sexual offence cases, they heightened judges' lack of trust in complainants and led to a stricter application of the rule of corroboration. The judges were usually careful in their public pronouncements (especially when there was no individualized suspicion against a complainant). However, the occasional denigrating remark slipped out, as in the minority opinion of Acting Supreme Court Justice Curry in the rape-cum-robbery case involving nineteen-year-old Rachel and her companions. Curry held that the evidence corroborating Rachel's rape testimony was inadequate. He further asserted that '[i]t is quite a common thing in this country for complainants to add a charge of rape to one of assault or robbery and it is not easy for an accused to defend himself successfully against such a fabricated charge'.[65]

The practice of corroboration in that setting epitomized British anxiety toward the dubious and threatening Orient, a world of loathsome sexuality, backward mentality and deceit. The fear of uncontrollable and perverted sexuality and its Siamese twin, the fear of false charges motivated by revenge or blackmail, intensified in the colonial context of the mysterious 'East'. Corroboration, as it was used in Mandate Palestine, incorporated mistrust

[64] Vol. 3A, John Henry Wigmore, *Evidence in Trials at Common Law* (Chadbourn rev. ed.), 10 vols. (Boston: Little, Brown, 1970), 736–737, section 924a. For a criticism of Wigmore, see Backhouse, *Carnal Crimes: Sexual Assault Law in Canada, 1900–1975*, 382–383.

[65] ISA Division 30 (Supreme Court Files), File B/441, original docket #Cr.A 31/47 *Fahed Kathem & Musa Ahmed* v. *A.G.* [1947].

toward local complainants in sexual assault cases not only on the basis of gender but also on the basis of ethnic origin. It is also evident that children were treated as much less credible than adults, an issue I explore further in Chapter 3.

In Palestine, judicial emphasis on the corroborative significance of medical and forensic evidence incorporated a narrative of the British instilling progress and modernization in the land entrusted to its care. Despite pervasive judicial rhetoric touting such evidence, however, in cases of sexual assault – even when such evidence was submitted and even when no individualized suspicion against the complainants existed – courts rejected victims' stories as insufficient to convict. The inflexible demand to corroborate the identity of the perpetrator (notwithstanding the improbability of a mistake when the accused was a familiar person) undermined the significance of the available medical and forensic evidence.

Palestine's British rulers represented themselves as the protectors of women and children, the weak inhabitants of the land. However, their explicit discourse was at odds with the actual practice of the courts and with their reluctance to believe local victims of sexual assaults, most notably children. The view of corroboration as a simple evidentiary tool in sexual cases relied on an array of social stereotypes about plausible scenarios of sexual assault and their fabrication and was predicated on the perceived inferiority and unreliability of local witnesses, especially the young, in cases of sexual assault. While claiming to proffer superior moral values and expressing repulsion toward allegedly widespread sexual immorality in Palestine, the British judiciary adopted an evidentiary standard of corroboration that was often hard to meet. In many cases, including severe sexual assaults of children, the demand for corroboration led to the acquittal of the accused.

The corroboration rule demonstrates how socially and culturally constructed elements of plausibility (such as the identity of witnesses or the likelihood of their versions of events) are built into formal legal rules. The incorporation of the constituents of plausibility into formal evidentiary and procedural mechanisms disguises their socially constructed nature. Cultural assumptions, social beliefs and bias are camouflaged in rules and procedures with technical, neutral and objective appearance. Findings of fact based on these evidentiary rules and procedures seem to reflect objective truth and not conclusions based on what counts as socially valid knowledge. Insight into these hidden elements of plausibility is enabled by a 'law in action' approach that critically examines the application of the rules within a wide social and cultural context and exposes the gap between the actual manner in which evidentiary rules are deployed and the declared rationale of the 'law on the books'. Thus, on the explicit level, distrusting a witness just because the person belongs to a disreputable social category (such as 'women', 'children' or 'natives') would violate the principle of equality before the law. It would also run counter to the declared goal of protecting those groups. However, the application of the rule of corroboration allows implicit importation and perpetuation of social beliefs concerning the plausibility of witnesses belonging to such categories. As plausibility is assimilated into evidentiary and procedural mechanisms, the finding of fact relies on conventions and scripts of plausibility, albeit often implicitly.

# 7

# Implausible Counter-Narratives

Since the implausible is the obverse of the plausible, tracing the boundaries of plausibility is facilitated through the identification of implausible tales and claims. In this chapter, I examine two kinds of stories that were deemed implausible in the courts of Mandate Palestine. The first is the inter-ethnic love story, which, if not considered totally implausible, was viewed as less plausible than a story of sexual assault or of a 'fallen woman'. Using two rape cases involving relationships between teenage Jewish girls and young Arab men, I demonstrate how the circumstances highlighted in court proceedings presented such relationships as aberrations, as lying outside the scope of normality. The second kind of implausible story is a national counter-narrative that the Mandate-era judiciary readily dismissed or undermined. Focusing on a 1933 rape case, I reconstruct hidden transcripts alluded to by Arab defence attorneys who challenged British superiority through substantive, evidentiary and procedural claims neatly tailored in accordance with the conventions of common law. Beneath the facade of a criminal trial ran an undercurrent of stories about national identity. Although the stories and arguments that this chapter highlights were told in the process of proving sex offences, they were not simply stories about the criminal cases at hand but rather stories about national identity and the nature of the British Mandate justice system. This chapter demonstrates that the concept of plausibility is relevant not only to the content of particular crime stories but also to beliefs about the essence of normal sexual or romantic relations and of the justice system.

I illustrate the above points by examining the delicate and subtle ways the plausibility or implausibility of stories was constructed within the process of proof. In the first two cases I consider, the plausibility that an inter-ethnic couple could establish a romantic connection was contemplated, if implicitly. While the girls in these cases seem to have found this scenario plausible, other participants conveyed the perception that inter-ethnic romance was plausible only when the girls involved were 'bad' or problematic. The prism of criminal prosecution itself cast doubt on the normality of such relationships, as the events were necessarily described as leading to the tragic end of sexual assault. Local Arab lawyers in the third case I examine, which also involved rape, used the platform of the criminal trial to express resistance to colonial rule and, through the proceedings, were able to exhibit, shape and negotiate social identities. In analysing the gap between text and subtext in the formal legal documents in this case, I find James C. Scott's distinction between 'public' and 'hidden' transcripts useful. The former constitute the repertoire of acceptable public discourse between subordinated groups and their superiors, and the latter comprise the 'offstage' discursive acts of the dominated among themselves. I further argue that the dominant too engage in such 'offstage' discursive acts and, thus, produce hidden transcripts of their own. The hidden transcript is sometimes influenced by the public transcript, and, occasionally, it emerges, disguised, in the public transcript.[1] Court transcripts are formal expressions of a public transcript. However, behind the legal conventions and courtroom formalism, one may find hidden transcripts of both subordinate and dominant groups. I suggest here that hidden transcripts regarding the interaction between law and identity may be accessed by focusing on the process of proof.

## The Stories of Margalit and Yaffa

Prosecutors during the British Mandate period were committed to the norm of impartiality. The ethnic identities of both accused and victims were presumed to be irrelevant to criminal proceedings. Direct ethnic labelling was avoided. Nevertheless, use of evidence subtly portrayed teenage Jewish girls who had relationships with young Arab men as, on the one hand, wayward and, on the other hand, naive and easy to exploit. Such a characterization relied on the notion that a romantic relationship with an Arab man was an implausible option for a 'normal' Jewish girl.

Voluntary inter-ethnic sexual relations were rare and prompted social sanctions. Only a few of the cases reviewed for this study involved Jewish teenage girls who had romantic relationships with Arab men; in the two stories discussed in this chapter, the filing of sexual assault charges against the men places the stories in the realm of 'fallen women' narratives. In one case, fourteen-year-old Margalit, a Jewish girl from Haifa, testified in a manner that made it difficult for the court to convict her Arab suitor, nineteen-year-old Munir, of raping her:[2] on the witness stand, she contradicted herself on the question of penetration, and the court held that there was no case for Munir to answer.

Margalit, who was raised by her mother after her father passed away, testified that she met Munir one day when she was standing near the municipal garden. Munir stopped the taxi he was driving and offered her a ride.

[1] James C. Scott, *Domination and the Arts of Resistance: Hidden Transcripts* (New Haven, CT: Yale University Press, 1990), 2–5.

[2] ISA/RG 30/Law 2065 (original docket # Cr.C 321/47).

Apparently Margalit already knew who he was, as she stated that she asked him about his friend Malka, another Jewish girl. Margalit and Munir's two-hour drive that day was followed by a longer trip to Tiberias the following week. On their third date, Munir took Margalit to a restaurant and later drove her to Mount Carmel. There they sat in the car and talked to each other in what Margalit described as a loving manner. After night fell, they moved from the front to the back seat and started to kiss and embrace. At that point, according to Margalit, Munir began pressing for intercourse. He took off her pants and lay on top of her. She stated that he penetrated her but later contradicted herself on that point. Subsequently, they went to see a late movie and then drove back to Mount Carmel and slept in the car. In the morning, Munir dropped Margalit off at the house of her friend Miryam.

Margalit's mother had become extremely worried by her daughter's absence. The family's Arab neighbour Shafiqa had reported seeing Margalit with a person who might be a Muslim, which prompted the mother to look for her daughter in various places (including Munir's house).[3] A taxi driver drove Margalit's mother around during her nightly search. She finally found her at Miryam's house, where Margalit had stayed on previous occasions after rows with her mother. Margalit's mother made her daughter get in the taxi to return home with her. However, during the ride Margalit threw herself from the car. She testified that she jumped out because she was angry at her mother. While her action may reflect simple wilfulness, the facts leave room for other possible interpretations, related, for example, to her romantic feelings for Munir or to post-rape despair. If Margalit is presented in case records as a problematic teenager, Munir is portrayed as a sexual predator. Police inspector Baum, who testified at the preliminary enquiry, had harsh things to say about Munir's reputation. He described Munir as a bad character, as a habitual seducer, who had already caused one girl to burn herself because of him.[4] Whether or not that tragedy was still fresh in the mind of the judges, the inspector's testimony created a link between that incident and the events described by Margalit.

While romantic contact between the Jewish girl and the Arab boy was adversely viewed by both Margalit's mother and an Arab neighbour, this case demonstrates the connectedness and amicable coexistence of Jews and

[3] It is not clear how the mother knew to look for her daughter at Munir's house. Shafiqa specifically stated that she did not recognize the man she had seen with Margalit. Perhaps Shafiqa had reasons for not incriminating Munir, and perhaps the mother knew more about her daughter's relationship with Munir than she cared to share with the court.

[4] That girl, Malka-Martha, committed suicide on 2 August 1945. A contemporary Hebrew magazine, *Iton Meyuhad*, depicts the incident as the story of a young and naive Jewish girl tempted by a devious and attractive young Arab man, who left her broken-hearted after toying with her and sexually exploiting her. The police investigation, however, raises the possibility that Munir was a good friend of Malka-Martha and that he attempted to lift her spirits after friends told him about her depression and asked for his help. The police investigation exposes a years-long friendship between Munir and a group of Jewish girls. Deborah Bernstein, *Women on the Margins: Gender and Nationalism in Mandate Tel Aviv* [in Hebrew] (Jerusalem: Yad Izhak Ben Zvi, 2008), 156–157.

Arabs in other areas of life. Both Margalit and her mother testified in Arabic, a fact that implies they had multiple close connections with Arabs. The mother had an Arabic first name, suggesting that the family had immigrated to Mandate Palestine from an Arab country. They resided in a mixed neighbourhood in Haifa, and the mother seems to have had a close, supportive relationship with her Arab neighbour Shafiqa. Sexuality, however, was beyond the zone of legitimate Jewish-Arab contact.

Thirteen-and-a-half-year-old Yaffa from Hadera was another Jewish girl who was attracted to an Arab youth.[5] Yaffa had known twenty-year-old Issat for about six months prior to the events described here. Issat worked in the laundry room of the military hospital adjoining Yaffa's family's home, and he also delivered white bread to her family each morning and evening. The couple took care not to be seen together. Yaffa had a stormy relationship with her stepmother and occasionally slept at her girlfriends' houses. On Friday night, 28 January 1945, she stayed at a girlfriend's house after her stepmother had beaten her. On her way home, she suddenly decided to look for Issat. She found him at the hospital and asked him to take her to Syria and marry her, as he had promised. Yaffa testified that she stayed with Issat and spent the night in the same room with him, where he raped her.

In both of these cases, the girls' behaviour was characterized as irregular. They were both portrayed as girls from dysfunctional families, who stayed out all night without letting their parents know where they were. They were also depicted as naive and thus as likely to fall prey to young Arab men who exploited their inexperience. Voluntary inter-ethnic connections were plausible in cases of such 'bad girls'. Yaffa expressed especially 'abnormal' desires: not only did she have a relationship with an Arab man but she also asked him to take her to Syria, and Issat testified that she told him she wanted to convert to Islam.

Having sex with a girl under sixteen constituted the criminal offence of rape, regardless of the girl's consent. A romantic relationship, therefore, did not establish a defence. Nevertheless, as explained in previous chapters, cultural perceptions of victims' culpability could be damaging to the proof of rape charges, even when the complainant was a child. 'Bad girls' like Yaffa and Margalit are cases in point: Munir and Issat were both acquitted of rape.[6]

Both Yaffa and Margalit described the initial stages of their relationships as romantic. Yaffa met Issat in secret for months. They spoke to one another in Hebrew and English. Yaffa wanted Issat to take her to Syria and marry her. According to her testimony, they loved each other. She said that Issat kissed

[5] ISA/RG 30/Law 2041 (original docket # Cr.C 32/45).

[6] Munir was acquitted when the court concluded that there was no case to answer, and Issat was acquitted after the judges disagreed about his culpability. The Jewish judge, Shems, supported conviction, but the Arab judge, Baradey, accepted Issat's argument that he believed Yaffa was older than sixteen. Such controversy mandated acquittal. §6(1) of the Defence (Judicial) Regulations (2), 1942 (Supplement II to the Gazette No. 1209 of 13 July 1942, p. 1150).

her once, but she did not expect him to touch her. She testified that, to fend off Issat's sexual advances, she told him she was married to another man who served in the army. She further testified that she had been a virgin prior to intercourse with Issat. When confronted with the medical opinion that she had lost her virginity much earlier in her life, she speculated it might have occurred as the result of a sports accident at school. Margalit dated Munir three times, during which they had long conversations. Munir courted Margalit, travelled with her and took her to a restaurant before they had physical contact. Afterwards, they went to a movie and then spent the night on the top of Mount Carmel. Margalit's confused and contradictory testimony in court, five months after the event, may have been meant to rescue Munir from conviction. Yet the other participants in these two cases hardly seem to have been convinced by the girls' favourable interpretation. A voluntary inter-ethnic affair between a Jewish girl and an Arab man was plausible only if the girl was 'bad' or problematic. Otherwise, it made no sense.

## The Story of Magdalene

In 1933, nineteen-year-old Magdalene, a member of Jerusalem's Greek community, lived in the Katamon neighbourhood with her stepmother, Anna, and her sister, Angelique.[7] Her father had passed away four or five years earlier and was buried in Mount Zion. Magdalene was a telephone operator at the Jerusalem Exchange, where she had been employed since she was thirteen.[8] The year before the events described here, Magdalene had met Timothy Kassiliani from South Africa, and they had become engaged through correspondence. Another man, George Georgiades, was in love with Magdalene. George, thirty-four years old, was a Greek national (born in Rhodes) who lived in the old city of Jerusalem. He was the owner of a local bus company and had known Magdalene since she was sixteen. He believed she was in love with him, and he planned to marry her. He had been carrying two rings in his pocket for an entire year, hoping to use them in the wedding ceremony.

Magdalene was aware of George's feelings but did not share them. What George deemed courtship, Magdalene experienced as harassment and threat. Her distress drove her to initiate official complaints against George. It is noteworthy that Magdalene had access to senior British government officials, a fact that may be credited to her position as a telephone operator. The year before the events in question, Magdalene had complained to Margaret Nixon,

[7] Unless otherwise mentioned, the details of the case are taken from the trial transcripts of Crime No. 44/33, held in the District Court of Jerusalem, and from the files of Henry Cattan, who represented one of the defendants in the appeal to the Supreme Court. ISA/RG 66/M/188/33.

[8] During the 1920s and 1930s, many Greek nationals who were deported by Turkey immigrated to Jerusalem, and the Greek community there grew significantly. Many Greek residents of Jerusalem were employed by the British administration and held jobs in banks, the post office and various Christian welfare organizations. David Kroyanker, *The Neighborhoods of Jerusalem Talbiya, Katamon and the Greek Colony* [in Hebrew] (Jerusalem: Keter, 2002), 280, 282.

the government welfare inspector who had been commissioned to prepare a report about child labour in Palestine.[9] Nixon took Magdalene to Roy Spicer, the inspector general of police, who received her at his private house. Magdalene told him that George pestered her and that she was frightened for her honour and her life. She said she did not want her life ruined by this 'horrible old man' and that George had threatened to kill her unless she married him. Spicer passed the information on to the German Colony police station. Magdalene also complained about George to Edward Keith-Roach, the governor of Jerusalem.

Unfortunately for Magdalene, on 22 March 1933, her fears were realized. That day, she finished working at 8 p.m. As she was afraid of George, her stepmother and sister came to the post office to accompany her home. The three women were waiting for the bus when a friend, Yanni Papadopulos, stopped and offered them a ride home in his car. They accepted. Yanni's car broke down shortly thereafter, and he was forced to stop. Another car stopped behind his, and three men got out of it: George; Nicola Stimati Vassiliadis, one of his employees; and Jabra Yacoub Barham, George's friend and the driver of the car. One man held Magdalene's screaming stepmother and covered her eyes, while the others chased her sister (apparently mistaking her for Magdalene), who managed to escape from Yanni's car. However, after the sister cried 'I am not Magdalene, I am Angeli!', they left her and returned to the car. The sister would later testify that one of the men was holding a revolver. The men grabbed Magdalene, forced her from Yanni's car and pushed her into the back seat of their car, where she sat pinned between George and Nicola. After they drove away, Yanni, who had been pushed to the ground by the men, repaired his car and continued with Magdalene's stepmother and sister to the house of a Mrs Freeman and then on to the police.

Meanwhile, George and his confederates drove Magdalene through the Greek Colony and then along a side road to Ras, near Beit Jala. There, they stopped the car and turned off the headlights. Before the two men left Magdalene alone with George in the darkness, Nicola threatened her with a gun and told her that unless she 'married' George within two hours, he would kill her. George tried to rape Magdalene, but she managed to resist. Two hours later, at around 3 a.m., Nicola returned, once more threatened Magdalene and then disappeared again. Magdalene told the court that, at that point, 'I lost all my power after struggling for so long. He opened my dress and raped me in the back way. I was screaming.' Magdalene's torn drawers were presented as Exhibit 'A' and her torn coat as Exhibit 'B'. George told the court that the sexual act in the car was consensual and that it was not sodomy. George blew the car's horn and his friends returned. Jabra secured a room at a fellaheen

[9] Margaret Nixon was created a dame of the Order of St John in 1919 and was appointed government welfare inspector in 1921. Marcella Simoni, 'At the Roots of Division: A New Perspective on Arabs and Jews, 1930–1939', *Middle Eastern Studies* 36, no. 3 (2000): 56.

house near a compound containing a monastery and a girls' school built by the Russian Orthodox Church, and the group went there to spend the night, the men all sitting awake by Magdalene's side until morning. Magdalene told the court she cried non-stop. The owner of the house brought them coffee, and Nicola offered Magdalene whiskey, which she refused. She also refused the simple breakfast of milk, bread and eggs brought to the group in the morning. George and his associates then took her to another house, this time within the Russian compound. There, Magdalene said, she was left alone in a room with George, who shut the windows, closed and locked the door, put the key in his pocket and raped her again, this time 'from the front'. She resisted at first, but then gave up, letting him do what he wanted.

Meanwhile, Nicola went to look for a priest to marry the couple. This was no easy task, since it was a fast day right before Easter, when, under Greek Orthodox canon law, no marriage is to be celebrated. Vassili Karpapas, a member of the Greek community whom George knew to be a friend of Archimandrite Theodoritas, tried to obtain the latter's permission for the marriage. Theodoritas held the office of chief dragoman of the Greek Orthodox patriarchate and also presided over the ecclesiastical court when the president of the court was unavailable.[10] During the time of the fast, marriage required the approval of the bishop or his locum tenens.[11] Theodoritas asked Karpapas whether George had violated Magdalene's virginity and, learning that he had, consulted his locum tenens (the bishop being in Jericho at the time) about the permissibility of conducting a marriage ceremony on a fast day under these circumstances. Being advised to obtain the girl's mother's permission, Theodoritas sent Karpapas to bring Magdalene's stepmother to him. Karpapas returned to Theodoritas and said the stepmother would not come. Theodoritas summoned Elias Saliba Bibi, the chief clerk of the ecclesiastical court, who went with Karpapas to look into the matter. About 4.30 p.m. three men, all of whom would later become defendants in this case, arrived at the Russian compound: Elias Saliba Bibi, Vassili Karpapas and Hanna Stawridis (Father John), the father superior of the convent in Beit Jala. Magdalene later reported that Bibi pressured her to marry George, especially after realizing George had had sexual contact with her. Bibi inscribed a document in Greek affirming her consent and asked her to sign it. Magdalene did so but added the words 'by force'. Bibi said this would not do and wrote a new document. However, he copied the words 'by force' onto it and then crossed them out. After Magdalene signed the document, the three men left. Bibi took the document to Theodoritas, who noticed the crossed-out words. Bibi explained that he had purposely written them down to verify Magdalene's real intentions and that she was the one who had crossed them out. Thereupon, Theodoritas gave his consent to the marriage, and the three men

10 A dragoman is an interpreter. While archimandrite is an ecclesiastical rank, the office of dragoman in the Greek Orthodox Church is an executive one that can be held by churchmen of different ranks.

11 The authority in the Church in the bishop's absence.

returned to the Russian compound at around 6.30 p.m. with an Arab priest. Yennavia Dighelawa, a woman residing in the Russian compound, recognized him as 'the priest of Beit Jala' and approached him to receive his blessing. Earlier, Dighelawa had noticed that Magdalene was weeping. All of the men entered the room where Magdalene was being held. At some stage, Dighelawa asked what was going on, and Bibi told her they were about to have a marriage ceremony and asked her to get a sprig for a wedding wreath. She became suspicious and inquired if they had permission from the Russian authorities to conduct the wedding. Unsatisfied with the priest's answer, and, so, determined not to allow the ceremony, she made it clear that unless they left she would notify the Russian authorities. The group then moved to another house. There, the Arab priest asked Magdalene if she wanted to marry George, to which all the other men called out 'yes', and the priest performed the ceremony. The priest gave George the ring. Magdalene later reported that 'there was no woman present when the ceremony was performed. Elias Bibi acted as best man on the request of Georgiades. No one acted as bridesmaid for me as there was no woman present.' After the ceremony was completed, the group went to the Greek convent in Beit Jala, where food was served. Magdalene then wrote some letters. She gave Nicola and Karpapas letters to take to her mother, and she gave Jabra a letter to her supervisor at the post office. The men departed, and Magdalene was left alone with George. About 10.30 p.m. there was a knock at the door. The police had arrived together with Magdalene's aunt and cousin. Magdalene and George were taken to a police station in Jerusalem. Magdalene returned to her stepmother's house about 2 a.m., about thirty hours after she was abducted.

In the aftermath of this episode, six men were brought to trial. George, Nicola and Jabra were convicted of abduction by force under Article 206 of the OPC and of rape and sodomy under Sections 3 and 4 of the CLAO.[12] George was sentenced to fifteen years of penal servitude, and Nicola and Jabra were each sentenced to five years. Elias Bibi, Vassili Karpapas and Abbot Hanna Stawridis, all of whom arranged the marriage, were convicted as accessories after the fact and were sentenced, respectively, to one year, three years' and three months' imprisonment. All except Stawridis appealed to the Supreme Court. The Supreme Court ruled that the act of sodomy was not a probable consequence of the common intention of George's accomplices and acquitted them of that charge. On similar grounds, Bibi and Karpapas were acquitted of being accessories to an act of sodomy. However, the rape-related charges were affirmed.[13] Karpapas's sentence was subsequently reduced to one year, the equivalent of Bibi's. The other sentences remained intact.

[12] The sections numbers, as modified in subsequent amendments, were 89 in the CLAO ( amendment no. 30, 1934) and 152 in the CCO (1936).

[13] Cr.A 36/33, *George Georgiades and Others* v. *The Attorney General*, in *Collection of Judgments of the Courts of Palestine 1919–1933. Vol. II*, ed. Max D. *Friedman and Leon Rotenberg* (Tel Aviv: L.M. Rotenberg – Law Publishers, 1935), 584.

The case was reported in the criminal sections of the Hebrew press. An account on 27 March related that a young Greek man aided by two of his friends had performed a daring abduction of his beloved before her mother's eyes.[14] The article detailed the events that took place before Magdalene was found and included an update on George's arrest and the illegal marriage ceremony. It noted that the abduction occurred after Magdalene had become engaged to another man, hinting at a crime of passion. A headline the following day was far more dramatic: 'What's New in Our Capital? Misery of Love around Katamon. Seven accused regarding the rape of the Greek maiden, including three priests.'[15] The related article covered the magistrate's preliminary investigation and reported that the proceeding attracted a large crowd of Jerusalemites, including both Greeks and Christian Arabs. It reported the names of the accused, the names of the attorneys and the nature of the charges – rape, sodomy and abduction and being accessories thereto. It also noted that three priests were suspected of assisting the offence.[16] The coverage continued on 29 March with details about the witnesses who had been investigated in the preliminary enquiry.[17] The appeal was also covered by the Hebrew newspapers, which provided many legal details, including the sentences of the appellants, the names of the attorneys and their grounds for appeal. Apparently, defence counsel got substantial time to make oral arguments, which were heard over three consecutive days.[18] The hearing of the appeal was reported on at length in the *Palestine Post*, an English-language daily, which provided many legal details (including an exact reference to the case, the identities of the judges and lawyers, the precise grounds for appeal and issues of substantive law, procedure and evidence).[19] The *Palestine Post* also published a detailed abstract of the judgment.[20]

The nuanced legal arguments of the defence in the case of the abduction and rape of Magdalene masked a threefold challenge to the British justice system. The arguments did not blatantly attack British principles. On the contrary, they adhered to the tenets of the common law. Yet the grounds of the defence appeal questioned the superiority of British jurisdiction and statute and the importance of British officials. The disguised, yet consistent, line of argumentation constituted a hidden transcript of resistance. One of the grounds of the

[14] 'A Young Woman Abducted under Gun Threats', *Davar*, 27 March 1933, p. 3. During the Mandate era, *Davar* was perceived as the official voice of the Jewish establishment and had a major impact on Jewish public opinion. Historical Jewish Press, www.jpress.org.il/publications/davar-he.asp.

[15] 'What's New in Our Capital?', *Doar Hayom*, 28 March 1933, p. 4. *Doar Hayom* (Palestine Daily Mail) was founded by Ithamar Ben Avi and his father, Eliezer Ben Yehuda. Ben Avi, the editor, was inspired by the popular European press, which published sensational items and novels. Historical Jewish Press, www.jpress.org.il/publications/DHY-he.asp.

[16] *Doar Hayom*, 28 March 1933, p. 4.

[17] *Doar Hayom*, 29 March 1933, p. 4.

[18] *Doar Hayom*, 16 May 1933, p. 4; 17 May 1933, p. 4; 18 May 1933, p. 4. The Arab priest mentioned as having performed the marriage ceremony was not ultimately indicted.

[19] *Palestine Post*, 16 May 1933, p. 4; 18 May 1933, p. 4.

[20] *Palestine Post*, 29 May 1933, p. 4.

appeal suggested that an Ottoman legal provision should have been applied to the case and not the British prohibitions of rape and sodomy. As noted, the indictment against George, Nicola and Jabra included charges of abduction by force under Article 206 of the Ottoman OPC and of rape and sodomy under Sections 3 and 4 of the British CLAO.[21] Under OPC Article 206 (abduction for the purpose of an 'abominable act'), a rapist was to be punished by a minimum term of five years in a hard-labour penal institution, a much less severe punishment than that specified in the British provisions, that is, a maximum term of fifteen years' imprisonment for rape or sodomy (and, indeed, George was sentenced to fifteen years of penal servitude by the District Court). The OPC offered additional mitigation when the abduction was followed by marriage, recognizing the custom of kidnapping girls to overcome parental objection to consensual marriage and allowing the woman or her guardian, if she was younger than fifteen, to waive the right to demand criminal prosecution of the offender. Although George forced Magdalene into marriage, he might still have had hope that she would eventually relent (the record of the trial reflects George's unrealistic hopes). In the appeal, George and Jabra were represented by the famous Arab lawyer, Naseeb Abcarius Bey, who submitted that only OPC Article 206 was applicable to the case. He argued, that, when several articles apply to the same offence, the accused should get the benefit of the doubt and, if convicted, be punished under the more favourable article. Despite its sophistication, his argument, which suggested favouring an Ottoman article over British provisions of law, was rejected. The Supreme Court reasoned that had the appellants been convicted of rape and sodomy alone, the British provisions would have applied and that they could not expect a lesser penalty since they were convicted of an additional offence.[22]

A claim of inadmissibility was made in relation to the testimony of two prosecution witnesses, Margaret Nixon, the government welfare inspector, and Roy Spicer, the inspector general of police. George Salah, Nicola's attorney, argued that Magdalene's statements to these witnesses had been made too long before the offence occurred (a year) for them to have been admissible.[23] Nixon and Spicer were not the only British officials who testified for the prosecution; others included police officers and the physicians who examined Magdalene. However, both stood out as high-ranking officials of the British government. Both testified that Magdalene had complained to them that

[21] The three were also charged with (and convicted by the District Court for) conspiracy to commit an offence punishable by penal servitude for a term of three years or more.

[22] Cr.A 36/33, *George Georgiades and Others* v. *The Attorney General*, in *Collection of Judgments of the Courts of Palestine 1919–1933*, 583.

[23] Attorney Salah objected to Mr Spicer's testimony in the District Court on the ground that Magdalene's complaint to him was hearsay. The court overruled that objection, holding that the defence was consent, and the testimony was therefore allowed. See the transcripts of the District Court at ISA/RG 66/M/188/33, 11.

George was following her. Mr Salah made no claim against the reliability or credibility of these two witnesses. However, had he been successful in his argument, the statements of two highly respected and prominent British officials would have been rendered inadmissible. Such a result was avoided both in the District Court and in the Supreme Court. The judgment of the latter reasoned that the statements were permissible, as the prosecution was allowed to contradict the defence claim of consent. The statements Magdalene made to Nixon and Spicer enabled the prosecution to prove her state of mind, that is, that she feared George would molest her and sought protection from him.[24] The ruling was not personal in the sense of referring to specific attributes of the witnesses, but it preserved their status, affirming that their testimony was significant and valuable. Thus, the ruling on an evidentiary matter served, albeit indirectly, to preserve the status of high-ranking British officials.

A third challenge to British judicial superiority was the claim that the District Court lacked jurisdiction to find that the marriage between Magdalene and George was invalid. Marital rape did not constitute a criminal offence in Mandate Palestine, but George was accused of raping Magdalene before marrying her, so he could not claim a marital exemption. However, he tried to claim that Magdalene's marriage to him made her an incompetent witness. The validity of the marriage, therefore, had to be determined. Jurisdiction, the defence claimed, was exclusively vested in the Greek Orthodox religious court.[25] Archimandrite Theodoritas testified that, according to Byzantine law, the marriage was valid as long as it was not declared void by the ecclesiastical court. The defence maintained that Magdalene, as George's wife, could not testify against him. The Supreme Court rejected the defence argument. First, it held under Article 47 of the Palestine Order-in-Council, 1922 that a civil court could determine a question of personal status that arose incidentally during a legal proceeding when such determination was necessary to resolve the matter under dispute. It also held that, even if the marriage was valid, Magdalene remained a competent witness.[26] Under the Evidence Ordinance, spouses were incompetent to testify against each other, except in cases of adultery and of 'bodily injury or violence' inflicted by one or the other – and George was accused of a forcible rape.[27]

[24] Cr.A 36/33, *George Georgiades and Others* v. *The Attorney General*, in *Collection of Judgments of the Courts of Palestine 1919–1933*, 583.

[25] The claim rested on Articles 54 or 64 of the Palestine Order-in-Council, 1922.

[26] Cr.A 36/33, *George Georgiades and Others* v. *The Attorney General*, in *Collection of Judgments of the Courts of Palestine 1919–1933*, 582.

[27] Article 5(1) of the Evidence Ordinance. It was further held that no evidence was presented before the District Court as to the applicable rules of personal law in this case (George was a Greek citizen, and the law of Greece applied to him; the law of the Orthodox Church was the personal law of Magdalene; and the Archimandrite Theodoritas testified as to the applicability of the Byzantine law). Cr.A 36/33, *George Georgiades and Others* v. *The Attorney General*, in ibid., 583.

The Supreme Court thus tackled three indirect attacks on the superiority of the British legal system: the challenge to the jurisdiction of the District Court, the attempt to exclude the testimony of high-ranking British officials and the claim that the British prohibition of rape and sodomy should be set aside in favour of an Ottoman provision that was more applicable to the circumstances of the case. Separately, these challenges hardly make coherent statements. Cumulatively, though, they transmit a message of resistance and refusal to unquestioningly acknowledge British superiority. The challenges were made within accepted British legal conventions, with reference to appropriate provisions in Mandate legislation and precedents in the common law. Yet all three points were decided in a manner that preserved British power. Their potentially subversive message met with a hegemonic response. The Supreme Court held that the British judges of the District Court were entitled to make a decision about the validity of the marriage, that the testimony of Nixon and Spicer was admissible and that the British prohibitions of rape and sodomy were applicable. George's penalty, fifteen years of penal servitude, was therefore affirmed.[28]

The local (non-British) lawyers in this case appeared to be complying with the legal norms imposed by the British. However, a close reading of the case demonstrates that they engaged in subtle forms of resistance. The position of lawyers in the colonial justice system was complex. They were licensed by the colonial regime to practise in the local courts and were committed to the norms and conventions of the legal profession.[29] Yet they could also deploy their professional role to challenge colonial rule and express national identity both through direct activism or the representation of national protagonists and causes[30] and through more subtle and covert action. The latter form of resistance is the subject of this chapter. As discussed in the previous chapter, the facade of evidentiary and procedural rules powerfully disguises notions and beliefs predicated on plausibility. I further argue that counter-narratives may be similarly veiled. To achieve insight into counter-narratives and their challenge to dominant (plausible) social and cultural narratives, I call for critical inspection of the process of proof.

The criminal rape case recounted in the above pages had no political dimension. That is, it was not an inter-ethnic Jewish-Arab case. The rapist and victim were both members of the Greek community in Jerusalem. Yet the legal proceedings were underpinned by subversive national themes. The Arab lawyers who represented the accused in this case shot thin but sharp counter-

28 George's application to remit part of his sentence was later denied by the High Commissioner.

29 According to Bourdieu, lawyers extend loyalty not only to the professional requirements of the bar but also to the social circles that they, as legal professionals, help to reproduce. Pierre Bourdieu, 'The Force of Law: Toward a Sociology of the Juridical Field', *Hastings L.J.* 38 (1987).

30 For references to literature on lawyers as anti-colonial activists, see Mitra Sharafi, 'A New History of Colonial Lawyering: Likhovski and Legal Identities in the British Empire', *Law & Social Inquiry* 32, no. 4 (2007): 1060.

narrative arrows at the British justice system, and the British judges recognized and deflected their challenges. In using the term 'narrative', I do not imply that these subversive 'stories' about the justice system necessarily took the form of temporally ordered accounts of past events, with a beginning, middle and end.[31] On the contrary, they were messages that could be hidden in supposedly plotless arguments about fine legal points. Nonetheless, they conveyed socially derived ideas about the British justice system. Judicial rejection of such subversive ideas as if they made no sense defined the border between the implausible and the plausible. The judgment in the rape case under discussion upheld the superiority of British law, witnesses and jurisdiction and implicitly rejected as implausible the subversive options suggested by the defence lawyers. I suggest that a focus on the dynamics of proof provides important insights into 'hidden transcripts' in courtroom performance. The notion of plausibility, this chapter demonstrates, relates not only to crime stories but also to characterizations of the justice system. Furthermore, the study of plausibility, which is integral to the process of proof, calls on a theoretical framework that brings together substantive norms, evidentiary rules, tactics of practice and socio-cultural interactions. This framework constitutes a powerful tool for investigating the complex interrelationship between law and identity.

## Conclusion

Delineating the implausible can help outline the plausible. As these concepts rely on socially constructed meanings, the line between them can be negotiated and debated. Yaffa and Margalit framed the initial stages of their relationships with Issat and Munir as consensual and romantic. Yet other participants in their cases framed stories of inter-ethnic affairs as plausible only when they involved gullible and errant girls. The arguments made by the Arab lawyers who represented the men convicted of the sexual assault of Magdalene contested British superiority and vented anti-colonial political sentiments irrelevant to the case at hand. It is no wonder, therefore, that they met with consistent rejection by the hegemonic decision makers.

Statements are made and stories are told for the purpose of achieving some goal or advancing some interest. In the words of Ewick and Silbey, 'story telling is strategic'.[32] This dictum is certainly apt in the case of lawyers, who explicitly aspire to present their cases in the most persuasive manner to the benefit of their clients. Yet both lawyers and other participants in criminal proceedings also use the process of proof as a platform to achieve goals and communicate

[31] Synthesizing various definitions of 'narrative', Ewick and Silbey set forth three minimal requirements: (1) selective appropriation of past events and characters, (2) temporal ordering and (3) emplotment, a structural relation between events and characters. Patricia Ewick and Susan S. Silbey, 'Subversive Stories and Hegemonic Tales: Toward a Sociology of Narrative', *Law & Society Review* 29, no. 2 (1995): 200.

[32] Ibid., 208.

messages that may be incidental or irrelevant to the main issues of the trial. Thus Magdalene's case, a criminal and non-political one, served as a platform for Arab attorneys to implicitly air subversive messages and for colonial justices to tacitly reinforce views of British superiority. And in Yaffa's and Margalit's cases, the plausibility of their accounts of voluntary romantic inter-ethnic contact was contested, despite the irrelevance of their view on the voluntariness of the relationships to the determination of criminal responsibility, since both girls were under the age of consent.

As a close analysis of defence attorneys' arguments in the rape of Magdalene reveals, beneath the obvious rhetorical level, political sentiments and aspirations were vented. Their provocative nature, however, was well disguised. In form, these arguments adhered to conventional common-law formulae. In content, they were tailored to the peculiar circumstances of the case (the forced marriage, the unusual access of Magdalene to high-ranking British officials). This particularity obscured the general and overarching structure of the hidden transcript created by the repetition of arguments undermining British superiority. None of these arguments individually conveyed a story that challenged mainstream perceptions of the colonial justice system. It was the accumulation and coherence of repeated themes that made them subversive. Likewise, the plausibility of voluntary inter-ethnic romance was not explicitly discussed in the cases involving Margalit and Yaffa, but the insinuations of the witnesses and the circumstances that they highlighted formed a hidden transcript that rendered such a relationship implausible where 'good' or 'normal' girls were concerned.

The Arab advocates who represented the accused in Magdalene's case did not prevail. Their sophisticated legal arguments were rejected. The subversive if well-hidden implications of their arguments and motions were, of course, no real threat to the British Mandate justice system. Even so, the sharp little arrows aimed at that system by the advocates who practised under its auspices demonstrated these actors' resilience and encoded hidden transcripts of national identity. The Arab lawyers were neither despised collaborators nor heroic national freedom fighters. Sharafi warns against mistaking the methodological aim of reconstructing the perspective of the colonized with the substantive claim for agency.[33] The judges of the British Mandate courts had the power to decide proceedings, and they consistently rejected Arab lawyers' attempts at subversion. The judges addressed only explicit legal issues and ignored (if they even noticed) 'hidden transcripts'. By failing to acknowledge a possible connection between case-specific arguments made by particular advocates and the social organization of their experience as lawyers under colonial rule, judicial arguments hid 'the grounds of their own plausibility and thus help[ed] reproduce the taken-for-granted hegemony'.[34]

[33] Sharafi, 1064. [34] Ewick and Silbey, 222.

There was nothing essentially 'Arab' in the acerbic arguments made by the Arab lawyers in Magdalene's case. The national agenda that one can find in the well-hidden transcripts behind their objections was based on resistance to British hegemony but did not offer an alternative ethnic or religious order, certainly not an essentially Arab alternative order. Legal professionals who wished to practise in a colonial justice system had to adopt the normative colonial order. Even explicit legal protest needed to be framed with reference to existing substantive law and procedure. Nonetheless, as Sharafi claims, Anglicization did not necessarily bolster identification with British rule.[35]

Two major conclusions can be drawn from the hidden transcripts in the rape cases discussed in this chapter: First, implausible ideas and suggestions help to define the plausible. In the cases involving Margalit and Yaffa, it was plausible that a wayward and gullible Jewish girl would engage in romantic contact with an Arab youth, and it was implausible that a 'good girl' would have a voluntary inter-ethnic affair. Although from a doctrinal point of view consent was irrelevant when the victims were younger than sixteen, the voluntariness of the relationship was culturally relevant as part of a hidden transcript of what constitutes 'real rape'. The voluntary inter-ethnic affair was another variation on the rape myth of victim blameability. In the case of Magdalene's rape, it was implausible to British jurists that an Ottoman penal section or an ecclesiastical tribunal should be preferred over British law or jurisdiction or that high-ranking British officials could be disqualified as witnesses, and it was self-evident that British justice was indeed superior to any local forms and was thus a 'precious gift' to the inhabitants of Palestine. Thus, the arguments of Arab defence attorneys were dismissed in their entirety.

Second, plausibility is contingent on power relations. Yaffa and Margalit, who suggested that relations between Jewish girls and Arab men could include romantic friendship, were held in low esteem. Their interpretation was heavily qualified, and limited only to cases of marginalized girls. Their testimony was thus considered highly suspect, reflecting their marginalization. In Magdalene's case, the British judges clearly rejected every argument that undermined British justice. Tracing counter-, or subversively implausible, narratives may require exhuming hidden transcripts that acquire their meaning on the power grid of dominant–subordinate relations.

[35] Mitra Sharafi, *Law and Identity in Colonial South Asia: Parsi Legal Culture, 1772–1947* (New York: Cambridge University Press, 2014), 5.

# Conclusion

What makes one crime story convincing and another a wrong story to tell in and outside the courtroom? That question lies at the heart of this book. I approach it through a historical analysis of the plausibility of stories about sex offences, focusing mainly on those told in the courtroom and during the investigative process but also taking into account those told outside the judicial sphere. I argue that examining the constitution and expression of plausible crime stories sheds new light on the process of proof and its embeddedness within broad socio-cultural settings. Plausibility is contingent on the particularities of the surrounding culture and social institutions. Therefore, any endeavour to uncover the elements of plausibility must concentrate on a specific historical and social context. This book examines the proof of sex offences in Mandate Palestine, a context of intense intercultural encounters between Arabs, Jews and Britons, of modernity and tradition and of an empire in decline amid rising nationalities.

The plausibility of a story or an argument, that is, its potential to convince and to make sense, is not the outcome of an arithmetic formula. The question of whether testimony or a legal argument makes sense cannot be answered merely through strict application of formal evidentiary rules such as admissibility, credibility and weight. Plausibility, rather, is woven from social and cultural perceptions of prototypical narratives, the socially constructed identity of narrators and of listeners, the interaction between these parties and the emotions that accompany or are absent from a story's telling. The chapters of this book explore different facets of plausibility. This thematic division serves the convenience of analysis, but readers can easily trace how intertwined these facets are.

These elements take shape within specific cultural and social circumstances, reflecting the operation of culture as a shared system of meaning.[1] Yet this meaning is not monolithic and static. It is shaped in the course of social interaction, it motivates and shapes social action and it can be debated and negotiated.

[1] On the definition of culture as a shared system of meaning, see Clifford Geertz, *The Interpretation of Cultures: Selected Essays* (New York: Basic Books, 1973), 5, 144–145.

Nafiseh's story of having been assaulted by her neighbour while she slept on the roof (see the introduction chapter) was met with judicial disbelief despite ample corroborating evidence (both physical and testimonial). Her story was deemed implausible by Judge Curry, who reasoned that although such a story was not impossible, it was 'strange'. It did not make sense to him that a man would show up at the house of his female neighbour in the middle of the night unless he had been encouraged to do so.[2] The case demonstrates some of the central traits of plausibility as it pertains to crime stories told in court. One is its opaqueness. Judge Curry explicitly stated that Nafiseh's story was 'strange', but he did not spell out why. The factors that rendered her story implausible to him (possibly his or Nafiseh's gender, ethnicity and socio-economic status or British views of Arab sexual norms) remained obscure, perhaps even to him. Second, the case illustrates that plausibility is a product of cultural interpretation and, thus, that social players who do not share the same system of meaning may disagree about what makes sense. Judge Curry's interpretation of what made sense clearly diverged from that of Nafiseh and her relatives. Third, the case shows that a plausible crime story may differ from one constructed through strict application of formal evidentiary rules and it may be inconsistent with the evidence on record. Judge Curry concluded that Nafiseh's story was implausible despite sufficient evidence to support the charges against her neighbour. Attention to these aspects of plausibility and the way they interconnect can enhance understanding of the process of proof.

The plausibility of a certain crime story derives, to a large extent, from the nature of the knowledge in which the story is grounded and from social and cultural perceptions of how the world operates. A cluster of hidden assumptions forms a system of tacit cultural knowledge that seems obvious to actors who share it while remaining obscure to actors outside the system. No explanation or articulation is necessary to support the conclusions that rest upon such shared assumptions within a given cultural framework. Their opaqueness renders the elements of plausibility potent in a number of ways.

Actors' unawareness of the hidden dimensions of plausibility makes certain stories appear natural and obvious. This is especially true when these hidden elements are embedded in formal procedures and evidentiary techniques (e.g. the British demand for corroborative evidence, which in practice incorporated doubt toward 'suspicious' categories of witnesses). The use of formal rules creates a facade of explicit, transparent and objective fact finding. Yet underlying the process of proof is a tacit understanding of how the world operates, and it may inform the finding of facts and judicial determination of admissibility, competence, credibility, weight and sufficiency in an uninformed or indirect way. The audience hearing the stories that are told inside and outside

[2] See the judgment given 16 December 1944, ISA/RG 30/Law 2036 (original docket # Cr.C 208/44).

the courtroom may not be aware of the elements that motivate them to accept these stories as convincing and plausible.

Such lack of awareness may be due in part to the role of emotions in establishing plausibility. Emotions play a significant part in legal reasoning, the conduct of legal actors and the operation of the justice system.[3] Nevertheless, their importance is often overlooked, and they are typically regarded as antithetical to analytical reasoning. The non-verbal character of emotional sensations and expressions gives them the appearance of natural instincts, even though they are subject to considerable social construction. Recent academic scholarship calls for the study of emotions as part of a cultural and social context in which they are expressed and given meaning.[4] Such an endeavour can benefit from extralegal sources of information that provide insight into the emotional worlds of legal actors.[5] Sources that relate to the display of emotion outside the courthouse can improve understanding of the process of proof by helping to elucidate which emotions are restrained in court and which inhibit the filing of official complaints, thus preventing some cases from even reaching the proof stage.

A plausibility perspective provides a useful analytical frame for the study of law and emotions. Emotional displays and their absence can both be sources of insight.[6] If victims of rape are expected to demonstrate anguish, then a calm reaction might render a complainant unbelievable. In my study of emotion, I used both legal and extralegal sources. In addition, I interpreted the meanings of silence and the emotions it conveyed. Articles in the Hebrew press and the actions of paramilitary organizations to avenge inter-ethnic rape expressed considerable anger. These extrajudicial registers shed light on emotions that are difficult to detect in court files but that significantly informed local views of inter-ethnic rape. A victim's silence or refusal to file a complaint thus might express an emotion such as shame, a possibility that must be considered when attempting to understand the social meaning of rape and which stories about rape make sense.

The chapters in this book reveal that telling a convincing story depends on the interface of the various elements that create plausibility. The complex way the elements of plausibility interweave differs in each individual case. Thus, as exemplified in the rape case of Rachel from Kibbutz Eilon (Chapter 4), a woman's trustworthiness could be assessed differently depending on whether she testified about rape or robbery.[7] Another example of this variable interweaving pertains to the plausibility of child witnesses. The identity of the

[3] Merridee L. Bailey and Kimberley-Joy Knight, 'Writing Histories of Law and Emotion', *The Journal of Legal History* 38, no. 2 (2017): 125.

[4] Laura Kounine, 'Emotions, Mind, and Body on Trial: A Cross-Cultural Perspective', *Journal of Social History* (2017): 9.

[5] Bailey and Knight, 125. [6] Kounine, 7.

[7] Deborah Tuerkheimer, 'Incredible Women: Sexual Violence and the Credibility Discount', *University of Pennsylvania Law Review* 166, no. 1 (2017): 13.

narrator as a native child affected the rhetorical merit of his or her testimony as perceived by the judges, yet other elements of identity, such as ethnicity, could also influence the plausibility of the story. The power of a child witness to convince rested in part on the consistency of the narrative with prevalent cultural scripts about sexual assault of children. In addition, the suspicion toward children's testimony was, in practice, rooted in the formal evidentiary rule that required corroboration. The diverse manifestations of the complex intersectionality of the elements of plausibility may offer an additional explanation for the opacity of the mechanism. It is hard to pinpoint a phenomenon with multiple, highly context-bound manifestations.

The rhetorical achievement of telling a plausible story derives not only from the content of the story and related statements but also from contextual circumstances. The meaning of rape and sodomy stories is rooted in the surrounding culture. When courts inquire whether a story is a convincing one, the verbal content of the testimony in terms of its internal coherence and consistency with other evidence often takes centre stage. The cultural circumstances that determine the plausibility of the story tend to stay in the background and are often left unverbalized, given their obvious nature to the players in a given social setting. Within a given system of meaning, the invisibility of the implicit elements of plausibility reinforces their ability to convince. Remaining unarticulated, the elements of plausibility escape scrutiny and doubt.

What characterizes plausibility is thus both opaque and context bound. Therefore, a study that aims to reveal what crime stories make sense focuses on actual practices and discourse rather than on the letter of the law. Such a study delves into the gap between the formal legal plane and that of the law 'in action' and calls attention to the socially and culturally embedded character of the law. It highlights values and cultural dispositions that are disguised within what seems to be the neutral, objective and technical application of legal rules. Such an approach is open to examining diverse and even conflicting cultural influences.

In Mandate Palestine, for example, a wide gap existed between the declared goal of protecting children and actual practices in cases of sexual crimes involving children. Consequently, the plausibility of crime stories told by children in court was questioned, diminishing the chances of obtaining convictions based on their testimony. The substantive criminal prohibitions of rape and sodomy explicitly aimed to protect children and purportedly facilitated proof when the victims were under sixteen years of age, thus making it unnecessary to prove the use of force. However, cultural notions of children's qualified plausibility were embedded in other evidentiary and procedural mechanisms. These included the precondition of oath, which often resulted in children's unsworn (and therefore less valuable) testimony, medical opinions about children's sexual past that cast doubt on their accounts, the willingness to charge children with perjury and a strict demand for corroboration. A parallel gap existed in Mandate Palestine between the explicit legislative claim of protecting children and the actual reality of child employment, girls' servitude and child brides.[8] This gap, grounded in the British ambition to legitimize their rule and in their self-perception as bearers of progress,[9] also characterized the protection of children from sexual offences.

Furthermore, despite exact numerical specification of the age of consent (sixteen), the narratives that unfolded in court revealed an ambiguous image of children – as both pure and sexual, innocent and blameable, unable to give consent and tempting, passive victims and active agents. This ambiguity implied a hazy distinction between 'child' and native 'adult', a distinction that went beyond child testimony in court. The colonial approach likened 'natives' to children, and therefore the use of 'child' as a historical category is helpful in exposing colonial attitudes toward natives in general. Children were perceived as immature, inept and in need of supervision (as the analysis of the plausibility of their stories demonstrates), and they therefore quintessentially epitomized the cultural role of the native.

Another major gap existed between explicit statutory goals and perceptions of plausible scenarios of male-to-male sex that shaped the enforcement and process of proof 'in action'. The British claimed to adopt criminal prohibitions that would improve the standards of moral hygiene in Palestine, a country entrusted to their care by international charter. They laid out various prohibitions regulating prostitution, outlawed sexual contact between males, even if consensual, and specified severe punishments for these offences. Nevertheless, the stories that unfolded in court seem to reflect other views. The official British rhetoric condemning male-to-male sex, for instance, encountered local perception of male sex as stratified interaction, in which a socially better positioned older man penetrated a younger, less privileged one, often in exchange for payment. The practice of enforcement was relatively lenient. Unlike their counterparts in England, the authorities of Palestine did not initiate raids or crackdowns on sites of homosexual activity, and the few cases of consensual male sex that were eventually brought to trial were thrust upon the police, either through a complaint or actual discovery of a male couple having sex. The explicit goal of criminalizing and rooting out sexual relationships between males was compromised by scenarios about male sex in Palestine that were considered plausible by both British rulers and locals.

The relatively tolerant colonial attitude toward consensual male sex may have rested on several grounds. First, the stratified local view of male sex was congruent with the British penetrator–penetrated dichotomy engrained in the wording of the criminal code. Second, the local status-based perception of male-to-male sex was less threatening to masculinity than the view of

[8] Assaf Likhovski, *Law and Identity in Mandate Palestine*, ed. Thomas A. Green and Hendrik Hartog, Studies in Legal History (Chapel Hill: University of North Carolina Press, 2006), 84–105.

[9] Ibid., 104–105.

homoerotic desire as gender transformative (i.e. as exposing the woman from within). A penetrator's masculinity remained intact, whether his partner was a female or a young male. The penetrated man, even a 'habitual' one, did not necessarily become effeminized. The local experience of male-to-male sex was not as disruptive to the institution of the heteronormative family as a model of same-sex partnership based on romantic love or mutual desire. Third, the colonial context mitigated the threat posed to British identity by male passion. Male–male sex was the 'habit' of Eastern locals, who were not expected to share British moral standards and sensitivities. Fourth, the British view of prostitution possibly informed their relatively temperate attitude toward male sex when payment was involved (which was often the case).

The scope of prostitution in general and youth prostitution in particular broadened with the presence of British troops in Palestine.[10] Academic research on prostitution in Mandate Palestine has focused on female prostitution.[11] My findings demonstrate that prostitution involving young men was not rare and that it ranged from occasional sexual contacts for money to institutionalized sex work in brothels. Prostitution was often used in legal proceedings as a mitigating factor, to justify lesser charges (unnatural offences rather than sodomy) or more lenient punishments (as in the case of Abdalla from Acre, discussed in Chapter 2, who not only engaged in male-to-male sex but also transgressed gender norms and employed female prostitutes in his brothel). Prostitution was acknowledged by the British authorities as an unavoidable reality. To mitigate the harm it did and out of concern for the health and safety of their troops in Mandate Palestine, the authorities adopted administrative and criminal prohibitions that regulated the operation of brothels.[12] Prostitution itself was never criminalized by the British in Palestine. Criminal prohibitions targeted incidental activities such as the operation of brothels, solicitation, living on the earnings of prostitutes and so

[10] Especially in the aftermath of the First World War and during the Second World War. Margalit Shilo, 'Women as Victims of War: The British Conquest (1917) and the Blight of Prostitution in the Holy City', *Nashim: A Journal of Jewish Women's Studies & Gender Issues*, no. 6 (2003): 73; Tammy Razi, '"My Daughter Burns Like Fire": Mothers and Daughters in Tel Aviv During the 1930s and 1940s', in *Gender in Israel: New Studies on Gender in the Yishuv and State*, ed. Margalit Shilo and Gideon Katz (Sde Boker: Ben Gurion University, Ben Gurion Research Institute, 2011), 147.

[11] Deborah Bernstein, 'Gender, Nationalism and Colonial Policy: Prostitution in the Jewish Settlement of Mandate Palestine, 1918–1948', *Women's History Review* 21, no. 1 (2012); *Women on the Margins: Gender and Nationalism in Mandate Tel Aviv* [in Hebrew] (Jerusalem: Yad Izhak Ben Zvi, 2008), 172–207; Tammy Razi, *Forsaken Children: The Backyard of Mandate Tel Aviv* [in Hebrew] (Tel Aviv: Am Oved, 2009), 238–239, 254–268, 289.

[12] Shilo, 73; Bernstein, *Women on the Margins: Gender and Nationalism in Mandate Tel Aviv*, 218–230. On 27 June 1928, in the early days of the British occupation, the Occupied Enemy Territories Authority set forth an ordinance regulating the operation of brothels and the behaviour of prostitutes. The ordinance delimited zones in which the operation of brothels was allowed. The ordinance was repealed three years later, but the lenient policy remained in effect, possibly because policemen were among the clients. Razi, *Forsaken Children: The Backyard of Mandate Tel-Aviv*, 262.

on.[13] This practical approach toward prostitution, both male and female, must have compromised British ardour for combating male-to-male sex.

Enforcement and proof were also influenced and undermined by rape myths, which constitute a category of plausible stories. While laws against unnatural offences were not enforced with zeal, prosecution of sodomy was relatively common. Although sodomy aimed to criminalize non-consensual male sex, the criminal prohibition was most commonly enforced in cases of child victims, for which lack of consent was not an element of the crime. This pattern alludes to a rape myth underpinning the law's enforcement: that it is practically impossible to rape an adult man. The myth of the impossibility of male rape was manifested in different ways, such as scrutiny of the victim's sexual past and his subjection to medical examination. Past involvement in male sex cast blame on the victim, insinuating some level of cooperation in the act. Medical conclusions as to whether a child victim was a 'habitual sodomist' were drawn, despite the lack of need to prove the use of force. The receipt of payment from the penetrator could also cast blame on the penetrated, regardless of age. It implied consent and negated the use of force.

Plausibility is founded on extrajudicial cultural knowledge. This may account for the persistence of rape myths and the failure of evidentiary reforms related to the offence of rape.[14] In addition, the stories told in court are just the tip of the iceberg, as most sexual assaults do not reach litigation. Stories that are deemed implausible by police investigators or prosecutors stand less chance of reaching the courthouse.[15] This may reflect police investigators' or prosecutors' own scepticism or their anticipation of defence arguments, jurors' assessments or the low probability of getting a guilty verdict.[16]

The ethnically, socially, nationally and religiously diverse social players in Mandate Palestine told each other stories about sexual assaults during legal proceedings as well as outside the courthouse, both within their own social milieu and to members of other groups. The meanings of these stories were the product of complex social dynamics, interaction and negotiation. The negotiation of meaning within the courthouse is formalized and ritualized. Witnesses and lawyers attempt to construct meanings that will serve their interests and at the same time appeal to judges. Judges explicate meanings that will satisfy the parties to proceedings, the public and the instance of appeal. Stories that are told outside the court, whether by the press or among friends,

[13] For the relevant criminal prohibitions, see CCO §§ 161–174 in the Appendix.

[14] Tuerkheimer, 27. For discussion of the failure to implement rape reforms, see Gregory M. Matoesian, *Law and the Language of Identity Discourse in the William Kennedy Smith Rape Trial* (Oxford: Oxford University Press, 2001); Andrew E. Taslitz, *Rape and the Culture of the Courtroom* (New York: New York University Press, 1999); Stephen J. Schulhofer, *Unwanted Sex: The Culture of Intimidation and the Failure of Law* (Cambridge, MA: Harvard University Press, 1998), 17–46.

[15] Tuerkheimer, 28–41.

[16] Lisa Frohmann, 'Convictability and Discordant Locales: Reproducing Race, Class, and Gender Ideologies in Prosecutorial Decisionmaking', *Law & Society Review* 31, no. 3 (1997): 531, 536.

also create and reproduce shared meanings. The purpose of telling stories about sex offences, as I have demonstrated in this book, is not merely to prove guilt or innocence but also to construct identity, maintain social boundaries and reproduce social hierarchies.

Criminal files provide a rich portrait of the lives of the inhabitants of Mandate Palestine, of humble social actors who happened to be involved in criminal cases, whether as perpetrators, victims or witnesses, of rural and urban life, of relationships between actors and communities and of contemporary dispositions and beliefs. One notable recurrent theme in both legal documents and other archival sources is the relationship between and the boundaries demarcating the Jewish and Arab communities. The materials I examined reflect tense inter-ethnic situations. Hebrew newspapers, for instance, warned against Arab rapists and reported on paramilitary resistance organizations that avenged the rape of Jewish women by Arab men. Arab defendants expressed awareness of the nationalistic implications of inter-ethnic rape. Nonetheless, the documentary evidence also reflects various meeting points between the Jewish and Arab collectives in Palestine, areas of neighbourly relations, professional coexistence and social ties.

The degree of separation between Arab and Jewish communities in Mandate Palestine has been debated by historians and sociologists. During the late 1970s, Israeli sociologist Dan Horowitz and political scientist Moshe Lissak coined the term 'dual society' in referring to the high degree of separation between Jewish and Arab communities.[17] Their model envisioned two communities living in separate social, cultural and economic spheres, with distinct systems of stratification, income and political representation, separate educational systems and different international allegiances. Separation was also physical, manifested in enclave neighbourhoods, even within mixed cities.[18] An alternative model that emerged in the literature in the 1980s framed the relationship between Arabs and Jews in Mandate Palestine as colonizing, with the latter dominating the former. Under this model, the two communities do not reside 'side by side', but rather one held a monopoly on power and possessed disproportionately greater resources. This model retains the view of segregated groups but situates them hierarchically. A third model, which also emerged in the 1980s, focused on everyday life rather than military and political conflict and emphasized personal and social connections and the common social ground Jews and Arabs shared vis-à-vis their British rulers.[19]

[17] Dan Horowitz and Moshe Lissak, *Origins of the Israeli Polity: Palestine under the Mandate*, ed. Moshe Lissak, trans. Charles Hoffman (Chicago: University of Chicago Press, 1978).

[18] Aviva Halamish, 'Mandatory Palestine: A Dual Society or Colonial Reality?' [in Hebrew], *Zmanim*, no. 92 (2005).

[19] For an outstanding example of a study of the multiple connections between Jews and Arabs, see Menachem Klein, *Lives in Common: Arabs and Jews in Jerusalem, Jaffa and Hebron*, trans. Haim Watzman (London: Hurst & Company, 2014).

On the basis of occurrences documented in primary sources, I argue that whether one views Mandate-era Jewish and Arab communities as separated or connected depends on the aspect of life under study and that separation or connection was also a matter of degree, depending on social circumstances. Sexuality, for example, was for both groups a well-guarded sphere, whereas boundaries around other areas of life, such as work and residence, were often thinner and more porous.

With respect to sexuality, the criminal files and contemporary press accounts demonstrate active and deliberate constitution of boundaries between the Jewish and Arab communities in Palestine. For example, the Hebrew press issued both explicit and implied warnings against the sexual dangerousness of Arabs, and Jewish men engaged in violent reprisals against Arab men accused of raping Jewish women. There are numerous indications that many social players, both Arabs and Jews, did not view those outside their communities as legitimate partners for sex. This is true even with respect to non-consensual sex. Sexual offences were most commonly committed within the bounds of the community; inter-ethnic offences were exceptional aberrations.

Perhaps the most striking finding of my investigation of ethnicity and sexual offences is the absence of any material suggesting that rape was part of the conventional warfare repertoire of the Jewish-Arab national conflict. Throughout its history, the Israeli-Palestinian conflict has often been violent, with the two neighbouring groups fighting over one small territory. One might expect to encounter in this history of violence a systematic use of military and paramilitary rape. Yet there is no evidence that either side has ever endorsed rape as a tactic, and there is little documented evidence of sexual offences having resulted as a 'side effect' of the friction between military forces and civilians.[20] This is not to say that there have been no inter-ethnic rapes. Such incidents, however, have mostly been 'ordinary' criminal sexual assaults rather than combat-related or military-orchestrated crimes. The rarity of rape as a standard warfare measure in the Israeli-Palestinian conflict seems to have roots in the Mandate period. Did the geographical proximity and resemblance

[20] Incidents have occurred, but historians disagree about how widespread they have been. Allegations often rely on hearsay and are unsubstantiated by direct evidence. Hillel Cohen reviews contradictory statements about the rape of Jewish women by Arabs during the 1929 disturbances in Hebron and concludes that the only official documentation of such incidents is the testimony of the Hebron police commander, Raymond Cafferata, who shot an Arab policeman whom he had seen standing over a bloody woman and holding a dagger. Another famous incident on which historians diverge is the rape of Arab women during the conquest of Dayr Yasin in 1949. For more on these and other reports, see Cynthia Cockburn, *The Space between Us: Negotiating Gender and National Identities in Conflict* (London: Zed Books, 1998), 128; Nur al-Din Masalha, *The Palestine Nakba: Decolonising History, Narrating the Subaltern, Reclaiming Memory* (London: Zed, 2012), 82–83; Tal Nitzan, '"Controlled Occupation": The Rarity of Military Rape in the Israeli Palestinian Conflict' (MA thesis, The Hebrew University, 2006), 23–25; Hillel Cohen, *1929: Year Zero of the Jewish-Arab Conflict* (Jerusalem: Keter, 2013), 199–200.

between the two Semitic nations render inter-ethnic rape an illegitimate military tool?

The rarity of systematic rape in military contexts does not mean, however, that sexual offences committed in non-military contexts lack a national and ethnic dimension. Quite the opposite. As I have argued in this book, ethnic and national identity is negotiated and interpreted in civilian criminal cases of both inter-ethnic and intra-ethnic sexual assaults.

Stories of voluntary inter-ethnic sex were plausible only when located at the social fringes of the two communities. Prostitution is a case in point. In Abdalla's shabby brothel in Acre, both Jewish and Arab prostitutes served an ethnically mixed clientele (Chapter 2). Another plausible inter-ethnic sexual meeting point emerged in narratives about 'fallen women'.[21] Even the stories of Margalit from Haifa and Yaffa from Hadera (Chapter 7), the Jewish teenagers who had supposedly voluntary romantic liaisons (at least initially) with young Arab men, adhere to this pattern. Rape in these instances is described, in retrospect, as the tragic, predestined end of wayward teenagers from dysfunctional families.

Some areas of life were less segregated, and vignettes from the criminal files reveal areas of interaction. Jewish Yehodit, the mother of Arie, was a maid for the household of the Arab man accused of molesting her young son Arie (Chapter 3).[22] Another accused Arab sex offender, seventeen-year-old Sharif, was employed by Jewish Musa Goldenberg in Hadera.[23] Twelve-year-old Victor, a Jewish boy from Safad, worked in an Arab-owned blacksmith shop and had contact with Arab boys.[24] Arab Issat brought bread to Yaffa's Jewish family twice a day (Chapter 7).[25] Arab Mohammad and Jewish Ishaq were neighbours for about four years before Mohammad sodomized Ishaq.[26] The incident happened after Ishaq accepted Mohammad's invitation to go out with him. Arabs and Jews interacted with each other in various situations, but sexual relations between them were taboo and occurred mainly along the social fringes, as reflected in prostitution and in instances of rebellious teenage conduct.

The social embeddedness of legal proof, the dependency of stories' and statements' plausibility on extrajudicial dispositions and beliefs, necessarily invokes questions relating to justice. A plausible story may not necessarily be

21 Bernstein, *Women on the Margins: Gender and Nationalism in Mandate Tel Aviv*, 149, 155–158.

22 ISA/RG 30/Law 2050 (original docket # Cr.C 24/46).

23 He assaulted and stabbed a Jewish woman he saw at his employer's house when he went there to collect his wages. ISA Division 30 (Supreme Court Files), File B/183/34, original docket # Cr.A 19/34.

24 Victor testified that the accused, a seventeen-year-old Arab boy, visited him several times at the shop. Other Arab boys testified that Victor took a walk with another Arab youth to a nearby fortress before being sodomized by the accused. ISA/RG 30/Law 2015 (original docket # Cr.C 50/42).

25 ISA/RG 30/Law 2041 (original docket # Cr.C 32/45).

26 ISA/RG 30/Law 2043 (original docket # Cr.C 159/45).

true. A conviction based upon a plausible yet untruthful story is a wrongful one. The philosopher Karen Jones analyses epistemic injustice resulting from prejudice against the trustworthiness of certain categories of testifiers.[27] Focusing on accounts she dubs 'astonishing', Jones argues that those belonging to suspicious social categories and whose stories stray from mainstream formulae suffer double discounting, first, on account of who they are, and, second, on account of what they have to tell.[28] As a consequence, their stories are painstakingly scrutinized for any sign of inconsistency, irrationality or untruthfulness. Yet it is unrealistic to assume that self-warnings against bias when estimating the truthfulness of a witness who belongs to a 'suspicious' social category would suffice to 'calibrate' prejudicial patterns of trust and distrust and overcome possible predisposition against narrators from that social category.[29] Witnesses, lawyers and judges can consciously attempt to convince or make sense to others and tailor what they deem to be a 'good' story. However, such attempts are not necessarily conscious or transparent, and narrators can tell stories that make sense to them without their realizing why they find them plausible. Of course, power relations are not symmetrical. Judges are social players who have the power to make decisions according to the meaning that seems plausible to them.

Evidence law is part of a broader social context. Examination of the rules set forth in law books and by judicial precedents alone cannot explain the actual operation of proof. The socio-legal history of plausibility offered in this book highlights the socially constructed nature of the supposedly neutral and technical mode of factual determination. While the multiple elements that constitute the plausibility of stories and other utterances may not always be easy to identify, aspiring to achieve that goal and thus to gain better insight into the gap between the law 'on the books' and the law 'in action' is clearly in the interest of justice. Such an understanding leaves room for claims about bias and unjust discounting of testimonies that would not be tolerated by an intrinsic doctrinal approach. Taking plausibility into account entails an acknowledgement of the way human knowledge is formed and influenced and of its limitations.

27 Tuerkheimer, 16–17; Karen Jones, 'The Politics of Credibility', in *A Mind of One's Own: Feminist Essays on Reason and Objectivity*, ed. Louise Antony and Charlotte Witt (Boulder, CO: Westview Press, 2002).

28 Ibid., 159.

29 Jones suggests adopting three rules to overcome epistemic injustice: (1) assess separately the trustworthiness of the witness and the plausibility of the story; (2) examine whether it is reasonable to distrust one's sense of the veracity of narrators belonging to suspicious social categories; (3) demand change in the level of corroborative evidence, depending on how reasonable one's confidence is in such a witness. However, the actual implementation of these rules is hard to exercise in practice, and the standard of 'reasonableness' makes it impossible to escape the social embeddedness of the assessment of the trustworthiness of witnesses. Ibid., 159, 164–165.

# List of Legal Cases

## Case Name, Year (Charges), Source

1. A.G. *v.* Georgiades and Others, 1933 (rape, sodomy, abduction), Henry Cattan's file. ISA/RG 66/M/188/33.
2. A.G. *v.* Kaiser Mikhael Daniel, 1934 (sodomy with a boy under sixteen), ISA/RG 30/Law 2043 (draft inside original docket # Cr.C 380/45).
3. A.G. *v.* Sharif Anis Amir, 1934 (attempted rape and attempted murder), ISA Division 30 (Supreme Court Files), File B/183/34 (original docket # Cr.A 19/34).
4. A.G. *v.* Adel Haj Ahmad Sara, 1934 (attempted sodomy), ISA Division 30 (Supreme Court Files), File B/183/34 (original docket # Cr.A 22/34).
5. A.G. *v.* Ibrahim el Haj Yusef el Ata, 1934 (sodomy), ISA Division 30 (Supreme Court Files), File B/183/34 (original docket # Cr.A 30/34).
6. A.G. *v.* Ali Mahmud Sukkar, 1934 (rape), ISA Division 30 (Supreme Court Files), File B/183/34 (original docket # Cr.A 31/34).
7. A.G. *v.* Mas'ud Khalil Mansour, Deeb Ibrahim Mansour, Abed Khalil Mansour, 1934 (rape – intercourse with a girl under sixteen), ISA Division 30 (Supreme Court Files), File B/186/40 (original docket # Cr.A 40/34).
8. A.G. *v.* Fusilier Hedley and Subhi Aref Faraon, 1936 (aiding to rape), Henry Cattan's file. ISA/RG 66/M/197/22.
9. A.G. *v.* Diban Ibn Ali Il Assad of Abssiyya, 1937 (rape), ISA/RG 30/Law 2002 (original docket # Cr.C 21/37).
10. A.G. *v.* Anis Mohammad Ilyyan, 1937 (rape – intercourse with a girl under sixteen), ISA/RG 30/Law 2003 (original docket # Cr.C 152/37).
11. A.G. *v.* Saleh Abdallah Ikhbian, 1937 (rape – intercourse with a girl under sixteen), ISA/RG 30/Law 2004 (original docket # Cr.C 259/37).
12. A.G. *v.* Ahmed Nimer Said el Nijem, 1937 (attempted rape – intercourse with a girl under sixteen), ISA/RG 30/Law 2024 (original docket # Cr.C 272/37).
13. A.G. *v.* Shafiq George Halaby, 1938 (attempted rape) ISA/RG 30/Law 268 + Henry Cattan's file. ISA/RG 66/M/196/37 (original docket # Cr.A 54/38).

14. A.G. *v.* Mohammad Abdul Ghani el Yusef, 1938 (sodomy – a boy under sixteen), ISA Division 30 (Supreme Court Files), File B/269/71 (original docket # Cr.A 71/38).
15. A.G. *v.* Mahmoud Odeh Esh Sheikh Khalil, 1938 (rape – intercourse with a girl under sixteen and sodomy), ISA Division 30 (Supreme Court Files), File B/269/79 (original docket # Cr.A 79/38).
16. A.G. *v.* Sa'ado Mahmoud Abu Salem, 1939 (two counts of sodomy – a boy under sixteen), ISA/RG 30/Law 2006 (original docket # Cr.C 59/39).
17. A.G. *v.* Shmuel Abraham Taksir, 1939 (attempted rape – a girl under sixteen), ISA/RG 30/Law 2006 (original docket #Cr.C 127/39).
18. A.G. *v.* Muhammad Huseiny, 1939 (sodomy – a boy under sixteen), ISA/RG 30/Law 2007 (original docket # 131/39).
19. A.G. *v.* Khadar Abdul Razek Abdul Aziz and Said Mohd. Haikal, 1939 (attempted sodomy), ISA/RG 30/Law 2007 (original docket # 137/39).
20. A.G. *v.* George Salim Bakouri, 1939 (152 (a, c) sexual intercourse and attempt to forcible rape), ISA/RG 30/Law 2032 (original docket # Cr.C 78/44).
21. A.G. *v.* Khalil Hamed Muhammad ash-Shatta, 1940 (rape – a girl under sixteen), ISA/RG 30/Law 2008 (original docket # Cr.C 134/40).
22. A.G. *v.* Mansour Sulaiman Brakh, 1940 (rape – a girl under sixteen), ISA/RG 30/Law 2008 (original docket # Cr.C 135/40).
23. A.G. *v.* Husein Salim abu en Neel, 1940 (sodomy – a boy under sixteen), ISA/RG 30/Law 2009 (original docket # Cr.C 147/40).
24. A.G. *v.* Mustafa Eissa El Sharif, 1940 (attempted rape and entering upon property to commit an offence), ISA/RG 30/Law 2009 (original docket # Cr.C 149/40).
25. A.G. *v.* Suleiman el Haj Husein Ibrahim el Qut and Raja Mohammad Eid, 1940 (attempted sodomy – a boy under sixteen), ISA/RG 30/Law 2009 (original docket # Cr.C 168/40).
26. A.G. *v.* Subhi Ibn Lutof Cotran (aka Dallou'ah), 1940 (attempted rape – a girl under sixteen), ISA/RG 30/Law 2009 (original docket # Cr.C 170/40).
27. A.G. *v.* Charles Keys, Edwin Passmore, 1940 (indecent act by force and assault), ISA/RG 30/Law 2009 (original docket # Cr.C 173/40).
28. A.G. *v.* Yousef Ahmad Eissa, 1940 (rape – a girl under sixteen), ISA/RG 30/Law 2010 (original docket # Cr.C 187/40).
29. A.G. *v.* Hasan Oqlah Qawash, 1940 (attempted sodomy – a boy under sixteen), ISA/RG 30/Law 2010 (original docket # Cr.C 194/40).
30. A.G. *v.* Rashid Ibrahim ad Dreakh, 1940 (sodomy – a boy under sixteen), ISA/RG 30/Law 2010 (original docket # Cr.C 195/40).
31. A.G. *v.* Rashid Hamed Awadeh, 1940 (sodomy – a boy under sixteen), ISA/RG 30/Law 2010 (original docket # Cr.C 198/40).
32. A.G. *v.* Ahmad Attallah Ismail, 1940 (rape by deception), ISA/RG 30/Law 298 (original docket # Cr.A 104/40).

33. A.G. *v.* Said Okleh el Mahmoud, 1940 (attempted rape and two additional charges of entering dwelling (tent) to commit felony), ISA/RG 30/Law 2011 (original docket # Cr.C 253/40).
34. A.G. *v.* Mohammad Khneifis El Ayadet, 1940 (attempted rape), ISA/RG 30/Law 2012 (original docket # Cr.C 290/40).
35. A.G. *v.* Nayef Mohammad Hamad Abu Dakdoukah, 1941 (burglary, robbery, rape), ISA/RG 30/Law 2012 (original docket # Cr.C 298/40).
36. A.G. *v.* Hassan Mustafa El Zamel and Mahmoud Mohd. Abdul Karim, 1941 (indecent act by force), ISA/RG 30/Law 2012 (original docket # Cr. C 307/40).
37. A.G. *v.* Ahmad al Haj Isa Qaddoura, 1942 (sodomy – a boy under sixteen), ISA/RG 30/Law 2015 (original docket # Cr.C 50/42).
38. A.G. *v.* Sadek Abdullat el Kurd, 1942 (attempted rape of insane girl), ISA Division 30 (Supreme Court Files), File B/334/52 (original docket # Cr.A 52/42).
39. A.G. *v.* Shehadeh Said Fares Abu El Sakan, 1942 (sodomy – a boy under sixteen), ISA/RG 30/Law 2015 (original docket # Cr.C 66/42).
40. A.G. *v.* Ali Ahmad Kaddourah, 1942 (sodomy – a boy under sixteen), ISA/RG 30/Law 2015 (original docket # Cr.C 80/42).
41. A.G. *v.* Mohammad Hafez el Qeisi, 1942 (rape), ISA/RG 30/Law 2017 (original docket # Cr.C 117/42).
42. A.G. *v.* Muhammad Husni Abdul Qadar, 1942 (attempted rape), ISA/RG 30/Law 2017 (original docket # Cr.C 126/42).
43. A.G. *v.* Mohammad Said Muhammad Hasan, 1942 (sodomy), ISA/RG 30/Law 2017 (original docket # Cr.C 133/42).
44. A.G. *v.* Muhammad Ahmad al Qawwas, 1941 (rape – a girl under sixteen), ISA/RG 30/Law 2018 (original docket # Cr.C 150/42).
45. A.G. *v.* Mohammad Abu Zeid, 1942 (rape), ISA Division 30 (Supreme Court Files), File B/335/118 (original docket # Cr.A 118/42).
46. A.G. *v.* Salah Hussein el Khaldi, 1942 (sodomy – a boy under sixteen), ISA/RG 30/Law 2019 (original docket # Cr.C 218/42).
47. A.G. *v.* Subhi Jubran el Jubran, 1942 (sodomy – a girl under sixteen), ISA/RG 30/Law 2022 (original docket # Cr.C 444/42).
48. A.G. *v.* Ibrahim Mohammad Hussein, 1942 (attempted indecent act), ISA/RG 30/Law 2022 (original docket # Cr.C 447/42).
49. A.G. *v.* Mohammad Hassan Mislimani, 1942 (sodomy), ISA/RG 30/Law 2023 (original docket # Cr.C 471/42).
50. A.G. *v.* Mahmoud Hassan Ghattas, Elias Tomeh Salloun Hayek, 1942 (unnatural offences), ISA/RG 30/Law 2023 (original docket # Cr.C 481/42).
51. A.G. *v.* Mustafa Jamil al-Halabi, 1942 (sodomy – a boy under sixteen), ISA/RG 30/Law 2017 (original docket # Cr.C 509/42).
52. A.G. *v.* Mohammad Qasem Mabruk, 1942 (rape – a girl under sixteen) ISA/RG 30/Law 2023 (original docket # Cr.C 515/42).

53. A.G. *v.* Mustafa Ahmad Ghazal, Hanna Tannnous Hayem, 1942 (unnatural offences), ISA/RG 30/Law 2023 (original docket # Cr.C 519/42).
54. A.G. *v.* Zaki Ibn Rasheed Tabanji, 1943 (rape – a girl under sixteen), ISA/RG 30/Law 2024 (original docket # Cr.C 7/43).
55. A.G. *v.* Mohammad Ali Hassan, 1943 (sodomy – a boy under sixteen), ISA/RG 30/Law 2024 (original docket # Cr.C 8/43).
56. A.G. *v.* Khaled Ben Abd Ez-Zu'ibi, 1943 (carnal knowledge of an animal), ISA/RG 30/Law 2027 (original docket # Cr.C 131/43).
57. A.G. *v.* Malek Shaker Karam, 1943 (unnatural offences), ISA/RG 30/Law 2028 (original docket # Cr.C 140/43).
58. A.G. *v.* Mohammad Daoud Abu Wardeh, 1943 (unnatural offences), ISA/RG 30/Law 2028 (original docket # Cr.C 141/43).
59. A.G. *v.* Mohd. Mahmoud Abu Deeb and Deeb Ahmad Kassem, 1943 (sodomy), ISA/RG 30/Law 2028 (original docket # Cr.C 146/43).
60. A.G. *v.* Abdalla Mohd Shukeiri, 1943 (unnatural offences, keeping brothel, living on earnings of prostitutes), ISA/RG 30/Law 2028 (original docket # Cr.C 154/43).
61. A.G. *v.* Abdulhamid Mohd. Abdulkarim Awad, 1943 (attempted sodomy – a boy under sixteen), ISA/RG 30/Law 2028 (original docket # Cr.C 157/43).
62. A.G. *v.* Mohammad Hassan Agha, 1943 (rape – a girl under sixteen), ISA Division 30 (Supreme Court Files), File B/353/122 (original docket # Cr. A 118/42).
63. A.G. *v.* Rushdi Aref Abu Shamat, 1943 (unnatural offences), ISA/RG 30/Law 2029 (original docket # Cr.C 211/43).
64. A.G. *v.* Shehadi Moh'd Hussein Zeitouni, 1943 (rape), ISA/RG 30/Law 2029 (original docket # Cr.C 214/43).
65. A.G. *v.* Mustafa Abed Zahran, 1943 (sodomy – a boy under sixteen), ISA/RG 30/Law 2029 (original docket # Cr.C 221/43).
66. A.G. *v.* Mohd. Subhi el Sunji, 1943 (perjury), ISA/RG 30/Law 2029 (original docket # Cr.C 221/43).
67. A.G. *v.* Mustafa Naif, 1943 (perjury), ISA/RG 30/Law 2029 (original docket # Cr.C 222/43).
68. A.G. *v.* Zaki Mahmoud Ka'aty, 1943 (sodomy – a boy under sixteen), ISA/RG 30/Law 2029 (original docket # Cr.C 225/43).
69. A.G. *v.* Elias Jad Hawa and Mohamad Ameen Sarhan, 1943 (unnatural offences), ISA/RG 30/Law 2030 (original docket # Cr.C 227/43).
70. A.G. *v.* Mohammad Said Serouji and Hassan Ali Kharbutly, 1943 (unnatural offences), ISA/RG 30/Law 2030 (original docket # Cr.C 230/43).
71. A.G. *v.* Ali Hadi, 1943 (rape – a girl under sixteen), ISA/RG 30/Law 2030 (original docket # Cr.C 236/43).
72. A.G. *v.* Mohammad Said Ajal, 1943 (sodomy – a boy under sixteen), ISA/RG 30/Law 2030 (original docket # Cr.C 252/43).

73. A.G. *v.* Muhammad Suleiman Mutalibeh, 1943 (attempted rape), ISA/RG 30/Law 2030 (original docket # Cr.C 257/43).
74. A.G. *v.* Khalil Ibrahim Sharkawi, 1944 (rape – a girl under sixteen), ISA/RG 30/Law 2031 (original docket # Cr.C 4/44).
75. A.G. *v.* M'aruf Rashid Hanqir, 1944 (sodomy – a boy under sixteen), ISA/RG 30/Law 2032 (original docket # Cr.C 50/44).
76. A.G. *v.* Zafer Sa'id Ahmad, 1944 (sodomy – a boy under sixteen), ISA/RG 30/Law 2032 (original docket # Cr.C 76/44).
77. A.G. *v.* Ahmed Ali Mohammad, 1944 (rape), ISA/RG 30/Law 2032 (original docket # Cr.C 78/44).
78. A.G. *v.* Fawzi Jarwas el Asali, 1944 (sodomy – a boy under sixteen), ISA/RG 30/Law 2033 (original docket # Cr.C 85/44).
79. A.G. *v.* Ali Abdul Rahimn Ibrahim, 1944 (attempted indecent act), ISA/RG 30/Law 2033 (original docket # Cr.C 88/44).
80. A.G. *v.* Nader Takiy Iddin Afaft, 1944 (sodomy), ISA/RG 30/Law 2034 (original docket # Cr.C 156/44).
81. A.G. *v.* Strati Foto, 1944 (sodomy – a boy under sixteen), ISA Division 30 (Supreme Court Files), File B/374/151 (original docket # Cr.A 151/44).
82. A.G. *v.* Mohmad Hussein Ashmawi, 1944 (sodomy – boy under sixteen), ISA/RG 30/Law 2034 (original docket # Cr.C 154/44).
83. A.G. *v.* Ali Mohamad Kiwan, 1944 (rape – a girl under sixteen), ISA/RG 30/Law 2034 (original docket # Cr.C 159/44).
84. A.G. *v.* Youssef Cattan, 1944 (unlawful intercourse with unmarried girl 16–21), ISA Division 30 (Supreme Court Files), File B/374/143 (original docket # Cr.A 143/44).
85. A.G. *v.* Hussein Ali Musleh, 1944 (indecent act with force), ISA/RG 30/Law 2035 (original docket # Cr.C 181/44).
86. A.G. *v.* Lutfi Abdul Hamid Jawdat, 1944 (rape – a girl under sixteen), ISA/RG 30/Law 2035 (original docket # Cr.C 184/44).
87. A.G. *v.* Said Hassan Saad, 1944 (rape – a girl under sixteen), ISA/RG 30/Law 2036 (original docket # Cr.C 197/44).
88. A.G. *v.* Ahmed Mustafa Abdo, 1944 (sodomy – a boy under sixteen), ISA/RG 30/Law 2036 (original docket # Cr.C 200/44).
89. A.G. *v.* Nimer Mohd Abdul Razzek, 1944 (attempted indecent act), ISA/RG 30/Law 2036 (original docket # Cr.C 208/44).
90. A.G. *v.* Hassan Kassem Zein, 1944 (attempted rape and robbery), ISA/RG 30/Law 2036 (original docket # Cr.C 213/44).
91. A.G. *v.* Mohamad Salim Bakheet, 1944 (sodomy – a boy under sixteen), ISA/RG 30/Law 2036 (original docket # Cr.C 234/44).
92. A.G. *v.* Bannnoura Mohammad, 1944 (perjury), ISA/RG 30/Law 2037 (original docket # Cr.C 248/44).
93. A.G. *v.* Mahmoud Ahmad Mohammad, 1944 (sodomy – a boy under sixteen), ISA/RG 30/Law 2037 (original docket # Cr.C 257/44).

94. A.G. *v.* Mustafa Mohammad Haj Ali, 1944 (sodomy), ISA/RG 30/Law 2037 (original docket # Cr.C 262/44).
95. A.G. *v.* Hamdan Yusef Arrabi, 1944 (sodomy), ISA/RG 30/Law 2038 (original docket # Cr.C 286/44).
96. A.G. *v.* Abdel Rahim Ibrahim Abdul Rahim, 1944 (attempted indecent act), ISA/RG 30/Law 2039 (original docket # Cr.C 315/44).
97. A.G. *v.* Jamil Abdallah Nuri, 1944 (sodomy – a girl under sixteen), ISA/RG 30/Law 2039 (original docket # Cr.C 325/44).
98. A.G. *v.* Issat Amin, 1945 (rape – a girl under sixteen), ISA/RG 30/Law 2041 (original docket # Cr.C 32/45).
99. A.G. *v.* Ibrahim Abdul Kerim Shatila, 1945 (sodomy – a boy under sixteen), ISA/RG 30/Law 2043 (original docket # Cr.C 92/45).
100. A.G. *v.* Aref Ben Ahmad Esh Sharida, 1945 (attempted rape, attempted indecent act), ISA/RG 30/Law 2043 (original docket # Cr.C 104/45).
101. A.G. *v.* Zeinab Ayoub, 1945 (perjury), ISA/RG 30/Law 2043 (original docket # Cr.C 111/45).
102. A.G. *v.* Suleiman Ahmed, 1945 (indecent act with force – a girl under sixteen), ISA/RG 30/Law 2045 (original docket # Cr.C 156/45).
103. A.G. *v.* Mohamad Salim Tahhan, 1945 (sodomy and wounding), ISA/RG 30/Law 2043 (original docket # Cr.C 159/45).
104. A.G. *v.* Mohammad Suleiman el Matalibi, 1945 (attempted rape and indecent act), ISA/RG 30/Law 2045 (original docket # Cr.C 167/45).
105. A.G. *v.* Fawzi Taher, 1945 (indecent act with force), ISA/RG 30/Law 2046 (original docket # Cr.C 206/45).
106. A.G. *v.* Mohammad Nazal Khalil, 1945 (attempted unnatural offences), ISA/RG 30/Law 2046 (original docket # Cr.C 211/45).
107. A.G. *v.* Sa'do Mahmoud Abu Salem, 1945 (sodomy – a boy under sixteen), ISA/RG 30/Law 2047 (original docket # Cr.C 264/45).
108. A.G. *v.* Hassan Mohammad Hassan, 1945 (indecent act with force), ISA/RG 30/Law 2047 (original docket # Cr.C 283/45).
109. A.G. *v.* Hussein Ali Mahmoud el Juma'a, 1945 (attempted rape), ISA/RG 30/Law 2047 (original docket # Cr.C 284/45).
110. A.G. *v.* Hassan Hussein Salem, 1945 (rape – a girl under sixteen), ISA/RG 30/Law 2048 (original docket # Cr.C 307/45).
111. A.G. *v.* Emil Naddi and Munjid Faris, 1945 (rape), ISA/RG 30/Law 2048 (original docket # Cr.C 320/45).
112. A.G. *v.* Yacoub Shukri Lapajian, 1945 (attempted rape), ISA/RG 30/Law 2049 (original docket # Cr.C 343/45).
113. A.G. *v.* Ali Darwish, 1945 (attempted rape), ISA/RG 30/Law 2049 (original docket # Cr.C 380/45).
114. A.G. *v.* Mustafa Qassem Es Sayed, 1946 (indecent act committed upon child), ISA/RG 30/Law 2050 (original docket # Cr.C 24/46).

115. A.G. *v.* Khaled Ahmad Sa'd El-Din (Abu Ahmad El-Shawish), 1946 (attempted sodomy – a boy under sixteen), ISA/RG 30/Law 2051 (original docket # Cr.C 64/46).
116. A.G. *v.* Mahmoud Darwish Habush, 1946 (perjury), ISA/RG 30/Law 2051 (original docket # Cr.C 65/46).
117. A.G. *v.* Mohammad Abdul Fattah El-Moghraby, 1946 (perjury), ISA/RG 30/Law 2051 (original docket # Cr.C 66/46).
118. A.G. *v.* Ali Saleh Muhamad El Ali, 1946 (rape, abduction and manslaughter), ISA/RG 30/Law 2053 (original docket # Cr.C 120/46).
119. A.G. *v.* Hassan Atieh Abu Ismeili, 1946, 152(1)(c) (intercourse with a girl under sixteen), ISA/RG 30/Law 2053 (original docket # Cr.C 139/46).
120. A.G. *v.* Hassan Khaizaran, 1946 (sodomy – a boy under sixteen), ISA/RG 30/Law 2054 (original docket # Cr.C 155/46).
121. A.G. *v.* Mahmud el Jubein, 1946 (attempted sodomy – a boy under sixteen), ISA/RG 30/Law 2054 (original docket # Cr.C 175/46).
122. A.G. *v.* Muhammad Ibrahim Abdul Rahman, 1946 (sodomy – a boy under sixteen and carrying dagger), ISA/RG 30/Law 2055 (original docket # Cr.C 181/46).
123. A.G. *v.* Mahmud Saleh Bushnak, 1946 (sodomy and theft 270), ISA/RG 30/Law 2055 (original docket # Cr.C 183/46).
124. A.G. *v.* Muhammad El-Haj Mahmud Makkawi, 1946 (perjury), ISA/RG 30/Law 2055 (original docket # Cr.C 184/46).
125. A.G. *v.* Hassan Musbah Johara, 1946 (attempted sodomy and wounding), ISA/RG 3/M/713/14 (original docket # Cr.C 202/46).
126. A.G. *v.* Husni Yousef Hassan, 1946 (attempted sodomy), ISA/RG 30/Law 2057 (original docket # Cr.C 253/46).
127. A.G. *v.* Akel Mohammad Mustafa, Fares Kassem Mohammad el Fares, Abd el Haj, 1946 (sodomy), ISA/RG 30/Law 2057 (original docket # Cr.C 261/46).
128. A.G. *v.* Ali Ramadan Mubarak, 1946 (sodomy and attempted sodomy), ISA/RG 30/Law 2057 (original docket # Cr.C 275/46).
129. A.G. *v.* Yousef Mordokhai Mizrahi, 1946, (sodomy – a girl under sixteen), ISA/RG 30/Law 2057 (original docket # Cr.C 276/46).
130. A.G. *v.* Fahd Jum'an el-Musa and Musa Diab Qassem el-Ahmed, 1947 (rape and robbery), ISA Division 30 (Supreme Court Files), File B/441/31 (original docket # Cr.A 31/47).
131. A.G. *v.* Khaled Issa Saffarini' Ahmad Nayif Ahmad Zarini, 1947 (robbery and attempted rape), ISA/RG 30/Law 2061 (original docket # Cr.C 124/47).
132. A.G. *v.* Manahel Hassan Habib, 1947 (perjury), ISA/RG 30/Law 2061 (original docket # Cr.C 132/47).
133. A.G. *v.* Suleiman Tewfik Abdallah Hadeed, 1947 (rape – a girl under sixteen), ISA/RG 30/Law 2061 (original docket # Cr.C 133/47).

134. A.G. *v.* Salim Hamdan Islim, 1947 (sodomy – a boy under sixteen), ISA/RG 30/Law 2062 (original docket # Cr.C 179/47).
135. A.G. *v.* Subhi Hussein el Kasem, 1947 (sodomy – a boy under sixteen), ISA/RG 30/Law 2062 (original docket # Cr.C 180/47).
136. A.G. *v.* Mahmud Hamid Ali, 1947 (rape – a girl under sixteen), ISA/RG 30/Law 2062 (original docket # Cr.C 186/47).
137. A.G. *v.* Qasem Ass'ad el-Kut, Muhammad Ibrahim el-Kut, 1947 (rape – a girl under sixteen and abduction), ISA/RG 30/Law 2063 (original docket # Cr.C 208/47).
138. A.G. *v.* Muhammad Said Abdalla Tabbara, 1947 (sodomy – a boy under sixteen), ISA/RG 30/Law 2063 (original docket # Cr.C 221/47).
139. A.G. *v.* Asa'ad Mahmud Saleh, 1947 (sodomy – a boy under sixteen), ISA/RG 30/Law 2063 (original docket # Cr.C 228/47).
140. A.G. *v.* Mustafa Yusuf Mustarahi, 1947 (attempted indecent act), ISA/RG 30/Law 2064 (original docket # Cr.C 247/47).
141. A.G. *v.* Said Asa'ad Sharqiya, Abed Asa'ad Sharqiya, 1947 (abduction and rape – a girl under sixteen), ISA/RG 30/Law 2067 (original docket # Cr.C 259/47).
142. A.G. *v.* Mohammad Mustafa Er Rifa'i, 1947 (sodomy – a boy under sixteen), ISA/RG 30/Law 2065 (original docket # Cr.C 306/47).
143. A.G. *v.* Naji Abdul Fattah Abu Isba, 1947 (sodomy), ISA/RG 30/Law 2065 (original docket # Cr.C 307/47).
144. A.G. *v.* Munir Tewfiq el Haj Ibrahim, 1947 (rape – a girl under sixteen), ISA/RG 30/Law 2065 (original docket # Cr.C 321/47).
145. A.G. *v.* Ibrahim Badi Shikho, Hassan Badi Shikho, 1947 (rape), ISA/RG 30/Law 2066 (original docket # Cr.C 331/47).
146. A.G. *v.* Khalil Abd El-Mughrabi, 1947 (sodomy – a boy under sixteen), ISA/RG 30/Law 2066 (original docket # Cr.C 355/47).
147. A.G. *v.* Wajih Salim Awas Nahfani, 1947 (rape – a girl under sixteen), ISA/RG 30/Law 2067 (original docket # Cr.C 417/47).

# Appendix
# Relevant Criminal Legislation

Models of criminal prohibitions relating to sexuality during the first half of the twentieth century:
The Ottoman Penal Code, 1913
Criminal Law Amendment Ordinance No. 2 1927
Criminal Law Amendment Ordinance No. 30 1934
Criminal Code Ordinance, 1936
The Indian Penal Code, 1860
Queensland Criminal Code Act 1899
Offences against the Person Act 1861 (24 & 25 Vict., c. 100)
Criminal Law Amendment Act 1885 (48 & 49 Vict., c. 69)

## Ottoman Penal Code, 1913[1]

### CHAPTER FIRST PART XIII

### Article 139

From the person who contrary to public morals prints or causes to be printed or publishes in verse or in prose any things relative to jest or satire or indecent pictures or images a fine of from one Mejidieh gold piece to five Mejidieh gold pieces is taken and he is imprisoned for from twenty-four hours to one week.

### CHAPTER SECOND PART II

### The Punishment Provided for Persons Causing Abortion, Selling Adulterated Drinks, or Poisons Without Surety

Article 192~~If a person becomes the cause of the miscarriage of a pregnant woman by beating her or by any other act he is after recovery of the Diyet under the sher' law placed in kyurek temporarily of this violence of his has been on purpose~~. (repealed in 1911 and replaced by a new article as follows)

The woman miscarrying her foetus by making use, or by giving her consent for the making use by another, of special means, is imprisoned for from six months to three years.

The individual causing a woman to miscarry her foetus by preparing special means with her consent, is condemned to imprisonment for from one year to three years. If as the result of such miscarriage of foetus, or in consequence of the means made use for

[1] The sections are cited from the English translation by Strachey Bucknill and Utidjian, footnotes omitted. John A. Strachey Bucknill and Haig Apisoghom S. Utidjian, eds., *The Imperial Ottoman Penal Code* (London: Oxford University Press, 1918). Repealed parts of earlier versions appear strikenthrough. For explanation about the kyurek see fn. 45 on page 26.

miscarriage, destruction of person comes about, he is put in kyurek for from four years to seven years.

If a person, without the consent of a woman of whose pregnancy he is aware brings about miscarriage by making use of special means, or by beating, wounding, or committing other acts, he is condemned to kyurek for from three years to ten years.

If as a result of such miscarriage, or in consequence of the means made use of the miscarriage the woman dies, the punishment is kyurek for not less than fifteen years.

If the individuals committing these acts are one of the physicians, or health officers or persons practising under Government supervision such as midwives, the specified punishment is increased by one-sixth.

**Art. 193**

If in order to make a pregnant woman make a miscarriage whether with her consent or without her consent she is treated with drugs, or the requirements or means for it are indicated and the miscarriage is brought about by the effect thereof, the person who has been the cause of this is imprisoned for from six months to two years; and if the person who has been the cause of this is a physician, surgeon or druggist he is placed in kyurek temporarily.

## PART III

## Sets Forth the Punishment for Persons who Violate Honour

**Art. 197**

~~Whoever does the abominable act to a child under eleven years of age is punished with the punishment of temporary imprisonment for not less than six months~~. (repealed in 1911 and replaced by a new article as follows)

Whoever does the abominable act to a child who has not completed the age of fifteen years is put in kyurek temporarily. If this act takes place by the exercise of compulsion or violence the punishment of kyurek cannot be less than seven years.

**Art. 198**

If a man does the abominable act to a person, that is to say violates his honour, by force he is placed in kyurek temporarily.

Art. 198 was amplified by an addendum dated 3 Jemazi'ul-Akhir 1277 (17 December 1860). The text of the addendum is as follows:

Where one has attempted to commit such abominable act by force but it has not come into effect by the intervention of impediments not under his control he is punished with the punishment of imprisonment for not less than three months.

**Art. 199**

If the commission of the abominable act by force takes place on the part of the instructors or guardians of the victims over whom they have authority or on the part of their salaried servants punishment of temporary kyurek for not less than five years is awarded.

**Art. 200**

If such abominable act by force takes place with regard to a girl who has not yet been married to a man, the person who has dared to do this further becomes liable to pay compensation in addition to such punishment of kyurek.

Art. 200 was amplified by an addendum dated 3 Jemazi'ul-Akhir 1277 (17 December 1860). The text of the addendum is as follows:

The person who deceives a virgin who has attained the age of puberty saying that he will take her to wife and does away with her virginity and afterwards refuses to take her is, after compensation has been recovered from him for loss of virginity, imprisoned for from one week to six months; but the issuing of the sentence depends on either the male's confessing and admitting the deceit by promise of marriage or the girl's side proving it.

**Art. 201**

Whoever dares to behave contrary to public decency by making it a habit to incite and entice young persons from amongst males of females to obscenities by perverting or deceiving them or facilitating the means of the coming about thereof is punished with imprisonment for from one month to one year; and if this matter of perverting or deceiving in this manner proceeds from persons who are the father or mother or guardian they are punished with imprisonment for from six months to one year and a half.

Art 201 was amplified by an addendum dated 3 Jemazi'ul-Akhir 1277 (17 December 1860). The text of the addendum is as follows:

~~The right to proceed against a woman for honour belongs absolutely to her husband or to her guardian if she has not got a husband; and the woman whose having committed the abominable act of adultery is proved upon such proceedings is punished with imprisonment for not less than three months or more than two years; provided that the husband can defeat the effect of this punishment consenting to take again his wife.~~

~~The person also who is the partner in such adultery of a woman convicted thereof is likewise punished with imprisonment for from three months to two years and apart from this a fine of from five Mejidieh gold pieces to one hundred Mejidieh gold pieces is taken from him; and the proof which may be admissible against such partner in the offence can be deduced from the actual performance of the said act or further from presence in the harim of a Mussulman or from letters and papers written by him.~~

~~And as the operation of this article depends entirely on a woman's committing the abominable act of adultery and proceedings of honour taking place on the part of her husband or guardian, the Police Regulations of the Imperial Ottoman Government now in force with regard to such obscenities will apply as heretofore in ordinary cases, and this does not affect them at all. A husband in the habit of committing the hideous act of adultery with another woman in the house wherein he is living with his wife and whose commission of the said act is proved on complaint made by his wife is punished by taking a fine from five Mejidieh gold pieces to one hundred Mejidieh gold pieces.~~

The above addendum was repealed and re-issued in an amended form on 6 Jemazi'ul-Akhir 1329 (4 June 1911). The text of the addendum is as follows:

The taking of proceedings against a woman in respect of adultery committed by her voluntarily with another individual depends, if matrimony is existent between them or until the end of four months from the taking place of divorce, on a complaint being made by her husband or by her guardian if she has no husband; and upon such complaint the woman who it is proved has committed adultery is punished with imprisonment for from three months to two years.

The individual too who is the partner of the woman in this act is imprisoned for from three months to two years if he is married or for from one months to one year if he is unmarried. Apart from this a fine of from five Ottoman gold pieces is taken from him. The proof which may be admissible in this respect can be deduced from being found in the state performing the said act or in the harim of a Mussulman, or from letters or papers written by him. Provided that if, either before or after sentence, the husband or guardian desists from prosecuting or the husband takes again his wife, the right to proceed and the punishment drop both as regards the wife and the accomplice; and if the complainant dies during the enquiries and trial, likewise no proceedings are taken as regards the others.

A husband the commission by whom of the hideous act of adultery with a woman in a house wherein he is residing with his wife is proved on complaint made by his wife is punished with imprisonment for from three months to two years and by taking a fine of from five Ottoman gold pieces to one hundred Ottoman gold pieces.

**Art. 202**

The person who dares to commit the abominable act publicly contrary to modesty and sense of shame is imprisoned for from three months to one year and a fine of from one Mejidieh gold piece to ten Mejidieh gold pieces is taken.

Art 202 was amended by an addendum dated 3 Jemazi'ul-Akhir 1277 (17 December 1860). It was further revised and amended on 6 Jemazi'ul-Akhir 1329 (4 June 1911).The text of the addendum is as follows:

Those who address impertinent innuendos ~~to young persons either males or females~~[2] *to females or to young persons of the male sex*[3] are imprisoned for from one week to one month and those who act outrageously with their hands for from one month to three months.

Those who in female attire enter places which are the abode of women are, for this act alone, imprisoned for from three months to one year and if after their so entering in disguise they have set themselves to do a Jinayet or Junha legally necessitating a more severe punishment then this punishment they are punished with the punishment for such act.

*If, with the intention of committing obscenities contrary to public decency, women are made to dance in open places, or in semi-open places such as vineyards and gardens which the people may easily become aware of, the persons who make them dance and the women who voluntarily so dance are punished with imprisonment for from one month to one year.*[4]

## PART IV

## Shameful Act of Imprisoning or Detaining Persons Contrary to Rule, of Stealing Infants or Murahiqs and of Abduction of Girls

**Art. 206**

~~Whoever, by force or fraud, carries away a child who has not attained the age of puberty is imprisoned for from three months to one year; and if the child thus carried away is a girl who has not attained the limit of puberty the abducting person is placed in kyurek temporarily; and if the abominable act has been committed on the abducted girl the maximum of the punishment provided for that act is inflicted on those who have perpetrated this, and, if marriage has taken place in the case in which a girl is carried away, action is taken according to the requirement of the Sher' in the matter.~~

Art 206 was amplified by an addendum dated 3 Jemazi'ul-Akhir 1277 (17 December 1860). The text is as follows:

~~Whoever forcibly removes and carries away a female who has attained puberty is imprisoned for from three months to three years but if she has a husband the abducting person is placed in kyurek temporarily.~~

~~Whoever assists the man carrying away a female who has attained puberty or a female who has not attained puberty in the affair of her forcible removal and carrying away, is imprisoned for from one month to six months.~~

The Amended Art 206 was repealed and replaced by a new article on 6 Jemazi'ul-Akhir 1329 (4 June 1911). The text of the new article is as follows:

Whoever by force or fraud carries away a person whether of the male or female sex, is punished in manner following:

If the person carried away is of the male sex and has not completed the age of fifteen years the offender is imprisoned for the following:

If the person carried away is of the male sex and has not completed the age of fifteen years the offender is imprisoned for from one year to three years. If the child in this manner carried away is of the female sex offender is put in kyurek temporarily, and if

[2] As revised on 4 June 1911. [3] As added on 4 June 1911. [4] As added on 4 June 1911.

the abominable act has taken place punishment of kyurek for not less than ten years is awarded to him.

If the person whether of the male or female sex carried away has completed the age of fifteen years the offender is imprisoned for from two years to three years.

If marriage has taken place with regard to the girl carried away and the girl too has completed the age of fifteen years the case for general rights lapses by her desistance, or by that of her guardian if she has not completed that age, from proceeding.

If the woman carried away has a husband or if the abominable act has taken place the offender is placed in kyurek for not less than five years.

If the person carried away has been, within forty eight hours at the most and without any aggression of any kind having taken place, spontaneously left at some safe place whence it is possible for him to be taken by his family the punishment is imprisonment from one month to one year.

## Criminal Law Amendment Ordinance No. 2 1927

An Ordinance to amend the Law concerning offences against Women and Children and against Decency.

### Interpretation

2. For the Purpose of this Ordinance –
   (a) any house, room or set of rooms in any house which is occupied or frequented by two or more females for the purpose of prostitution shall be deemed to be a brothel.
   (b) where the context permits, words used to import the masculine shall be deemed also to import the feminine.

### Rape, etc.

3. Any person who –
   (a) has unlawful sexual intercourse with a female against her will by the use of force or threats of death or severe bodily harm, or when she is in a state of unconsciousness or otherwise incapable of resisting, or
   (b) commits an act of sodomy with any person against his will by the use of force or threats of death or severe bodily harm, or when he is in a state of unconsciousness or otherwise incapable of resisting, or
   (c) has unlawful sexual intercourse or commits an act of sodomy with a child under the age of sixteen years,

   Shall be liable on conviction to penal servitude for a term not exceeding fifteen years.

### Rape by Deception, etc.

4. Any person who has unlawful sexual intercourse with a female whom he knows to be insane or imbecile, or with a female whose consent has been obtained by threats or deception as to the nature of the act or as to the person committing it, shall be liable on conviction to penal servitude for a term not exceeding ten years.

### Attempt to Commit Rape, etc.

5. Any person attempting to commit an offence under either of the two preceding sections shall be liable on conviction to penal servitude for a term not exceeding seven years.

### Illicit Relation with Unmarried Girl

6. Any person who has unlawful sexual intercourse, or aids or abets another to have such intercourse, with an unmarried girl who is above the age of sixteen and under the age of twenty one years and is his descendant or the descendant of his wife, or his ward, or has been entrusted to him for the purpose of education or supervision, shall be liable on conviction to penal servitude for a term not exceeding five years.

### Indecent Act, with Force, etc.

7. Any person who commits, or attempts to commit, an indecent act upon the person of another against his will by the use of force or threats, or when he is in a state of unconsciousness or otherwise incapable of resisting, or by use of force or threats compels a person to commit, or to submit to any indecent act, shall be liable on conviction to penal servitude for a term not exceeding five years.

### Indecent Act without Force

8. Any person who commits or attempts to commit, an indecent act upon the person of another without his consent, but without force or threats, or where consent is obtained by deception as to the nature of the act or as to the person by whom it is committed, or induces, or attempts to induce, any person whom he knows to be insane or imbecile to commit, or to submit to any indecent act, shall be liable on conviction to imprisonment for a term not exceeding two years or a fine not exceeding £E.100.[5]

### Indecent Act Committed upon Child

9. Any person who commits an indecent act upon any child under the age of sixteen years shall be liable on conviction to imprisonment for a term not exceeding five years.

### Public Indecency

10. Any person who does or makes any indecent act or gesture in a public place or public gathering or in such a way that it may be seen by a person in a public place shall be liable on conviction to imprisonment for a term not exceeding six months or a fine not exceeding £E.50.

### Procuration for Immoral Purposes

11. Any person who –
    (a) Procures, or attempts to procure, any female under the age of 20 years, not being a common prostitute or of known immoral character, to have unlawful sexual intercourse, either within or without Palestine, with any other person, or
    (b) Procures or attempts to procure, any female to become, either within or without Palestine, a common prostitute, or
    (c) Procures, or attempts to procure, any female to leave Palestine, with intent that she may become an inmate of, or frequent, a brothel elsewhere, or
    (d) Procures, or attempts to procure, any female to leave her usual place of abode in Palestine, such place not being a brothel, with intent that she may, for the purpose of prostitution, become an inmate of, or frequent, a brothel, within or without Palestine,

Shall be liable on conviction to imprisonment for a term not exceeding three years.

[5] The Palestine Pound was yet to be introduced later in 1927. When this ordinance was promulgated, the Egyptian Pound still retained legal tender status in Palestine. Clauson, Gerard LM, 'The British colonial currency system', *The Economic Journal* 54, no. 213 (1944): 1, 14.

## Procuring Defilement of Females by Threats, Fraud or Administering Drugs

12. Any person who –
    (a) by threats or intimidation, procures or attempts to procure, any female to have unlawful sexual intercourse within or without Palestine, or
    (b) by false pretences or false representations, procures any female, not being a common prostitute or of known immoral character, to have any unlawful sexual intercourse either within or without Palestine, or
    (c) applies or administers to, or causes to be taken by, any female any drug, matter or thing with intent to stupefy or overpower, so as thereby to enable any person to have unlawful sexual intercourse with such female,

Shall be liable on conviction to imprisonment for a term not exceeding three years.

## Keeping of Brothel

13. Any person who –
    (a) keeps or manages, or acts or assists in the management of, a brothel, or
    (b) being the tenant or person in charge of any premises, knowingly permits such premises or any part thereof to be used as a brothel or for the purpose of habitual prostitution, or
    (c) being the landlord of any premises or the agent of such landlord, lets the premises or any part thereof with the knowledge that such premises or some part thereof are or is to be used as a brothel or is wilfully a party to the continued use of such premises or any part thereof as a brothel,

Shall be liable on conviction to imprisonment for a term not exceeding three months or a fine not exceeding £E. 100, and on a second or subsequent conviction, to imprisonment for a term not exceeding six months or a fine of not exceeding £E. 250, or in any such case to both such penalties.

## Determination of Tenancy of Premises on Conviction for Permitting Use of Brothel

14. (1) Upon the conviction of the tenant of any premises for knowingly permitting the premises or any part thereof to be used as a brothel, the landlord shall be entitled to require the person so convicted to assign the lease or other contract under which the said premises are held by him to some person approved by the landlord, which approval shall not be unreasonable withheld, and, in the event of the person so convicted failing within three months to assign the lease or contract, the landlord shall be entitled to determine the lease or other contract, but without prejudice to the rights or remedies of any party to such lease or contract accrued before the date of such determination: if the landlord should so determine the lease or other contract of tenancy, the Court which has convicted the tenant shall have power to make a summary order for delivery of possession to the landlord.

    (2) If the landlord after such conviction has been brought to his notice, fails to exercise his rights under the foregoing provisions of this Section, and subsequently, during the subsistence of the lease or contract, any such offence is again committed in the respect of the premises, the landlord shall be deemed to be a party to the continued use of the premises as a brothel, unless he proves that he had taken all reasonable steps to prevent the recurrence of the offence.

(3) Where a landlord determines a lease or other contract under the powers conferred by this Section, and subsequently grants another lease or enters into another contract of tenancy to, with, or for the benefit of, the same person, without causing to be inserted therein all reasonable provisions for the prevention of a recurrence of any such offence, he shall be deemed to have failed to exercise his rights under the foregoing provisions of this Section; and any such offence committed during the subsistence of the subsequent lease or contract shall be deemed, for the purpose of this Section, to have been committed during the subsistence of the previous lease or contract.

## Permitting Child to Reside in Brothel

15. Any person, having the custody or care of a child between the ages of two and sixteen years, who allows the child to reside in or frequent a brothel shall be liable on conviction to a fine not exceeding £E.25 or imprisonment for a term not exceeding six months.

## Living on Earning of Prostitute

16. (1) Any male person who lives wholly or in part on the earnings of a female as a prostitute shall be liable on conviction to imprisonment for a term not exceeding three years.

(2) Where a male person is proved to live with, or to be habitually in the company of, a prostitute, or is proved to have exercised control or influence over the movements of a prostitute in such a manner as to show that he is aiding, abetting or compelling her prostitution with any other person or generally, he shall, unless he can satisfy the court to the contrary, be deemed to be knowingly living on the earnings of a prostitute.

## Solicitation

17. (1) Any person who, by word or gesture, solicits for immoral purposes any person who is in a public street, or in any other place to which the public has access shall be liable on conviction to imprisonment for a term not exceeding one month or a fine not exceeding £E.5.

(2) The parent or guardian of a child under the age of sixteen years, or any other person entrusted with the charge or care of such child, who aids or abets such child to commit the offence mentioned in this Section shall be liable on conviction to imprisonment for a term not exceeding six months or a fine not exceeding £E. 50.

## Repeals

21 (1) Articles 197, 198, 199, 200 and the Addendum to Article 200 dated 3rd Jamazi Akhir, 1277, and Article 202 of the Ottoman Penal Code will cease to have effect; provided, that nothing herein shall affect the Addendum of Article 200 dated 19th Rabi Akhir, 1332, A.H.

(2) The Criminal Law Amendment Ordinance, 1925, is hereby repealed.

(3) The Public Notices issued by the Occupied Enemy Territory Administration concerning disorderly houses at Jerusalem, Jaffa, Gaza, Beersheba, Ramleh, Bethlehem and Haifa dated 1918 and 1919, and the Public Notice dated 3rd February, 1921, amending those Notices are repealed.

## Criminal Law Amendment Ordinance No. 30 1934

Offences against Women and Children, etc.

### Interpretation

88. For the Purpose of sections 89 to 106 –
   (a) any house, room or set of rooms in any house which is occupied or frequented by two or more females for the purpose of prostitution shall be deemed to be a brothel.
   (b) where the context permits, words used to import the masculine shall be deemed also to import the feminine.

### Rape, etc.

89. Any person who –
   (a) has unlawful sexual intercourse with a female against her will by the use of force or threats of death or severe bodily harm, or when she is in a state of unconsciousness or otherwise incapable of resisting, or
   (b) commits an act of sodomy with any person against his will by the use of force or threats of death or severe bodily harm, or when he is in a state of unconsciousness or otherwise incapable of resisting, or
   (c) has unlawful sexual intercourse or commits an act of sodomy with a child under the age of sixteen years,

   Is guilty of an offence and is liable to penal servitude for fifteen years.

### Rape by Deception, etc.

90. Any person who has unlawful sexual intercourse with a female whom he knows to be insane or imbecile, or with a female whose consent has been obtained by threats or deception as to the nature of the act or as to the person committing it, is guilty of an offence and is liable to penal servitude for ten years.

### Attempt to Commit Rape, etc.

91. Any person attempting to commit an offence under either of the two preceding sections is guilty of an offence and is liable to penal servitude for seven years.

### Illicit Relation with Unmarried Girl

92. Any person who has unlawful sexual intercourse, or aids or abets another to have such intercourse, with an unmarried girl who is above the age of sixteen and under the age of twenty one years and is his descendant or the descendant of his wife, or his ward, or has been entrusted to him for the purpose of education or supervision, is guilty of an offence and is liable to penal servitude for five years.

### Indecent Act, with Force, etc.

93. Any person who commits, or attempts to commit, an indecent act upon the person of another against his will by the use of force or threats, or when he is in a state of unconsciousness or otherwise incapable of resisting, or by use of force or threats compels a person to commit, or to submit to, any indecent act, is guilty of an offence and is liable to penal servitude for five years.

### Indecent Act without Force

94. Any person who commits or attempts to commit, an indecent act upon the person of another without his consent, but without force or threats, or where consent is obtained by deception as to the nature of the act or as to the person by whom it is committed, or induces, or attempts to induce, any person whom he knows to be insane or imbecile to commit, or to submit to any indecent act, is guilty of an offence and is liable to imprisonment for two years or a fine of one hundred pounds.

### Indecent Act Committed upon Child

95. Any person who commits an indecent act upon any child under the age of sixteen years is guilty of an offence and is liable to imprisonment for five years.

### Public Indecency

96. Any person who does or makes any indecent act or gesture in a public place or public gathering or in such a way that it may be seen by a person in a public place is guilty of an offence and is liable to imprisonment for six months or a fine of fifty pounds.

### Procuration for Immoral Purposes

97. Any person who –
    (a) Procures, or attempts to procure, any female under the age of twenty years; not being a common prostitute or of known immoral character, to have unlawful sexual intercourse, either within or without Palestine, with any other person, or
    (b) Procures or attempts to procure, any female to become, either within or without Palestine, a common prostitute, or
    (c) Procures, or attempts to procure, any female to leave Palestine, with intent that she may become an inmate of, or frequent, a brothel elsewhere, or
    (d) Procures, or attempts to procure, any female to leave her usual place of abode in Palestine, such place not being a brothel, with intent that she may, for the purpose of prostitution, become an inmate of, or frequent, a brothel, within or without Palestine,

Is guilty of an offence and is liable to imprisonment for three years.

### Procuring Defilement of Females by Threats, Fraud or Administering Drugs

98. Any person who –
    (a) by threats or intimidation, procures or attempts to procure, any female to have unlawful sexual intercourse within or without Palestine, or
    (b) by false pretences or false representations, procures any female, not being a common prostitute or of known immoral character, to have any unlawful sexual intercourse either within or without Palestine, or
    (c) applies or administers to, or causes to be taken by, any female any drug, matter or thing with intent to stupefy or overpower, so as thereby to enable any person to have unlawful sexual intercourse with such female,

Is guilty of an offence and is liable to imprisonment for three years.

### Keeping of Brothel

99. Any person who –
    (a) keeps or manages, or acts or assists in the management of, a brothel, or

(b) being the tenant or person in charge of any premises, knowingly permits such premises or any part thereof to be used as a brothel or for the purpose of habitual prostitution, or

(c) being the landlord of any premises or the agent of such landlord, lets the premises or any part thereof with the knowledge that such premises or some part thereof are or is to be used as a brothel or is wilfully a party to the continued use of such premises or any part thereof as a brothel,

Is guilty of an offence and is liable to imprisonment for three months or a fine of one hundred pounds and, on a second or subsequent conviction, to imprisonment for six months or a fine of two hundred and fifty pounds or, in any such case, to both such penalties.

## Determination of Tenancy of Premises on Conviction for Permitting Use of Brothel

100. (1) Upon the conviction of the tenant of any premises for knowingly permitting the premises or any part thereof to be used as a brothel, the landlord shall be entitled to require the person so convicted to assign the lease or other contract under which the said premises are held by him to some person approved by the landlord, which approval shall not be unreasonable withheld, and, in the event of the person so convicted failing within three months to assign the lease or contract, the landlord shall be entitled to determine the lease or other contract, but without prejudice to the rights or remedies of any party to such lease or contract accrued before the date of such determination: if the landlord should so determine the lease or other contract of tenancy, the court which has convicted the tenant shall have power to make a summary order for delivery of possession to the landlord.

(2) If the landlord after such conviction has been brought to his notice, fails to exercise his rights under subsection (1) and subsequently, during the subsistence of the lease or contract, any such offence is again committed in the respect of the premises, the landlord shall be deemed to be a party to the continued use of the premises as a brothel, unless he proves that he had taken all reasonable steps to prevent the recurrence of the offence.

(3) Where a landlord determines a lease or other contract under the powers conferred by this section, and subsequently grants another lease or enters into another contract of tenancy to, with, or for the benefit of, the same person, without causing to be inserted therein all reasonable provisions for the prevention of a recurrence of any such offence, he shall be deemed to have failed to exercise his rights under subsection (1), and such offence committed during the subsistence of the subsequent lease or contract shall be deemed, for the purpose of this section, to have been committed during the subsistence of the previous lease or contract.

## Permitting Child to Reside in Brothel

101. Any person, having the custody or care of a child between the ages of two and sixteen years, who allows the child to reside in or frequent a brothel is guilty of an offence and is liable to imprisonment for six months or a fine of twenty five pounds.

## Living on Earning of Prostitute

102. (1) Any male person who lives wholly or in part on the earnings of a female as a prostitute is guilty of an offence and is liable to imprisonment for three years.

(2) Where a male person is proved to live with, or to be habitually in the company of, a prostitute, or is proved to have exercised control or influence over the movement of a prostitute in such a manner as to show that he is aiding, abetting or compelling her prostitution with any other person or generally, he shall, unless he can satisfy the court to the contrary, be deemed to be knowingly living on the earnings of a prostitute.

### Solicitation

103. (1) Any person who, by word or gesture, solicits for immoral purposes any person who is in a public street, or in any other place to which the public has access is guilty of an offence and is liable to imprisonment for one months or a fine of five pounds.

(2) The parent or guardian of a child under the age of sixteen years, or any other person entrusted with the charge or care of such child, who aids or abets such child to commit the offence mentioned in this section is guilty of an offence and is liable to imprisonment for six months or a fine of fifty pounds.

### Custody of Child in Case of Prosecution under Ordinance

104. (1) Where a person having the care or custody of a child under the age of sixteen years is convicted in respect of such child of an offence under this Ordinance, or has been committed for trial for any such offence, the court convicting the offender or the court before which the offender is committed for trial may, if satisfied that it is expedient, order that the child be committed to the care of a relative or of any other fit person or institution named in the order, such relative or person or the manager of such institution being willing to undertake such care, until he attains the age of sixteen years or for any shorter period: the court shall, in making such order, have regard to the religion professed by the parents of the child.

(2) If the child has a parent or legal guardian no order shall be made under this section unless such parent or legal guardian has been convicted of, or committed to trial, for an offence under this Ordinance, or is under committal for trial for having been, or has been proved to the satisfaction of the court making the order to have been, a party to, the offence, or cannot be found.

(3) The consent of any person to undertake the care of a child shall be proved in such manner as the court may think sufficient to bind him.

(4) Where an order is made under this section in respect of a person who has been committed for trial, if that person is acquitted of the charge, or if the charge is dismissed for want of prosecution, the order shall forthwith be void, except with regard to anything that may have been lawfully done under it.

(5) The court or any court of like jurisdiction may, on the application of any person interested, from time to time renew, vary or revoke any order made under this section.

### Jurisdiction

### No. 4 of 1930

105. Any charge under sections 96, 99, 101 and 103(2) shall be tried by a British magistrate.

### Search Warrant

106. (1) A magistrate may issue a search warrant authorising the person named in the warrant to make search in any house or premises if he has reason to believe that –
(a) such premises are being used for any purpose contrary to the provisions of this Ordinance, or
(b) any person is detained, concealed or present therein with regard to whom any offence under this Ordinance is believed to have been committed or to be in contemplation.
(2) If, upon such search, any person is found upon the premises with regard to whom an offence under the Ordinance is believed to have been committed or to be contemplated, such person may be detained by the police pending enquiries unless he shall give an address in Palestine satisfactory to the police.
(3) The provisions of sections 20 to 24 of the Criminal Procedure (Arrest and Searches) Ordinance shall apply to warrants issued under this section, but the provisions of section 19 shall not apply.
(4) For the purpose of this section the term 'premises' shall be deemed to include any ship, boat, railway train, carriage or other vehicle.

## Criminal Code Ordinance, 1936

CHAPTER XVII

Offences Against Morality

### Interpretation of Brothel

151. For the purpose of this chapter any house, room or set of rooms in any house which is occupied or frequented by two or more females for the purpose of prostitution shall be deemed to be a brothel.

### Sexual and Unnatural Offences

152.0 (1) Any person who:-
(a) has unlawful sexual intercourse with a female against her will by the use of force or threats of death or severe bodily harm, or when she is in a state of unconsciousness or otherwise incapable of resisting; or
(b) commits an act of sodomy with any person against his will by the use of force or threats of death or severe bodily harm, or when he is in a state of unconsciousness or otherwise incapable of resisting; or
(c) has unlawful sexual intercourse or commits an act of sodomy with a child under the age of sixteen years

Is guilty of a felony and is liable to imprisonment for fourteen years.

If such felony is committed under paragraph (a) hereof it is termed rape:

Provided that it shall be a sufficient defence to any charge of having unlawful sexual intercourse with a female under paragraph (c) of this sub-section if it shall be made to appear to the court before which the charge shall be brought that the person so charged had reasonable cause to believe that the female was of or above the age of sixteen years.

(2) Any person who:-
(a) has carnal knowledge of any person against the order of nature; or
(b) has carnal knowledge of an animal; or
(c) permits a male person to have carnal knowledge of him or her against the order of nature,

Is guilty of a felony, and is liable to imprisonment for ten years.

### Rape by Deception

153. Any person who has unlawful sexual intercourse with a female whom he knows to be insane or imbecile, or with a female whose consent has been obtained by threats or deception as to the nature of the act or as to the person committing it, is guilty of a felony, and is liable to imprisonment for ten years.

### Attempt to Commit Rape, etc.

154. Any person attempting to commit an offence under either of the two preceding sections is guilty of a felony and is liable to imprisonment for seven years.

### Illicit Relation with Unmarried Girl

155. Any person who has unlawful sexual intercourse, or aids or abets another to have such intercourse, with an unmarried girl who is above the age of sixteen and under the age of twenty-one years and is his descendant or the descendant of his wife, or is his ward, or has been entrusted to him for the purpose of education or supervision, is guilty of a felony and is liable to imprisonment for five years.

### Intercourse by Husband with Girl under Fifteen Years

156. (1) Any person who, being married to a girl under the age of fifteen years completed:-

(a) has sexual intercourse with her, or
(b) endeavours to facilitate such intercourse by any instrument or other physical means,

Is guilty of a misdemeanour and is liable to imprisonment for two years.

(2) It shall be a good defence to a charge brought under paragraph (a) of subsection (1) hereof that notwithstanding the fact that the female is under fifteen years completed,
 (i) She has reached puberty, and
 (ii) Prior to such intercourse, a certificate (which certificate shall be deemed to be a certificate within the meaning of section 12 of the Medical Practitioners Ordinance, 1928) had been obtained from a medical practitioner licensed to practice medicine under the Medical Practitioners Ordinance, 1928, that no physical ill effects would be likely to follow the consummation of the marriage by her.

### Indecent Act with Force, etc.

157. Any person who commits or attempts to commit an indecent act upon the person of another against his will by the use of force or threats, or when he is in a state of unconsciousness or otherwise incapable of resisting, or by use of force or threats compels a person to commit or to submit to any indecent act, is guilty of a felony and is liable to imprisonment for five years.

### Indecent Act without Force

158. Any person who commits or attempts to commit an indecent act upon the person of another without his consent, but without force or threats, or where consent is obtained by deception as to the nature of the act or as to the person by whom it is committed, or induces or attempts to induce any person whom he knows to be insane or imbecile, to commit or to submit to any indecent act, is

guilty of a misdemeanour and is liable to imprisonment for two years or to a fine of one hundred pounds.

### Indecent Act Committed upon Child

159. Any person who commits an indecent act upon any person under the age of sixteen years is guilty of a misdemeanour and is liable to imprisonment for three years.

### Indecency in Public

160. Any person does or makes any indecent act or gesture in a public place or public gathering or in such a way that it may be seen by a person in a public place, is guilty of a misdemeanour and is liable to imprisonment for six months or to a fine of fifty pounds or to both such penalties.

### Procuration for Immoral Purposes

161. Any person who:-
   - (a) procures or attempts to procure any female under the age of twenty years, not being a common prostitute or of known immoral character, to have unlawful sexual intercourse, either within or without Palestine, with any other person; or
   - (b) procures or attempts to procure any female to become, either within or without Palestine, a common prostitute; or
   - (c) procures or attempts to procure any female to leave Palestine, with intent that she become an inmate of or frequent a brothel elsewhere; or
   - (d) procures or attempts to procure any person under the age of sixteen years to commit sodomy; or
   - (e) procures or attempts to procure any female to leave her usual place of abode in Palestine, such place not being a brothel, with intent that she may, for the purpose of prostitution, become an inmate or frequent a brothel, within or without Palestine;

   Is guilty of a misdemeanour.

### Procuring Defilement of Females by Threats, Fraud or Administering Drugs

162. Any person who:-
   - (a) by threats or intimidation, procures or attempts to procure any female to have unlawful sexual intercourse within or without Palestine; or
   - (b) by false pretences or false representations, procures any female, not being a common prostitute or of known immoral character, to have any unlawful sexual intercourse either within or without Palestine; or
   - (c) applies, administers to, or causes to be taken by any female any drug, matter or thing with intent to stupefy or overpower, so as thereby to enable any person to have unlawful sexual intercourse with such female;

   Is guilty of a misdemeanour.

### Keeping of Brothel

163. Any person who:-
   - (a) keeps or manages, or acts or assists in the management of, a brothel; or
   - (b) being the tenant or person in charge of any premises, knowingly permits such premises or any part thereof to be used as a brothel or for the purpose of habitual prostitution; or

(c) being the landlord of any premises or the agent of such landlord, lets the premises or any part thereof with the knowledge that such premises or some part thereof are or is to be used as a brothel or is wilfully a party to the continued use of such premises or any part thereof as a brothel;

Is guilty of a misdemeanour and is liable to imprisonment for three months or a fine of one hundred pounds, or to both such penalties, and on a second or subsequent conviction, to imprisonment for six months or a fine of two hundred and fifty pounds, or to both such penalties.

### Determination of Tenancy of Premises on Conviction for Permitting Use of Brothel

164. (1) Upon the conviction of the tenant of any premises for knowingly permitting the premises or any part thereof to be used as a brothel, the landlord shall be entitled to require the person so convicted to assign the lease or other contract under which the said premises are held by him to some person approved by the landlord, which approval shall not be unreasonable withheld, and, in the event of the person so convicted failing within three months to assign the lease or contract, the landlord shall be entitled to determine the lease or other contract, but without prejudice to the rights or remedies of any party to such lease or contract accrued before the date of such determination: if the landlord should so determine the lease or other contract of tenancy, the court which has convicted the tenant shall have power to make a summary order for delivery of possession to the landlord.

(2) If the landlord after such conviction has been brought to his notice, fails to exercise his rights under the foregoing provisions of this section, and subsequently, during the subsistence of the lease or contract, any such offence is again committed in the respect of the premises, the landlord shall be deemed to be a party to the continued use of the premises as a brothel.

(3) Where a landlord determines a lease or other contract under the powers conferred by this section, and subsequently grants another lease or enters into another contract of tenancy to, with, or for the benefit of, the same person, without causing to be inserted therein all reasonable provisions for the prevention of a recurrence of any such offence, he shall be deemed to have failed to exercise his rights under the foregoing provisions of this section; and any such offence committed during the subsistence of the subsequent lease or contract shall be deemed, for the purpose of this section, to have been committed during the subsistence of the previous lease or contract.

### Permitting Child to Reside in Brothel

165. Any person, having the custody or care of a child between the ages of two and sixteen years, who allows the child to reside in or frequent a brothel is guilty of a misdemeanor and is liable to imprisonment for six months, or to a fine of twenty-five pounds.

### Living on Earning of Prostitute

166. (1) Any male person who lives wholly or in part on the earnings as a prostitute of a female is guilty of a misdemeanour.

(2) Where a male person is proved to live with, or to be habitually in the company of, a prostitute, or is proved to have exercised control or influence over the movements of a prostitute in such a manner as to show that he is aiding, abetting or compelling her prostitution with any other person or generally, he shall, unless he can satisfy the court to the contrary, be deemed to be knowingly living on the earnings of a prostitute.

## Solicitation

167. (1) Any person who, by word or gesture, solicits for immoral purposes any person who is in a public place, is guilty of a misdemeanour and is liable to imprisonment for one month or to a fine of five pounds.

(2) The parent or guardian of a child whether male or female under the age of sixteen years, or any other person entrusted with the chare or care of such child, who aids or abets such child to commit the offence mentioned in this section, is guilty of a misdemeanour and is liable to imprisonment for six months or to a fine of fifty pounds.

## Indecent Suggestions

168. Any person who addresses indecent suggestions to any person under the age of sixteen years or to any female is guilty of a misdemeanour and is liable to imprisonment for one month.

## Male Entering Women's Apartments in Female Dress

169. Any male who in female dress enters an apartment reserved for women is guilty of a misdemeanour and is liable to imprisonment for one year.

## Detention with Intent or in Brothel

170. Any person who detains any woman against her will-

(a) in or upon any premises with intent that she may have unlawful sexual intercourse with any man, whether any particular man or generally; or

(b) in any brothel;

Is guilty of a misdemeanour and is liable to imprisonment for two years.

## Constructive Detention by Withholding Clothes

171. (1) When a woman is in or upon any premises for the purpose of having any unlawful sexual intercourse or is in any brothel, a person shall be deemed to detain such woman in or upon such premises or in such brothel, if, with intent to compel or induce her to remain in or upon such premises or in such brothel, he withholds from such woman any wearing apparel or other property belonging to her, or where wearing apparel has been lent or otherwise supplied to such woman by or by the directions of such person, he threatens such woman with legal proceedings if she takes away with her the wearing apparel so lent or supplied.

(2) No legal proceedings, whether civil or criminal, shall be taken against any such woman for taking away or being found in possession of any such wearing apparel as was necessary to enable her to leave such premises or brothel.

## Search Warrant

172. (1) A Magistrate may issue a search warrant authorising the person named in the warrant to make search in any house or premises if he has reason to believe that:-

(a) such premises are being used for any purpose contrary to the provisions of this chapter; or
(b) any person is detained, concealed or present therein with regard to whom any offence under this chapter is believed to have been committed or to be in contemplation.

(2) if upon such search any person is found upon the premises with regard to whom an offence under this chapter is believed to have been committed or to be contemplated, such person may be detained by the police in a place of safety pending enquiries, or may by order of the Magistrate be delivered up to his or her parents or guardians or otherwise dealt with as circumstances may permit or require.

(3) The provisions of sections 18 to 22 inclusive of the Arrest of Offenders and Searches Ordinance, 1924, shall apply to warrants issued under this section, but the provisions of section 17 thereof shall not apply.

(4) For the purpose of this section the term 'premises' shall be deemed to include any ship, boat, railway train, carriage or other vehicle.

(5) A woman shall be deemed to be unlawfully detained for immoral purposes if she is so detained for the purpose of having unlawful sexual intercourse with any man, whether any particular man or generally, and:
(a) either is under the age of sixteen years; or
(b) if she is of or over the age of sixteen years and under the age of eighteen years, is so detained against her will or against the will of her father or mother or of any person having the lawful care or charge of her; or
(c) if she is of or over the age of eighteen years and is so detained against her will.

### Woman Aiding, etc., for Gain Prostitution of Another Woman

173. Every woman who is proved to have for the purpose of gain exercised control, direction or influence over the movements of a prostitute in such a manner as to show that she is aiding, abetting or compelling her prostitution with any person, or generally, is guilty of a misdemeanor.

### Conspiracy to Defile

174. Any person who conspires with another to induce any female, by means of any false pretence or other fraudulent means, to permit any person to have unlawful sexual intercourse with her, is guilty of a misdemeanor.

### Attempts to Procure Abortion

175. Any person who, with the intent to procure miscarriage of a woman, whether she is or is not with child, unlawfully administers to her or causes her to take any poison or other noxious thing, or uses any force of any kind, or uses any other means whatever, is guilty of a felony, and is liable to imprisonment for fourteen years.

### The Like by Woman Herself

176. Any person who, with intent to procure her own miscarriage, whether she is or is not with child, unlawfully administers to herself any poison or other noxious thing, or uses any force of any kind, or uses any other means whatever, or permits any such thing or means to be administered or used to her, is guilty of a felony, and is liable to imprisonment for seven years.

### Supplying Drugs or Instruments to Procure Abortion

177. Any person who unlawfully supplies to or procures for any person anything whatever, knowing that it is intended to be unlawfully used to procure the miscarriage of a woman whether she is or is not with child, is guilty of a misdemeanour.

### Knowledge of Age of Female Immaterial

178. Except as otherwise expressly stated, it is immaterial in the case of an of the offences committed with respect to a woman or girl under a specified age, that the accused person did not know that the woman or girl was under that age, or believed that she was not under that age.

### Obscene Publications

179. Any person who:-
   (a) sells or has in his possession for sale, hire or distribution, or prints or reproduces in any other manner for sale, hire, or distribution any obscene printed or written matter, or any obscene picture, photograph, drawing or model, or any other object tending to corrupt morals; or
   (b) expresses to view or distributes for exhibition in a public place any obscene picture, photograph, drawing or model, or any other object tending to corrupt morals; or
   (c) carries on or takes part in any business for the sale or publication or exhibition of any obscene printed or written matter, or picture, photograph, drawing or model, or other object tending to corrupt morals; or
   (d) advertises or makes known by any means whatsoever that a person is engaged in the sale, printing, reproduction, exhibition, or distribution of any such obscene matter or thing or that such obscene matter or thing can be procured either directly or indirectly from any person;

Is guilty of a misdemeanor and is liable to imprisonment for three months or to a fine of one hundred pounds, or to both such penalties.

## CHAPTER XVIII

## Offences Relating to Marriage and Domestic Obligations

### Fraudulent Pretence of Marriage

180. Any person who wilfully and by fraud causes any woman who is not lawfully married to him to believe that she is lawfully married to him and to co-habit or have sexual intercourse with him in that belief, is guilty of a felony and is liable to imprisonment for ten years.

## CHAPTER XXVIII

## Offences against Liberty

### Abducting in Order to Subject Person to Grievous Hurt

258. Any person who abducts any person in order that such person may be subjected or may be so disposed of as to be put in danger of being subjected, to grievous harm, or to the unnatural lust of any person, or knowing it to be likely that such person will be so subjected or disposes of, is guilty of a felony and is liable to imprisonment for ten years.

## The Indian Penal Code, 1860

### Unnatural Offences

377. Whoever voluntarily has carnal intercourse against the order of nature with any man, woman or animal shall be punished with [imprisonment for life],[6] or with imprisonment of either description for a term which may extend to ten years, and shall be liable to fine.

Explanation – Penetration is sufficient to constitute the carnal intercourse necessary to the offence described in this section.

## Queensland Criminal Code Act 1899

### CHAPTER XXII

### Offences against Morality[7]

#### Unnatural Offences

208. Any person who-
   (1) Has carnal knowledge of any person against the order of nature; or
   (2) Has carnal knowledge of an animal; or
   (3) Permits a male person to have carnal knowledge of him or her against the order of nature;

Is guilty of a crime, and is liable to imprisonment with hard labour for life.

#### Attempt to Commit Unnatural Offences

209. Any person who attempts to commit any of the crimes defined in the last preceding section is guilty of a crime, and is liable to imprisonment with hard labour for fourteen years.

The offender cannot be arrested without warrant.

#### Indecent Treatment of Boys under Fourteen

210. Any person who unlawfully and indecently deals with a boy under the age of fourteen years is guilty of a crime, and is liable to imprisonment with hard labour for seven years.

The term 'deal with' includes doing any act which, if done without consent, would constitute an assault as hereinafter defined.

#### Indecent Practices between Males

211. Any male person who, whether in public or private, commits any act of gross indecency with another male person, or procures another male person to commit any act of gross indecency with him, or attempts to procure the commission of any such act by any male person with himself or with another male person, whether in public or private, is guilty of a misdemeanour, and is liable to imprisonment with hard labour for three years.

#### Defilement of Girls under Twelve

212. Any person who has unlawful carnal knowledge of a girl under the age of twelve is guilty of a crime, and is liable to imprisonment with hard labour for life, with or without whipping.

[6] Changed from "transportation for life" by Act 26 of 1955.

[7] Sections 214 (attempt to abuse girls under ten), 215 (defilement of girls under fourteen and of idiots), 216 (indecent treatment of girls under fourteen) & 227 (indecent acts) are not transcribed here.

Any person who attempts to have unlawful carnal knowledge of a girl under the age of twelve years is guilty of a misdemeanour, and is liable to imprisonment with hard labour for three years, with or without whipping.

In the case of an offender whose age does not exceed sixteen years, the Court, instead of sentencing him to any term of imprisonment, may, in addition to the sentence of whipping, or without such sentence, order him to be sent to an industrial or reformatory school, and to be there detained for a period not exceeding three years.

A prosecution for either of the offences defined in this section must be begun within two months after the offence is committed.

A person cannot be convicted of either of the offences defined in this section upon the uncorroborated testimony of one witness.

The wife of the accused person is a competent but not a compellable witness.

### Householder Permitting Defilement of Young Girls on his Premises

213. Any person who, being the owner or occupier of any premises, or having, or acting or assisting in, the management or control of any premises, induces or knowingly permits any girl of such age as is in this section mentioned to resort to or be in or upon such premises for the purposes of being unlawfully carnally known by any man, whether a particular man or not, is guilty of an indictable offence.

If the girl is under the age of fourteen years, he is guilty of a misdemeanour, and is liable to imprisonment with hard labour for two years, with or without whipping.

If the girl is under the age of twelve years, he is guilty of a crime, and is liable to imprisonment with hard labour for life, with or without whipping.

It is a defence to a charge of any of the offences defined in this section to prove that the accused person believed, on reasonable grounds, that the girl was of or above the age of fourteen years.

The husband or wife of the accused person is a competent but not a compellable witness.

## CHAPTER XXXII[8]

## Assaults on Females: Abduction

### Definition of Rape

347. Any person who has carnal knowledge of a woman, not his wife, without her consent, or with her consent, if her consent is obtained by force, or by means of threats or intimidation of any kind, or by fear of bodily harm, or by means of false and fraudulent representations as to the nature of the act, or, in the case of a married woman, by personating as her husband, is guilty of a crime, which is called rape.

### Punishment of Rape

348. Any person who commits the crime of rape is liable to imprisonment with hard labour for life.

### Attempt to Commit Rape

349. Any person who attempts to commit the crime of rape is quilty of a crime, and is liable to imprisonment with hard labour for fourteen years.

The Offender cannot be arrested without warrant.

[8] Sections 351 & 352, which regulate the abduction of females for sexual purposes, marriage or gain are not transcribed here.

### Incedent Assaults on Females

350. Any person who unlawfully and indecently assaults a woman or girl is guilty of a misdemeanour, and is liable to imprisonment with hard labour for two years.

### Rules of Evidence

353. Upon a charge of any of the offences defined in this Chapter, the wife of the accused person is a competent but not a compellable witness.

## Offences against the Person Act 1861 (24 & 25 Vict., c. 100)

Unnatural Offences

### Sodomy and Bestiality

61. Whosoever shall be convicted of the abominable Crime of Buggery, committed either with Mankind or with any Animal, shall be liable, at the Discretion of the Court, to be kept in Penal Servitude for Life or for any Term not less than Ten Years.

### Attempt to Commit an Infamous Crime

62. Whosoever shall attempt to commit the said abominable Crime, or shall be guilty of any Assault with Intent to commit the same, or of any indecent Assault upon any Male Person, shall be guilty of a Misdemeanor, and being convicted thereof shall be liable, at the Discretion of the Court, to be kept in Penal Servitude for any Term not exceeding Ten Years and not less than Three Years, or to be imprisoned for any Term not exceeding Two Years, with or without Hard Labour.

### Carnal Knowledge Defined

63. Whenever, upon the Trial for any Offence punishable under this Act, it may be necessary to prove carnal Knowledge, it shall not be necessary to prove the actual Emission of Seed in order to constitute a carnal Knowledge, but the carnal Knowledge shall be deemed complete upon Proof of Penetration only.

## Criminal Law Amendment Act 1885 (48 & 49 Vict., c. 69).

CHAPTER 69

An Act to make further provision for the Protection of Women and Girls, the suppression of brothels, and other purposes [14 August 1885]. Be it enacted by the Queen's most Excellent Majesty, by and with the advice and consent of the Lords Spiritual and Temporal, and Commons, in this present Parliament assembled, and by the authority of the same, as follows:

### Short Title

1. This Act may be cited as the Criminal Law Amendment Act, 1885.

PART I

Protection of Women and Girls

### Procuration

2. Any person who –
   (1) Procures, or attempts to procure, any girl or woman under the age of twenty-one years of age; not being a common prostitute or of known immoral

character, to have unlawful carnal connexion, either within or without the Queen's dominions, with any other person or persons, or

(2) Procures or attempts to procure, any woman or girl to become, either within or without the Queen's dominions, a common prostitute, or

(3) Procures, or attempts to procure, any woman or girl to leave the United Kingdom, with intent that she may become an inmate of a brothel elsewhere, or

(4) Procures, or attempts to procure, any woman or girl to leave her usual place of abode in the United Kingdom (such place not being a brothel), with intent that she may, for the purposes of prostitution, become an inmate of a brothel, within or without the Queen's dominions,

Shall be guilty of a misdemeanour, and being convicted thereof shall be liable at the discretion of the court to be imprisoned for any term not exceeding two years, with or without hard labour.

Provided than no person shall be convicted of any offence under this section upon the evidence of one witness, unless such witness be corroborated in some material particular by evidence implicating the accused.

## Procuring Defilement of Women by Threats, Fraud or Administering Drugs

3. Any person who –

(1) By threats or intimidation, procures or attempts to procure, any woman or girl to have any unlawful carnal connexion within or without the Queen's dominions, or

(2) By false pretences or false representations, procures any woman or girl, not being a common prostitute or of known immoral character, to have any unlawful carnal connexion either within or without the Queen's dominions, or

(3) Applies or administers to, or causes to be taken by, any woman or girl any drug, matter or thing with intent to stupefy or overpower, so as thereby to enable any person to have unlawful carnal connexion with such woman or girl,

Shall be guilty of a misdemeanor, and being convicted thereof shall be liable on conviction to imprisonment for a term not exceeding three years, at the discretion of the court to be imprisoned for any term not exceeding two years, with or without hard labour.

Provided than no person shall be convicted of an offence under this section upon the evidence of one witness only, unless such witness be corroborated in some material particular by evidence implicating the accused.

## Defilement of Girl under Thirteen Years of Age

4. Any person who-

Unlawfully and carnally knows any girl under the age of thirteen years

Shall be guilty of felony, and being convicted thereof shall be liable at the discretion of the court to be kept in penal servitude for life, or for any term not less than five years, or to be imprisoned for any term not exceeding two years, with or without hard labour.

Any person who attempts to have unlawful carnal knowledge of any girl under the age of thirteen years shall be guilty of misdemeanor, and being convicted thereof shall be liable at the discretion of the court to be imprisoned for any term not exceeding two years, with or without hard labour.

Provided that in the case of an offender whose age does not exceed sixteen years, the court may, instead of sentencing him to any term of imprisonment, order him to be whipped, as prescribed by the Act of the twenty-fifth and twenty-sixth Victoria, chapter eighteen, intituled "An Act to amend the law as to the Whipping of Juvenile and other Offenders" and the said Act shall apply so far as circumstances admit, as if the offender had been convicted in manner in that Act mentioned; and if, having regard to his age and all the circumstances of the case, it should appear expedient, the court may, in addition to the sentence of whipping, order him to be sent to a certified reformatory school, and to be there detained for a period not less than two years and not more than five years.

The court may also order the offender to be detained in custody for a period of not more than seven days before he is sent to such reformatory school.

Where, upon the hearing of a charge under this section, the girl in respect of whom the offence is charged to have been committed, or any other child of tender years who is tendered as witness, does not, in the opinion of the court or justices, understand the nature of an oath, the evidence of such girl or other child of tender years may be received, though not given upon oath, if, in the opinion of the court or justices, as the case may be, such girl or other child of tender years is possessed of sufficient intelligence to justify the reception of the evidence, and understands the duty of speaking the truth: Provided that no person shall be liable to be convicted of the offence unless the testimony admitted by virtue of this section and given on behalf of the prosecution shall be corroborated by some other material evidence in support thereof implicating the accused: Provided also, that any witness whose evidence has been admitted under this section shall be liable to indictment and punishment for perjury in all respects as if he or she had been sworn.

Whereas doubt have been entertained whether a man who induces a married woman to permit him to have connexion with her by personating her husband is or is not guilty of rape, it is hereby enacted and declared that every such offender shall be deemed to be guilty of rape.

## Defilement of Girl between Thirteen and Sixteen Years of Age

5. Any person who-
   (1) Unlawfully and carnally knows or attempts to have unlawful carnal knowledge of any girl being or above the age of thirteen years and under the age of sixteen years; or
   (2) Unlawfully and carnally knows or attempts to have unlawful carnal knowledge of any female idiot or imbecile woman or girl, under circumstances which do not amount to rape, but which prove that the offender knew at the time of the commission of the offence that the woman or girl was an idiot or imbecile,

Shall be guilty of a misdemeanor, and being convicted thereof shall be liable at the discretion of the court to be imprisoned for any term not exceeding two years, with or without hard labour.

Provided that it shall be a sufficient defence to any charge under sub-section one of this section if it shall be made to appear to the court or jury before whom the charge shall be brought that the person so charged had reasonable cause to believe that the girl was of or above the age of sixteen years.

Provided also, that no persecution shall be commenced for an offence under sub-section one of this section more than three months after the commission of the offence.

## Householder, &c. Permitting Defilement of Young Girl on his Premises

6. Any person who, being the owner or occupier of any premises or having, or acting or assisting in, the management or control thereof-

Induces or knowingly suffers any girl of such age as is in the section mentioned to resort to or be in or upon such premises for the purpose of being unlawfully and carnally known by any man whether such carnal knowledge is intended to be with any particular man or generally,

(1) Shall, if such girl is under the age of thirteen years, be guilty of felony, and being convicted thereof shall be liable at the discretion of the court to be kept in penal servitude for life, or for any term not less than five years, or to be imprisoned for any term not exceeding two years with or without hard labour; and

(2) if such girl is of or above the age of thirteen and under the age of sixteen years, shall be guilty of a misdemeanor, and being convicted thereof shall be liable at the discretion of the court to be imprisoned for any term not exceeding two years with or without hard labour.

Provided that it shall be a sufficient defence to any charge under this section if it shall be made to appear to the court or jury before whom the charge shall be brought that the person so charged had reasonable cause to believe that the girl was of or above the age of sixteen years.

## Abduction of Girl under Eighteen with Intent to Have Carnal Knowledge

7. Any person who-

With intent that any unmarried girl under the age of eighteen years should be unlawfully and carnally known by any man, whether such carnal knowledge is intended to be with any particular man, or generally-

Takes or causes to be taken such girl out of the possession and against the will of her father or mother, or any other person having the lawful care or charge of her,

Shall be guilty of a misdemeanor, and being convicted thereof shall be liable at the discretion of the court to be imprisoned for any term not exceeding two years, with or without hard labour.

Provided that it shall be a sufficient defence to any charge under this section if it shall be made to appear to the court or jury that the person so charged had reasonable cause to believe that the girl was of or above the age of eighteen years.

## Unlawful Detention with Intent to Have Carnal Knowledge

8. Any person who detains any woman or girl against her will-

(1) In or upon any premises with intent that she may be unlawfully and carnally known by any man, whether any particular man, or generally, or

(2) In any brothel

Shall be guilty of a misdemeanor, and being convicted thereof shall be liable at the discretion of the court to be imprisoned for any term not exceeding two years, with or without hard labour.

Where a woman or girl is in or upon any premises for the purpose of having any unlawful carnal connexion, or is in any brothel, a person shall be deemed to detain such woman or girl in or upon such premises or in such brothel, if, with intent to compel or induce her to remain in or upon such premises or in such brothel, such person withholds from such woman or girl any wearing apparel or other property belonging to her, or, where wearing apparel has been lent or otherwise supplied to such woman or girl by or by the direction of such person, such person threatens such woman or girl with legal proceedings if she takes away with her the wearing apparel so lent or supplied.

No legal proceedings, whether civil or criminal, shall be taken against any such woman or girl for taking away or being found in possession of any such wearing apparel as was necessary to enable her to leave such premises or brothel.

### Power, on Indictment for Rape, to Convict of Certain Misdemeanors

9. If upon the trial of any indictment for rape, or any offence made felony by section four of this Act, the jury shall be satisfied that the defendant is guilty of an offence under section three, four, or five of this Act, or of an indecent assault, but are not satisfied that the defendant is guilty of the felony charged in such indictment, or of an attempt to commit the same, then and in every such case the jury may acquit the defendant of such felony, and find him guilty of such offence as aforsaid, or of an indecent assault, and thereupon such defendant shall be liable to be punished in the same manner as if he had been convicted upon an indictment for such offence as aforesaid or for the misdemeanor of indecent assault.

### Power of Search

10. If it appears to any justice of the peace, on information made before him on oath by any parent, relative, or guardian of any woman or girl, or any other person who, in the opinion of the justice, is bona fide acting in the interest of any woman or girl, that there is reasonable cause to suspect that such woman or girl is unlawfully detained for immoral purposes by any person in any place within the jurisdiction of such justice, such justice may issue a warrant authorizing any person named therein to search for, and when found, to take to and detain in a place of safety such woman or girl until she can be brought before a justice of the peace; and the justice of the peace before whom such woman or girl is brought may cause her to be delivered upon to her parents or guardians, or otherwise dealt with as circumstances may permit and require.

The justice of the peace issuing such warrant may, by the same or any other warrant, cause any person accused of so unlawfully detaining such woman or girl to be apprehended and brought before a justice, and proceedings to be taken for punishing such person according to law.

A woman or girl shall be deemed to be unlawfully detained for immoral purposes if she is so detained for the purpose of being unlawfully and carnally known by any man, whether any particular man or generally, and-

(a) Either is under the age of sixteen years; or
(b) If of or over the age of sixteen years, and under the age of eighteen years, is so detained against her will, or against the will of her father or mother or of any other person having the lawful care or charge of her; or
(c) If of or above the age of eighteen years is so detained against her will.

Any person authorized by warrant under this section to search for any woman or girl so detained as aforesaid may enter (if need be by force) any house, building, or other place specified in such warrant, and may remove such woman or girl therefrom.

Provided always, that every warrant issued under this section shall be addressed to and executed by some superintendent, inspector, or other officer of police, who shall be accompanied by the parent, relative, or guardian or other person making the information, if such person so desire, unless the justice shall otherwise direct.

### Outrages on Decency

11. Any male person who, in public or private, commits, or is a party to the commission of, or procures or attempts to procure the commission by any male person of, any act of gross indecency with another male person, shall be guilty of a misdemeanor, and being convicted thereof shall be liable at the discretion of the court to be imprisoned for any term not exceeding two years, with or without hard labour.

### Custody of Girls under Sixteen

12. Where on the trial of any offence under this Act it is proved to the satisfaction of the court that the seduction or prostitution of a girl under the age of sixteen has been caused, encouraged, or favoured by her father, mother, guardian, master, or mistress, it shall be in the power of the court to divest such father, mother, guardian, master, or mistress of all authority over her, and to appoint any person or persons willing to take charge of such girl to be her guardian until she has attained the age of twenty-one, or any age below this as the court may direct, and the High Court shall have the power from time to time to rescind or vary such order by the appointment of any other person or persons as such guardian, or in any other respect.

## PART II Suppression of Brothels

### Summary Proceedings against Brothel Keeper, &c

13. Any person who –
    (1) keeps or manages, or acts or assists in the management of, a brothel, or
    (2) being the tenant, lessee, or occupier of any premises, knowingly permits such premises or any part thereof to be used as a brothel or for the purpose of habitual prostitution, or
    (3) being the lessor or landlord of any premises or the agent of such lessor or landlord, lets the same or any part thereof with the knowledge that such premises or some part thereof are or is to be used as a brothel or is wilfully a party to the continued use of such premises or any part thereof as a brothel,

shall on summary conviction in manner provided by the Summary Jurisdiction Acts be liable –

(1) to a penalty not exceeding twenty pounds, or in the discretion of the court, to imprisonment for a term not exceeding three months, with or without hard labour, and

(2) on a second or subsequent conviction to a penalty not exceeding forty pounds, or, in the discretion of the court, to imprisonment for any term not exceeding four months, with or without hard labour;

and in case of third or subsequent conviction such person may in addition to such penalty or imprisonment as last aforesaid, be required by the court to enter into a recognizance, with or without sureties, as to the court seems meet, to be of good behaviour for any period not exceeding twelve months, and in default of entering into such recognizance, with or without sureties (as the case may be), such person may be imprisoned for any period not exceeding three months, in addition to any such term of imprisonment as aforesaid.

Any person on being summarily convicted in pursuance of this section may appeal to a court of general or quarter sessions against such conviction.

The enactments for encouraging prosecutions on disorderly houses contained in sections five, six, and seven of the Act passed in the twenty-fifth year of the reign of King George the Second, chapter thirty-six, as amended by the enactment contained in section seven of the Act passed in the fifty-eight year of the reign of King George the Third, chapter seventy, shall, with the necessary modifications, be deemed to apply to prosecutions under this section, and the said enactments shall, for the purposes of this section, be construed as if the prosecution in such enactments mentioned included summary proceedings under this section as well as prosecution on indictment.

# Bibliography


Aldrich, Robert. *Colonialism and Homosexuality*. London: Routledge, 2003.

Alroey, Gur. *An Unpromising Land: Jewish Migration to Palestine in the Early Twentieth Century*. Stanford, CA: Stanford University Press, 2014.

Alyagon Darr, Orna. *Marks of an Absolute Witch: Evidentiary Dilemmas in Early Modern England*. Farnham, UK: Ashgate, 2011.

'Relocated Doctrine: The Travel of the English Doctrine of Corroboration in Sex Offense Cases to Mandate Palestine'. *Yale Journal of Law & the Humanities* 26, no. 2 (2014): 185–209.

Amir, Menachem. *Patterns in Forcible Rape*. Chicago: University of Chicago Press, 1971.

Archbold, John Frederick, Sir John Jervis, Henry Delacombe Roome and Robert Ernest Ross. *Archbold's Pleading, Evidence & Practice in Criminal Cases*. London: Sweet & Maxwell, 1922.

Arondekar, Anjali. 'Without a Trace: Sexuality and the Colonial Archive'. *Journal of the History of Sexuality* 14, no. 1–2 (2005): 10–27.

Ashworth, Andrew. *Sentencing and Criminal Justice*. 6th ed. Cambridge: Cambridge University Press, 2015.

Avnoor, Hannah. 'Corroboration in Sexual Offences – What for'. [In Hebrew]. *Hapraklit* 26 (1970–1971): 79–84.

Backhouse, Constance. *Carnal Crimes: Sexual Assault Law in Canada, 1900–1975*. Toronto: Osgoode Society, 2008.

'The Doctrine of Corroboration in Sexual Assault Trials in Early Twentieth-Century Canada and Australia'. *Queen's Law Journal* 26 (2001): 297–338.

Bailey, Merridee L. and Kimberley-Joy Knight. 'Writing Histories of Law and Emotion'. *The Journal of Legal History* 38, no. 2 (2017): 117–129.

Bashar, Nazife. 'Rape in England between 1550 and 1700', in *The Sexual Dynamics of History*, edited by The London Feminist History Group. London: Pluto Press, 1983.

Bates, Victoria. *Sexual Forensics in Victorian and Edwardian England: Age, Crime and Consent in the Courts*. Basingstoke, UK: Palgrave Macmillan, 2016.

Ben-Naeh, Yaron. 'Moshko the Jew and His Gay Friends: Same-Sex Sexual Relations in Ottoman Jewish Society'. *Journal of Early Modern History* 9, no. 1–2 (2005): 79–105.

Ben-Yishai, Ayelet. *Common Precedents: The Presentness of the Past in Victorian Law and Fiction*. Oxford: Oxford University Press, 2013.

Bensinger, Gad J. 'Criminal Justice in Israel', in *Crime and Criminal Justice in Israel: Assessing Knowledge Base toward the Twenty-First Century*, edited by Robert R. Friedmann. Albany: State University of New York Press, 1998.

Bentham, Jeremy. *Of Sexual Irregularities, and Other Writings on Sexual Morality*. Penology and Criminal Law, Religion and the Church. Edited by Philip Schofield, Catherine Pease-Watkin and Michael Quinn. Oxford: Clarendon Press, 2014.

Bentwich, Norman. 'The New Criminal Code for Palestine'. *Journal of Comparative Legislation and International Law* 20, no. 1 (1938): 71–79.

Bernstein, Deborah. 'Gender, Nationalism and Colonial Policy: Prostitution in the Jewish Settlement of Mandate Palestine, 1918–1948'. *Women's History Review* 21, no. 1 (2012): 81–100.

*Women on the Margins: Gender and Nationalism in Mandate Tel Aviv* [in Hebrew]. Jerusalem: Yad Izhak Ben Zvi, 2008.

Bilsky, Leora. 'The City, the Woman and the Drifter: A New Reading of the Yaakobowitz Trial'. [In Hebrew]. *HaMishpat* 16 (2011): 131–172.

'"Rothstein's Affair": Nachum Guttman, Local Mythology and the First Attempted Rape in Tel Aviv'. [In Hebrew]. *Iyunei Mishpat* 26, no. 2 (2002): 391–449.

Blackstone, William. *Commentaries on the Laws of England*. 4 vols. Dublin: John Exshaw, Henry Saunders, Boulter Grierson, James Williams and John Milliken, 1769.

Blum, Binyamin. 'Evidence Rules and Colonial Difference(s): Reexamining the Complexities and Lessons of Legal Grafting'. *Paper presented at the Mandate Law Research Group*: Berg Institution of Law and History, Tel Aviv University, 2011.

'Evidence Rules of Colonial Difference: Identity, Legitimacy and Power in the Law of Mandate Palestine, 1917–1939'. JSD dissertation, Stanford University, 2011.

Bosworth, Clifford Edmund. 'Gerard Leslie Makins Clauson'. In *A Century of British Orientalists 1902–2001*, edited by Clifford Edmund Bosworth, 89–98. Oxford: Oxford University Press, 2001.

Bourdieu, Pierre. 'The Force of Law: Toward a Sociology of the Juridical Field'. *Hastings L.J.* 38 (1987): 805.

Brun, Nathan. 'Jaffa 1912: Rape of a Girl in Mea-Shearim Jerusalem'. [In Hebrew]. *Katedra*, no. 142 (2012): 75–112.

*Judges and Lawyers in Eretz Israel* [In Hebrew]. Jerusalem: The Magnes Press, 2008.

*Law, Passions and Politics: Judges and Lawyers between the British Mandate and the State of Israel* [In Hebrew]. Tel Aviv: Steimatzky, 2014.

Bumiller, Kristin. 'Rape as a Legal Symbol: An Essay on Sexual Violence and Racism'. *University of Miami Law Review* 42 (1988): 75–91.

Bunton, Martin. 'Inventing the Status Quo: Ottoman Land-Law During the Palestine Mandate, 1917–1936'. *The International History Review* 21, no. 1 (1999): 28–56.

Camps, Francis. 'Smith, Sir Sydney Alfred (1883–1969)'. *Oxford Dictionary of National Biography* (2004). Published electronically 23 September 2014. https://doi.org/10.1093/ref:odnb/36159.

Cermak, Bonni. 'Race, Honor, Citizenship: The Massie Rape/Murder Case'. In *Sex without Consent: Rape and Sexual Coercion in America*, edited by Merril D. Smith, 230–246. New York: New York University Press, 2001.

Childs, Mary, and Louise Ellison, eds. *Feminist Perspectives on Evidence*. London: Cavendish, 2000.

Clauson, Gerard LM, 'The British colonial currency system'. *The Economic Journal* 54, no. 213 (1944): 1–25.

Cockburn, Cynthia. *The Space between Us: Negotiating Gender and National Identities in Conflict*. London: Zed Books, 1998.

Cocks, H. G. 'Secrets, Crimes and Diseases, 1800–1914'. Chap. 4 in *A Gay History of Britain*, edited by Matt Cook, 107–144. Oxford: Greenwood World Publishing, 2007.

Cocks, Harry G. *Nameless Offences: Homosexual Desire in the Nineteenth Century*. London: I. B. Tauris, 2003.

Cohen, Claire. *Male Rape Is a Feminist Issue: Feminism, Governmentality and Male Rape*. Basingstoke, UK: Palgrave Macmillan, 2014.

Cohen, Daniel A. 'Social Injustice, Sexual Violence, Spiritual Transcendence: Constructions of Interracial Rape in Early American Crime Literature, 1767–1817'. *The William and Mary Quarterly* 56, no. 3 (1999): 481–526.

Cohen, Gamliel. *Under Cover* [In Hebrew]. Tel Aviv: Ministry of Defence, 2002.

Cohen, Hillel. *1929: Year Zero of the Jewish-Arab Conflict* [In Hebrew]. Jerusalem: Keter, 2013.

Cohen, L. Jonathan. *The Probable and the Provable*. Oxford: Clarendon Press, 1977.

Coughlin, Anne M. 'Sex and Guilt'. *Virginia Law Review* 84, no. 1 (1998): 1–46.

Crenshaw, Kimberle. 'Mapping the Margins: Intersectionality, Identity Politics, and Violence against Women of Color'. *Stanford Law Review* 43 (1991).

Damaska, Mirjan R. *Evidence Law Adrift*. New Haven, CT: Yale University Press, 1997.

Davis, Joseph E. *Accounts of Innocence: Sexual Abuse, Trauma, and the Self*. Chicago: University of Chicago Press, 2005.

Dennis, I. H. *The Law of Evidence*. 4th ed. Sweet & Maxwell: London, 2010.

Diamond, Michael. *Victorian Sensation, or, the Spectacular, the Shocking, and the Scandalous in Nineteenth-Century Britain*. London: Anthem Press, 2004.

Dikshtein, Paltiel. *Criminal Law* [In Hebrew]. Vol. 1, Tel Aviv: School of Law and Economics, 1938.

Edelstein, Laurie. 'An Accusation Easily to Be Made? Rape and Malicious Prosecution in Eighteenth-Century England'. *American Journal of Legal History* 42, no. 4 (1998): 351–390.

Egan, R. Danielle, and Gail L. Hawkes. 'Imperiled and Perilous: Exploring the History of Childhood Sexuality'. *Journal of Historical Sociology* 21, no. 4 (2008): 355–367.

Ehrlich, Susan. *Representing Rape: Language and Sexual Consent*. London: Routledge, 2001.

Elad, Nava, and Anita Weiner. *The History of Youth Probation and Services for Disadvantaged Delinquent Children in Israel* [in Hebrew]. Tel Aviv, Ramot: Tel Aviv University, 1995.

Estrich, Susan. *Real Rape*. Cambridge, MA: Harvard University Press, 1987.

Ewick, Patricia, and Susan S. Silbey. 'Subversive Stories and Hegemonic Tales: Toward a Sociology of Narrative'. *Law & Society Review* 29, no. 2 (1995): 197–226.

Farr, Samuel. *Elements of Medical Jurisprudence*. 1st ed. London: T. Becket, Pall-Mall, 1788.

Foucault, Michel. *The History of Sexuality: An Introduction*. Vol. 1, New York: Vintage Books, 1990.

Friedman, Max D., and Leon Rotenberg, eds. *Collection of Judgments of the Courts of Palestine 1919–1933*. Vol. II, Tel Aviv: L.M. Rotenberg – Law Publishers, 1935.

Frohmann, Lisa. 'Convictability and Discordant Locales: Reproducing Race, Class, and Gender Ideologies in Prosecutorial Decisionmaking'. *Law & Society Review* 31, no. 3 (1997): 531–556.

Gavey, Nicola. *Just Sex?: The Cultural Scaffolding of Rape*. New York: Routledge, 2004.

Geertz, Clifford. *The Interpretation of Cultures: Selected Essays*. New York: Basic Books, 1973.

Geis, Gilbert. 'Lord Hale, Witches, and Rape'. *British Journal of Law and Society* 5, no. 1 (Summer 1978): 26–44.

Geis, Gilbert, and Ivan Bunn. *A Trial of Witches: A Seventeenth-Century Witchcraft Prosecution*. London: Routledge, 1997.

Gilbert, Sir Geoffrey. *The Law of Evidence*. 3rd ed. London: W. Owen, 1769.

Gordon, Robert W. 'Critical Legal Histories'. *Stanford Law Review* 36, no. 1/2 (1984): 57–125.

Gupta, Alok, and Scott Long. 'This Alien Legacy: The Origins of "Sodomy" Laws in British Colonialism'. New York: Human Rights Watch, 2008. www.hrw.org/sites/default/files/reports/lgbt1208_web.pdf.

Habib, Samar. *Female Homosexuality in the Middle East: Histories and Representations*. New York: Routledge, 2007.

Halamish, Aviva. 'Mandatory Palestine: A Dual Society or Colonial Reality?'. [In Hebrew]. *Zmanim*, no. 92 (2005).

Hale, Sir Matthew. *Historia Placitorum Coronae. The History of the Pleas of the Crown, by Sir Matthew Hale ... Now First Published from His Lordship's Original Manuscript, and the Several References to the Records Examined by the Originals, with Large Notes. By Sollom Emlyn ... To Which Is Added a Table of the Principal Matters. In Two Volumes....* London: F. Gyles, T. Woodward and C. Davis, 1736.

Hale, Sir Matthew. *Pleas of the Crown*. London: William Shrewsbury and John Leigh, 1678.

Halley, Janet E. 'Reasoning about Sodomy: Act and Identity in and after Bowers V. Hardwick'. *Virginia Law Review* 79, no. 7 (1993): 1721–1780.

Han, Enze, and Joseph O'Mahoney. 'British Colonialism and the Criminalization of Homosexuality'. *Cambridge Review of International Affairs* 27 (2014): 268–288.

Harnon, Eliahu. *Law of Evidence* [in Hebrew]. Vol. 2, Jerusalem: Hebrew University of Jerusalem, Faculty of Law, 1977.

Harvey, A. D. 'Prosecutions for Sodomy in England at the Beginning of the Nineteenth Century'. *The Historical Journal* 21, no. 4 (1978): 939–948.

Hess, Tamar B. 'I Am Not Alone in the World: The Memoirs of Henya Pekelman'. In *The Life of a Worker in Her Homeland*, 219–235 [In Hebrew]. Or-Yehuda: Kinneret, Zmora-Bitan, Dvir, 2007.

Hinchy, Jessica. 'Obscenity, Moral Contagion and Masculinity: Hijras in Public Space in Colonial North India'. *Asian Studies Review* 38 (2014): 274–294.

Hirschi, Travis, and Michael Gottfredson. 'Age and the Explanation of Crime'. *American Journal of Sociology* 89, no. 3 (1983): 552–584.

Horowitz, Dan, and Moshe Lissak. *Origins of the Israeli Polity: Palestine under the Mandate*. Translated by Charles Hoffman. Edited by Moshe Lissak. Chicago: University of Chicago Press, 1978.

Houlbrook, Matt. *Queer London: Perils and Pleasures in the Sexual Metropolis, 1918–1957*. Chicago: University of Chicago Press, 2005.

Hughes, Matthew. 'The Banality of Brutality: British Armed Forces and the Repression of the Arab Revolt in Palestine, 1936–39'. *English Historical Review* 124, no. 507 (2009): 313–354.

Ilany, Ofri. 'A Fine Bequest from our Neighbors'. In *Another Sex: Selected Essays in Israeli Queer and LGBT Studies* [in Hebrew], edited by Aeyal Gross, Amalya Ziv and Yosef Raz, 281–313. Tel Aviv: Resling, 2016.

'An Oriental Vice: Representations of Sodomy in Early Zionist Discourse'. In *National Politics and Sexuality in Transregional Perspective: The Homophobic Argument*, edited by Achim Rohde, Christina von Braun and Stefanie Schüler-Springorum. Abingdon: Routledge, 2017.

Inbar, Zvi. *Scales and Sword: The Foundations of Military Law in Israel* [In Hebrew]. Tel Aviv: Ministry of Defense Publishing, 2005.

Jones, Karen. 'The Politics of Credibility'. In *A Mind of One's Own: Feminist Essays on Reason and Objectivity*, edited by Louise Antony and Charlotte Witt, 154–176. Boulder, CO: Westview Press, 2002.

Kantrovitch, H., ed. *The Law of Criminal Procedure in Palestine*. Tel Aviv: Mizpah, 1943.

Kaspi, Joshua. 'Prisons in Mandate Palestine'. [In Hebrew]. *Kathedra* 32 (1984): 141, 146.

Kassan, Shalom. *Convicted and Acquitted* [in Hebrew]. Tel Aviv: Dvir, 1960.

Kermack, S. G. *A Handbook of the Law of Criminal Procedure in Palestine*. Jerusalem: Tarbuth, 1928.

Kirby, Michael. 'The Sodomy Offence: England's Least Lovely Criminal Law Export?'. *Journal of Commonwealth Criminal Law* 1, no. 1 (2011): 22–43.

Klein, Menachem. *Lives in Common: Arabs and Jews in Jerusalem, Jaffa and Hebron*. Translated by Haim Watzman. London: Hurst & Company, 2014.

Kolsky, Elizabeth. '"The Body Evidencing the Crime": Rape on Trial in Colonial India, 1860–1947'. *Gender & History* 22, no. 1 (2010): 109–130.

'The Rule of Colonial Indifference: Rape on Trial in Early Colonial India, 1805–57'. *The Journal of Asian Studies* 69, no. 4 (2010): 1093–1117.

Kounine, Laura. 'Emotions, Mind, and Body on Trial: A Cross-Cultural Perspective'. *Journal of Social History* 51, no. 2 (2017): 219–230.

Kozma, Liat. 'Sexology in the Yishuv: The Rise and Decline of Sexual Consultation in Tel Aviv, 1930–39'. *International Journal of Middle East Studies* 42 (2010): 231–249.

Kroyanker, David. *The Neighborhoods of Jerusalem: Talbiya, Katamon and the Greek Colony*. Jerusalem: Keter, 2002.

LaFont, Suzanne. 'Very Straight Sex: The Development of Sexual Mores in Jamaica'. *Journal of Colonialism and Colonial History* 2, no. 3(2001).

LaFree, Gary D. 'Male Power and Female Victimization: Toward a Theory of Interracial Rape'. *American Journal of Sociology* 88, no. 2 (1982): 311–328.

Langbein, John H. *The Origins of Adversary Criminal Trial*. Oxford Studies in Modern Legal History. Oxford: Oxford University Press, 2003.

Lewin-Epstein, Eliyahu Zeev Halevi. *Memoirs* [In Hebrew]. Tel Aviv: Lewin-Epstein, 1932.

Likhovski, Assaf. 'Chasing Ghosts: On Writing Cultural Histories of Tax Law'. *UC Irvine Law Review* 1, no. 3 (2011): 843–892.

*Law and Identity in Mandate Palestine*. Studies in Legal History. Edited by Thomas A. Green and Hendrik Hartog. Chapel Hill: University of North Carolina Press, 2006.

Lindquist Dorr, Lisa. '"Another Negro-Did-It Crime": Black-on-White Rape and Protest in Virginia 1945–1960'. In *Sex without Consent: Rape and Sexual Coercion in America*, edited by Merril D. Smith, 247–264. New York: New York University Press, 2001.

Mack, Kathy. 'An Australian Perspective on Feminism, Race and Evidence'. *Southwestern University Law Review* 28 (1999): 367–388.

'Continuing Barriers to Women's Credibility: A Feminist Perspective on the Proof Process'. *Criminal Law Forum* 4, no. 2 (1993): 327–353.

Masalha, Nur al-Din. *The Palestine Nakba: Decolonising History, Narrating the Subaltern, Reclaiming Memory*. London: Zed, 2012.

Matoesian, Gregory M. *Law and the Language of Identity Discourse in the William Kennedy Smith Rape Trial* . Oxford: Oxford University Press, 2001.

McGuire, Danielle L. '"It Was like All of Us Had Been Raped": Sexual Violence, Community Mobilization, and the African American Freedom Struggle'. *The Journal of American History* 91, no. 3 (2004): 906–931.

Merin, Yuval. 'A Feminist Perspective on Evidence Law: The Gendered Truth and the Silencing of the Different Voice'. [In Hebrew]. *HaMishpat* 16 (2011): 97.

Mezey, Naomi. 'Law as Culture'. *Yale Journal of Law & the Humanities* 13, no. 1 (2001): 35–68.

Mnookin, Jennifer L. 'Expert Evidence, Partisanship, and Epistemic Competence'. *Brooklyn Law Review* 73, no. 3 (2008): 1009–1033.

'Fingerprint Evidence in an Age of DNA Profiling'. *Brooklyn Law Review* 67, no. 1 (2001): 13–70.

Morrison, Heidi. *Childhood and Colonial Modernity in Egypt*. Houndmills: Palgrave Macmillan, 2015.

Murray, Stephen O. 'Some Nineteenth-Century Reports of Islamic Homosexuals'. In *Islamic Homosexualities: Culture, History, and Literature*, edited by Stephen O. Murray and Will Roscoe, 204–221. New York: New York University Press, 1997.

'The Will Not to Know'. In *Islamic Homosexualities: Culture, History, and Literature*, edited by Stephen O. Murray and Will Roscoe, 14–54. New York: New York University Press, 1997.

Murray, Stephen O. and Will Roscoe, eds. *Islamic Homosexualities: Culture, History, and Literature*. New York: New York University Press, 1997.

Najmabadi, Afsaneh. *Women with Mustaches and Men without Beards: Gender and Sexual Anxieties of Iranian Modernity*. Berkeley: University of California Press, 2005.

Nelson, William. *The Law of Evidence*. 1st ed. London: B. Gosling, 1717.

Nevo, Amos. 'The Punishment' [In Hebrew]. *Yediot Ahronot*, 30 April 1993.

Nitzan, Tal. '"Controlled Occupation": The Rarity of Military Rape in the Israeli Palestinian Conflict' [In Hebrew]. MA thesis, The Hebrew University, 2006.

Orenstein, Aviva. '"My God!": A Feminist Critique of the Excited Utterance Exception to the Hearsay Rule'. *California Law Review* 85, no. 1 (1997): 159–223.

'No Bad Men!: A Feminist Analysis of Character Evidence in Rape Trials'. *Hastings Law Journal* 49 (1998): 663–716.

'The Seductive Power of Patriarchal Stories'. *Howard Law Journal* 58, no. 2 (2015): 411–436.

'Special Issues Raised by Rape Trial'. *Fordham Law Review* 76, no. 3 (2007): 1585–1608.

Palmer, Brian. 'How Do You Say Gay in Arabic?' *Slate* (2012). Published electronically 16 August 2012. www.slate.com/articles/life/explainer/2012/08/homosexuality_and_islam_how_do_you_say_gay_in_arabic_.html.

Paris, Leslie. 'Through the Looking Glass: Age, Stages, and Historical Analysis'. *The Journal of the History of Childhood and Youth* 1, no. 1 (2008): 106–113.

Paxton, Nancy L. 'Mobilizing Chivalry: Rape in British Novels About the Indian Uprising of 1857'. *Victorian Studies* 36, no. 1 (1992): 5–30.

Paz, Omri. 'Crime, Criminals, and the Ottoman State: Anatolia between the Late 1830s and the Late 1860s'. Ph.D. diss., Tel Aviv University, 2010.

Pedersen, Susan. 'Getting out of Iraq – in 1932: The League of Nations and the Road to Normative Statehood'. *The American Historical Review* 115, no. 4 (2010): 975–1000.

Pekelman, Henya M. *The Life of a Worker in Her Homeland* [In Hebrew]. Or-Yehuda: Kinnert, Zmora-Bitan, Dvir, 2007.

Peled, Kobi. *Noura's Dream: A Historical Portrait of a Bedouin Tribe* [In Hebrew]. Tel Aviv: University of Haifa Press, 2015.

Philipose, Elizabeth. 'Feminism, International Law, and the Spectacular Violence of the "Other": Decolonizing the Laws of War'. In *Theorizing Sexual Violence*, edited by Renee J. Heberle and Victoria Grace, 176–204. New York: Routledge, 2011.

Razi, Tammy. *Forsaken Children: The Backyard of Mandate Tel-Aviv* [in Hebrew]. Tel Aviv: Am Oved, 2009.

'Jewish-Arab Women? Ethnicity, Nationality and Gender in Mandate Tel Aviv'. [In Hebrew]. *Theory and Criticism*, no. 38–39 (2011): 137–160.

'"My Daughter Burns Like Fire": Mothers and Daughters in Tel Aviv During the 1930s and 1940s'. In *Gender in Israel: New Studies on Gender in the Yishuv and State*, edited by Margalit Shilo and Gideon Katz, 140–169. Sde Boker: Ben Gurion University, Ben Gurion Research Institute, 2011.

Reuveny, Jacob. *The Administration of Palestine under the British Mandate 1920–1948: An Institutional Analysis* [In Hebrew]. Ramat Gan: Bar Ilan University Press, 1993.

Reynold, Nick. *Britain's Unfulfilled Mandate for Palestine*. Lanham, MD: Lexington Books, 2014.

Roberts, Paul, and Candida Saunders. 'Piloting PTWI – a Socio-Legal Window on Prosecutors' Assessments of Evidence and Witness Credibility'. *Oxford Journal of Legal Studies* 30, no. 1 (20 March 2010): 101–141.

Robson, Laura. *Colonialism and Christianity in Mandate Palestine*. Austin: University of Texas Press, 2011.

Said, Edward W. *Orientalism*. New York: Vintage Books, 1979.

Salent, Ephraim. *Evidence Law: In Criminal Trials*. Tel Aviv: Israel Print, 1952.

Sanders, Douglas E. '377 and the Unnatural Afterlife of British Colonialism in Asia'. *Asian Journal of Comparative Law* 4 (2009): 1–19.

Sarat, Austin, and Thomas R. Kearns. 'The Cultural Lives of Law'. In *Law in the Domains of Culture*, edited by Austin Sarat and Thomas R. Kearns, 1–20. Ann Arbor: University of Michigan Press, 2001.

Schulhofer, Stephen J. *Unwanted Sex: The Culture of Intimidation and the Failure of Law*. Cambridge, MA: Harvard University Press, 1998.

Schwendinger, Julia R. and Herman Schwendinger. *Rape and Inequality*. Beverly Hills, CA: Sage, 1983.

Scott, James C. *Domination and the Arts of Resistance: Hidden Transcripts*. New Haven, CT: Yale University Press, 1990.

Sebba, L. 'The Requirement of Corroboration in Sex Offences'. *Israel Law Review* 3 (1968): 67–87.

Seikaly, May. *Haifa: Transformation of a Palestinian Arab Society 1918–1939*. London: I.B. Tauris, 1995.

Seltenreich, Yair. 'Masculinity, Respect and Body in the Pjca Settlements of the Galilee during the Settlement Period'. [In Hebrew]. *Israeli Sociology* 11, no. 1 (2009): 137–157.

Semerdjian, Elyse. *'Off the Straight Path': Illicit Sex, Law, and Community in Ottoman Aleppo*. New York: Syracuse University Press, 2008.

Sengoopta, Chandak. *Imprint of the Raj: How Fingerprinting Was Born in Colonial India*. London: Macmillan, 2003.

Shachar, Yoram. 'The Origins of the Criminal Code, 1936'. [In Hebrew]. *Iyunei Mishpat* 7 (1979): 75–113.

'The Reasonable Person and Criminal Law'. [In Hebrew]. *Hapraklit* 39, no. 1 (1989): 78–107.

Shamir, Ronen. *The Colonies of Law: Colonialism, Zionism, and Law in Early Mandate Palestine*. Cambridge: Cambridge University Press, 2000.

Shapiro, Barbara J. *Probability and Certainty in Seventeenth-Century England: A Study of the Relationships between Natural Science, Religion, History, Law, and Literature*. Princeton, NJ: Princeton University Press, 1983.

Sharafi, Mitra. *Law and Identity in Colonial South Asia: Parsi Legal Culture, 1772–1947*. New York: Cambridge University Press, 2014.

'A New History of Colonial Lawyering: Likhovski and Legal Identities in the British Empire'. *Law & Social Inquiry* 32, no. 4 (2007): 1059–1094.

Sharpe, Jenny. *Allegories of Empire: The Figure of Woman in the Colonial Text*. Minneapolis: University of Minnesota Press, 1993.

Shilo, Margalit. *Princess or Captive? Jewish Women in Jerusalem, 1840–1914* [in Hebrew]. Haifa: Haifa University Press, 2001.

'Women as Victims of War: The British Conquest (1917) and the Blight of Prostitution in the Holy City'. *Nashim: A Journal of Jewish Women's Studies & Gender Issues*, no. 6 (2003): 72–83.

Shoham, Hizky. 'From "Great History" to "Small History": The Genesis of the Zionist Periodization'. *Israel Studies* 18, no. 1 (2013): 31–55.

Silverstein, Richard. 'Amos Horev: Castrated Palestinian in Blood Vengeance'. www.richardsilverstein.com/2010/06/17/amos-horev-castrated-palestinian-in-blood-vengeance/.

Simoni, Marcella. 'At the Roots of Division: A New Perspective on Arabs and Jews, 1930–1939'. *Middle Eastern Studies* 36, no. 3 (2000): 52–92.

'A Dangerous Legacy: Welfare in British Palestine, 1930–1939'. *Jewish History* 13, no. 2 (1999): 81–109.

Smith, Sidney. *Forensic Medicine: A Text-Book for Students and Practitioners*. 8th ed. London: J & A Churchill, 1945.

Smithers, Gregory D. *Slave Breeding: Sex, Violence, and Memory in African American History*. Gainesville: University Press of Florida, 2012.

Stein, Alex. *The Foundations of Evidence Law*. Oxford: Oxford University Press, 2005.

Stewart, Christine. 'Men Behaving Badly: Sodomy Cases in the Colonial Courts of Papua New Guinea'. *Journal of Pacific History* 43, no. 1 (2008): 77–93.

Strachey Bucknill, John A., and Haig Apisoghom S. Utidjian, eds. *The Imperial Ottoman Penal Code*. London: Oxford University Press, 1918.

Strawson, John. *Partitioning Palestine: Legal Fundamentalism in the Palestinian-Israeli Conflict*. London: Pluto Press, 2010.

Tapper, Colin. *Cross & Tapper on Evidence*. 12th ed. Oxford: Oxford University Press, 2010.

Taslitz, Andrew E. *Rape and the Culture of the Courtroom*. New York: New York University Press, 1999.

Taylor, Alfred Swaine. *A Manual of Medical Jurisprudence*. 9th ed. London: J & A Churchill, 1874.

Temkin, Jennifer. *Rape and the Legal Process*. 2nd ed. Oxford: Oxford University Press, 2002.

Tidhar, David. *In My Homeland Service (1912–1960)* [in Hebrew]. Tel Aviv: Yedidim, 1961.

Tomlins, Christopher. 'How Autonomous Is Law?'. *Annual Review of Law & Social Science* 3, no. 1 (2007): 45–68.

Tracy, Larissa. 'Introduction: A History of Calamities: The Culture of Castration'. In *Castration and Culture in the Middle Ages*, edited by Larissa Tracy, 1–28. Cambridge: D.S. Brewer, 2013.

Tuerkheimer, Deborah. 'Incredible Women: Sexual Violence and the Credibility Discount'. *University of Pennsylvania Law Review* 166, no. 1 (2017): 1–58.

Turchik, Jessica A., and Katie M. Edwards. 'Myths About Male Rape: A Literature Review'. *Psychology of Men & Masculinity* 13, no. 2 (2012): 211–226.

Twining, William. 'Narrative and Generalizations in Argumentation about Questions of Fact'. *South Texas Law Review* 40 (1999): 351–365.

*Rethinking Evidence: Exploratory Essays*. Cambridge: Cambridge University Press, 2006.

Ullman, Sarah E. and Henrietta H. Filipas. 'Correlates of Formal and Informal Support Seeking in Sexual Assault Victims'. *Journal of Interpersonal Violence* 16, no. 10 (2001).

Volger, Richard. *A World View of Criminal Justice*. Aldershot, UK: Ashgate, 2005.

Wagenaar, Willem Albert, P. J. van Koppen and Henricus Florentine Maria Crombag. *Anchored Narratives: The Psychology of Criminal Evidence*. Hemel Hempstead, UK: Harvester Wheatsheaf, 1993.

Walker, Garthine. *Crime, Gender and Social Order in Early Modern England*. Cambridge: Cambridge University Press, 2003.

Wheatley, Natasha. 'Mandatory Interpretation: Legal Hermeneutics and the New International Order in Arab and Jewish Petitions to the League of Nations'. *Past & Present* 227, no. 1 (2015): 205–248.

Whitman, James O. *The Origins of Reasonable Doubt: Theological Roots of the Criminal Trial*. New Haven, CT: Yale University Press, 2008.

Wiener, Martin J. *Men of Blood: Violence, Manliness and Criminal Justice in Victorian England*. Cambridge: Cambridge University Press, 2004.

Wigmore, John Henry. *Evidence in Trials at Common Law*. (Chadbourn rev. ed.) 10 vols. Vol. 3A, Boston: Little, Brown and Company, 1970. 1923.

*Evidence in Trials at Common Law*. Wigmore on Evidence. 4th ed. 10 vols. Vol. 1, Boston: Little, Brown and Company, 1983. 1904.

Williams, Glanville. *The Proof of Guilt: A Study of the English Criminal Trial*. The Hamlyn Lectures. London: Stevens & Sons, 1955.

Yonay, Yuval, and Dori Spivak. 'Constructing the Identity of Homosexuals in the Israeli Legal Discourse, 1948–1988'. In *LGBT Rights in Israel*, edited by Alon Harel, Yaniv Lushinsky and Einav Morgenstern. Jerusalem: Hebrew University Press, Harry Sacher Institute, 2015.

Zander, Walter, rev. Robert Brown. 'Bentwich, Norman De Mattos (1883–1971)'. *Oxford Dictionary of National Biography* (2004). www.oxforddnb.com/view/article/30811.

Zeevi, Dror. 'Changes in Legal-Sexual Discourses: Sex Crimes in the Ottoman Empire'. *Continuity and Change* 16, no. 2 (2001): 219–242.

*Producing Desire: Changing Sexual Discourse in the Ottoman Middle East, 1500–1900*. Berkeley: University of California Press, 2006.

Ziff, William B. *The Rape of Palestine*. New York: Argus Books, Inc., 1946.

# Index